Living and Breathing the Psalms

Jim V Edwards

2018

Edwards Family Publishing

Living and Breathing the Psalms
Jim V. Edwards

ISBN-13: 978-1535590730
ISBN-10: 1535590734
Kindle ASIN: B01LOZL5MQ

www.amazon.co.uk/Living-Breathing-Psalms-Jim-Edwards/dp/1535590734

www.amazon.com/Living-Breathing-Psalms-Jim-Edwards/dp/1535590734

Cover design by Jim Edwards
Edited by Lisa J Lickel
1st Edition

Published by Edwards Family Publishing

	www.landbreathingt.com
Contact	landbreathingt@gmail.com
Facebook	https://tinyurl.com/facelandbt

Acknowledgements

Thank You King Jesus, Wonderful Holy Spirit, Mighty Papa God. This was never my idea, and yet this has been a most wonderful adventure. Thank You for how You value process. I and so many, value the end goal, and miss the importance and the value of the process. Thank You for such a huge reminder.

Thank You for Your insight, Your Wisdom, and above all, for Your Presence as I have worked through these Psalms.

And thank You Lord, for the encouragement of friends and family to press on through them all. Thank you Lisa Saville, Nicola Taylor, Lynn Donovan, Lorilyn Roberts, Tina Rizzo, Nancy Robinson, Heather Tremblay & Jonathan and Rachael – thank you so much for spurring me on.

And thank you Bill Johnson for your love of the Psalms and for sharing from them so readily. I'm deeply indebted to your heart and your wisdom on nearly every page here and all the family of Bethel Church in Redding. You have a very special place in Papa's heart, with your commitment to pursue His Presence, and to understand His ways in order to bring His Kingdom rule to this planet of ours—thank you—all of you. It has been a huge privilege to have been able to visit as often as I have—*Oh, thank YOU Jesus!*—and make such friendships there too. And thank You Lord for the gifts and surprises that You have given me on each and every visit.

And many thanks too, to Lisa Lickel for all your wonderful, helpful, and encouraging comments and help with editing. Your attention to detail is so re-assuring, and helpful—many, many thanks.

And last but by no means least, for my wife Val, thank you for understanding, as I have buried myself in this, grabbing every available moment to bring this to completion.

There are a number of translations I have drawn on in my walk here through the Psalms, so special thanks to BibleGateway for organising the different translations to be so readily accessible side by side. I have drawn much on the American Standard Version, and the New International Version. When I have found the need to dig deeper into the original Hebrew I have called up the Orthodox Jewish Bible, and also referred to 'The Book of Psalms' by Robert Alter, ISBN 978-0-393-33704-4 pbk, published by W.M. Norton & Company Inc. Other more modern paraphrases have also been very helpful, such as 'The Message', by Eugene Peterson and 'The Passion Translation' by Dr Brian Simmons.

Dedication

I dedicate this to Miss Reeves and Miss Fisher, who are now dancin' in Glory, before the throne of Grace. Founding pastors of Hockley Mission, in Birmingham (UK), they made every gathering a loud, tambourine swinging, occasion to dance, praise and worship King Jesus, and see Him redeem, heal and save. Val and I forever carry your legacy in our hearts—thank you.

Introduction

A contemporary Christian's thankful-hearted, intimate, prayer-walk through the Psalms.

This is simply my personal prayer journey through these old songs of worship. As I have journeyed through them, personalising them as my own prayer with our amazing Papa God, all sorts of facets have appeared that I would never have dreamed of.

Much changed at the cross. So how we relate to, understand, and draw from this pre-the-cross worship in a post-the-cross era is going to be different. However as I have drawn out the meanings and truths behind these Psalms, the changes are smaller than I would have imagined. In some places they make far more sense when understood this way!

I hope you find them helpful, and in them find expression for your own heart's cries to our High King. I hope and pray they lead you to a closer, more intimate and understanding relationship with each member of the Trinity.

So as you set out to read your favourite, enjoy and worship our Wonderful King Jesus. Please savour the moment and enjoy His Glorious Presence, rather than feeling you have to rush on to the next one. May they stir you in a fresh way to praise and wonder at the Lovingkindness, at the Faithfulness, at the Goodness and Grace extended to each and every one of us by our Saviour King—Jesus the Nazarene—Jesus the anointed one—the Christ.

This is not a book to be read from cover to cover—you will get serious indigestion if you try it! As Lisa my editor commented, "it is like a three layer fudge cake with thick buttercream cocoa frosting. One can stand only so much at a time and I found I had to step away from time to time."

But there are times and situations when each one of us

needs to hear Papa's voice afresh speaking words of life directly into our situation. I would recommend Bill Johnson's approach, which is to read Psalms until He speaks. Now that may be difficult with this version for the above reason, but having found Him speaking to you in another version, then's the time to pull this off the shelf and hear Him speaking fresh words of Hope, of Faith and of Life direct to your spirit, as you pray this psalm with me.

I personally struggle with many of the Psalms, particularly in the archaic language of the Bible I normally read. Most of the other books I can read and not get too bogged down by the language, but the Psalms in many places are almost unintelligible. I also have great difficulty in seeing how we relate to them in an age of Grace and God's amazing Mercy, as I have personally experienced. So this has been an eye-opening walk, and process for me.

Oh, thank You King Jesus that Your promises are true for thousands of generations, to all who turn to You, Your promises are Yes and Amen! And thank You so much for singling out even me, when I was so far from You.

***   ***   ***

But this caught me completely unawares. I needed Psalm 126 for another book, and no translation expressed it in the way I wanted to, so I made my own. Then another, and another and I suddenly realised this was something from Papa's own heart. And as I dared to embrace it, it came with an urgency and gripping on my heart and spirit to stop everything I possibly could in order to do them all. I have been surprised when turning back to other modern translations at how totally different my wording and approach is, and often how different are the truths I have found.

I have tried to set down my own heart's response in entering into what I understand the Psalmist to have been expressing. I am not suggesting that the Psalmists had the same comprehension of Papa God, of their Messiah, or of Holy Spirit that we have today, though there are many biblical instances that would indicate that they understood our perspective a lot more than we would normally think to give them credit for. But that is a discussion for elsewhere.

As God's word inspired by Holy Spirit and intended to bless and enrich our lives today[1], these were written for our benefit as much as for Old Covenant believers. In mulling over my heart's response, or in phrasing the issues expressed, I have often widened and expounded on the original intent. Many Psalms, but not all, are prayer to the Lord, and can be expressed directly this way. Some include or infer His response; after all, prayer is a two-way conversation. It is never intended to be a monologue. And where the Psalmist hints at Praise and Worship, I give that expression—not as something I will do one day, but turn my heart to enter into right now, in the context of the situation or heart of that moment, as I would encourage you to do in your daily walk.

With many I have struggled and wrestled as to how to approach and what line to take, when suddenly... So while those who know me may well say they recognise my wording and my style here, I know different—very different—thank You Holy Spirit. I hope I have done justice to Your incredible revelation and inspiration—to bring honour, praise and Glory to Jesus. *Oh,* thank You Jesus for all You are to me—You are so, so worth every honour I could bestow.

And I have been very surprised too, that no-one else has done anything even vaguely similar, that I have yet found[2].

---

[1] 2 Timothy 3:16

[2] As this whole project nears completion I have discovered some have come close. A search for 'Praying the Psalms' lists a number,

Once I got started, it seemed such an obvious way of expressing this facet of God's word, to unlock many of the truths interwoven and hidden in this poetry from another age and culture. With all of the translations now available on sites such as BibleGateway, it is not difficult to access the basic words with a good approach to much of their meaning. But this does not necessarily unlock the Psalmist's heart and spirit, or how we should now respond in the light of our New Covenant and New Covenant relationship with our mighty King and Saviour who these songs lift high in worship and praise. We are called to an intimacy (into-me-you-see) with Papa God, with King Jesus, and with Glorious Holy Spirit, that the Psalmists could scarcely dream of, though clearly King David and some of the sons of Korah knew them this closely from their time spent in such intimate worship. 'My heart and my flesh cry out for the living God[3]' comes from someone who has been a long time in that place of worship to a God they had come to know this closely.

So from this place of intimacy, there are times, sometimes consciously, sometimes unconsciously, when I am talking to one particular member of the Trinity, at other times, to them all, as one.

I hope these all read like they were written today—not 3,000 years ago. They are just as relevant today as they were then. I have tried to unravel, explain and expound so as to open them up for us in simple, everyday language.

---

such as that by Walter Bruegemann, Elmer Townes, Lloyd Hildebrand, Juanita Ryan, Rick Stedman and 'Psalms for Praying' by Nan Merrill [This is not exhaustive list.] I look forward to reading some of these once 'Living and Breathing the Psalms' is finally in print.

[3] Psalm 84:2

I do not believe that those who give their lives to our King Jesus enter into a family that replaces Israel, and that Israel therefore now has no special place in Papa's grand scheme of things. On the contrary, many promises were made specifically to Israel and we are seeing them coming to fruition in our day. However, everyone who accepts Jesus as their Lord and Saviour is adopted into the big Jewish family and grafted into the vine, with all of the accompanying promises that were made to Israel. So for many of the Psalms there can be no distinction between the heirs by promise or the heirs by adoption.

Notes

1/ Shalom—often simply translated as 'peace' but in Hebrew this covers so much more! This is peace of body, mind and spirit, so covers physical health and wholeness, relational health and wholeness, as well as spiritual health and wholeness, and a peace in relationship with our El Shaddai—our God who is more than enough.

So sometimes it is enough to translate this as 'peace' but there are times I have left this as 'Shalom'.

2/ Some Psalms read today like they were written today. Have a glimpse at the world news, and then take a read of Psalm 2, or Psalm 94, by way of example.

3/ 'Zion' is another word that is difficult to translate in this context. I have spelled out something of it in the beginning of Psalm 48. In Old Testament times, Zion was more than just the Temple Mount—it stood for the worshipping community of believers, often gathered there, with the Presence of the Lord at its very heart, in the Ark of the Covenant.

But this side of the cross, we are mindful of the New Jerusalem[4] that John saw in his vision on the island of Patmos, with the throne room of heaven at its heart, with the throne surrounded by the countless host of believers.

4/ Some Psalms I found very easy, and some I struggled with—aspects of many of them I did find difficult. I'm certainly not saying I have *the* definitive understanding of any of these Psalms! But equally, I believe what I have expressed here is a valid comprehension for us today, from our knowledge and understanding of ancient Hebrew, language, culture and belief, as is transformed through the cross of Jesus, the Mashiach.

5/ A couple of Psalms have a few verses here and there that express things that I really cannot reconcile to the 'Law of Love' that Jesus set out and exemplified for us. So please bear with me for these few instances.

Perhaps one of the hardest for me to approach was Psalm 29, which I know is quite a favourite for some. Holy Spirit really did surprise me here!

Then there are those few verses with words that make little sense in the Hebrew, and even less when strung together in English. A quick look at the different translations and everyone has their own—myself included. Here, I have tried to see the writer's heart and purpose over the whole Psalm. Psalm 68:10-16 is the one I remember the most.

6/ Capitalisation: much of this book is a conversation, so where I am addressing the Lord, I have capitalised Him as 'You' which, once you get used to it, you will find very helpful in understanding who I'm referring to. Similarly there are many facets or titles of our God where I have also chosen to capitalise; the Spirit of Peace, or Wonderful Counsellor being good examples. I hope this helps you realise just how much is

---

[4] Revelation 3:12, Revelation 21:2

addressed specifically to the Lord, and how Wonderful He is!

Enemies.

I think everyone has enemies! Everyone, wittingly or unwittingly, creates enemies as we walk through life. However, Jesus made it very clear that He expects us to love our enemies, and to bless those who hate and persecute us[5]. But in the unseen world there are also enemies—demon spirits who oppose the saints at every turn—however, these are subject to the Mighty name of Jesus. *We* are the ones called to resist them[6], and trample over them[7]—this is our responsibility as believers, and then to go on and set others free from their entanglement with them.

So for many of the Psalms, our enemies are primarily in the spirit world, but we are faced with a serious problem when a particular enemy epitomises evil, and is clearly very much driven under the influence of a demon, specifically targeting us. Under these circumstances, loving the sinner while hating their sin gets extremely difficult!

All of these facets have to be borne in mind in reading, translating, and praying through the Psalms.

      ***   ***   ***

What have I learned as a result of this prayer-walk through all of the Psalms? Perhaps the most surprising aspect is the appreciation and thankfulness of the Psalmists that God is a God of Truth and Justice, and has a particularly soft heart for the poor and needy. I add my Amen to that!

Oh what a sorry place this earth would be if Jesus had lost it along the way, or ducked out before it was finished. What a sorry place this would be if the king of this earth was the

---

[5] Matthew 5:44, Luke 6:27, Luke 6:35
[6] James 4:7
[7] Luke 10:19

adversary—a liar, a thief and a destroyer. As we see nations rage against Israel and Christianity, we glimpse something of what this would look like.

Oh, thank YOU King Jesus for going through with it right to the very end. How can we ever thank You enough?

But there is another aspect of our Papa God's nature that surprised me, though for any reader of the New Testament, it really shouldn't. And this is our Papa God's Joy and His love to party. Now what was the Prodigal Son's father's first reaction to the return of his son—to have a party! And who was the father representing in the story? And what did Jesus say happens in heaven when a sinner repents and has a change of heart?—it's party time! Aren't you glad that Papa is a God of JOY? I am! Just take a peep at the first few verses of Psalm 147, or the conclusion of Psalm 16 as two prize examples. This highlights the poignancy of Psalm 137, that their party songs were worship and praise to the Lord. I think we need to get a hold of the truth behind 1 Peter 1:8, "though we don't see Him right now, yet in our believing in Him, we rejoice with *joy* **unspeakable** *that is full of glory*" and Jude 24, "He is able to keep you and bring you absolutely faultless into the presence of His Glory with *exceeding joy.*"

Dignity is vastly over-rated—Steve Backlund.

Finally
Psalm 102— this is for you, Lou Engle.
"Now is the time."

Psalm 1

Thank You Lord for the Joy of knowing and following You. But it does seem strange that I forever find myself walking in the opposite direction to so many of those around me. I seem to keep having to step out of their way—and keep out of their way—as they mock You and all the things You hold dear. That grieves me, Papa.

Lord, it's Your blessing and Your direction I long for as I wake up. That wonderful privilege of knowing You and Your word and having Your Presence with me is what I think about as I go about my day, and Your love and peace enfold my thoughts as I settle down to sleep. Thank You so much! This way You help me to grow in favour with You and with those around me. You wash my heart clean from the muck and rubbish I was so entangled in before, and help my roots go deep into your life and love as I learn more about You and Your wonderful ways.

Lord, I want to grow strong like an oak or a cedar planted by a stream of water that never runs dry, even through what seems like the craziest drought—when Your hand of blessing is still evident to those around me—even when I've lost sight myself. I know my own frailty only too well—help me grow my roots so into You and Your ways and Your love that I always have things to thank You for.

I don't dare remember what I used to be like before You planted me into Your love. I was always being blown around with a guilty conscience. But You chose me and adopted me into Your family. You declared my sin forgiven and to be remembered no more[1] so I could stand before You as Your

---

[1] Jeremiah 31:34, Hebrews 8:12, Hebrews 10:17

beloved child—of Your Grace. Thank YOU so much!

Thank You Papa for how You watch over me and care for every aspect of my life, so that I grow strong in You. Thank You for saving me from myself and the path I would have taken without You, and Your wondrous love.

Psalm 2

Lord—I'm curious. Just why do so many set themselves against You and Your so obvious ways of peace and prosperity? I hear the news and it seems like so many nations and their leaders are not just dead set against You as they stir up trouble, but they're raging against You and Your ways! Just listening to them talk—it's clear they don't know You or in any way honour Your Son Jesus and the ways of Life He taught and demonstrated. All they seem to want to do is to grab power for themselves and dis everyone else, while bowing in political correctness to those who shout the loudest. It seems they have no respect for human life or the marriage vow, and twist the rule of law to their own ends.

And what do *You* do about it, Lord? What? Do I really catch You laughing at them—scoffing at them? *Oh,* You're going to pull the rug out from under them when they least expect it—bring it on, Lord, that'll get me laughing too! "They'll be terrified when their plans collapse on top of them"—such a shame they really can't see that ahead of time.

I'm so glad You set Your Son Jesus as King of Kings over all the nations. I love Your ways—He's so worthy of honour, of worship and the love of my heart. I remember how at His baptism You declared Him to be "Your Beloved Son in whom You were well pleased" and immediately following that in the wilderness He preferred to win His right to rule over the nations going Your way, rather than bowing to the adversary—Wow! that was a costly choice. So ALL the leaders and ALL the nations will bow the knee to You, Jesus, one day—willingly or unwillingly. I'll say my "Amen!" to that.

Oh you kings and leaders—would that you could see the destructive fruit you are growing by your hostility to King Jesus. It's not going to be long now and it will all descend catastrophically around your ears, with absolutely no way of escape, and you will be held accountable. No—neither we nor your subjects will be laughing at your demise, but we will be glad to see Righteousness rule in your place. *Oh* that you would turn to Jesus for His Wisdom and His way out of the holes you've dug for yourselves. He will show you, if you choose to ask Him. When He comes you will be flat on the floor with your nose in the dirt, in awe at His Glory, splendour and majesty. *Oh* that you would do that ahead of time.

But if you continue to refuse to listen, then His judgment of you will be fair and just, and you will reap all the pain and sorrow that you have caused others by your choices and actions. But you can save yourself from that now by turning to Him, and not only will you be blessed, but all those you lead or to whom you have to give account as well; everyone benefits.

Psalm 3

[A Psalm for James Bond.]

Sorry, David—I know you penned this at a very serious and painful point in your life, and I really don't mean this facetiously. But the situations Bond gets himself in exemplify this Psalm of David.

Lord—every way I turn I find enemies, either without or within. It looks like I'm totally hemmed in by them and completely incapacitated both physically and in spirit. I give up.

Lord I'm not just stuck, I'm out-of-it altogether.

It seems like all of them are singing in chorus that there's no escape and You are not going to do anything to help me, and my thoughts are joining in too… Aaaaaah!

But Lord!

Even though I can't see any way out, I trust YOU! In times past You always somehow delivered me and rescued me… even when I seriously messed up and even when it was all my fault, You still came through for me, and restored me, and amazingly increased my reputation.

"HELP, Lord! Help!"

I need more than just answers and nice words—I need action. I need You to *do* something! Thank You! Whether I see it or not, I say "Thank You!"

I'm not just worn out—I'm absolutely exhausted, and can't even keep my eyes open any longer. And when I sleep, my dreams are filled with pictures that wind me up further.

I give up, though I refuse to fear. If I've learned one thing, it's not to go down that path. And you enemies—"you can't threaten me with death—that just propels me into the presence of my King Jesus". I don't care how many of you there are tearing my guts out—"I will NOT fear!"

"HELP, Lord! Help"

When Jaws smiles his row of gold teeth at me and cracks his knuckles in gloating anticipation—You take him out for me. Thank You, Lord.

"Lord—I look to You and You alone for my rescue." Each time I say it, that glimmer of hope burns brighter inside, so I'll say it again, "Lord—I look to You and You alone for my rescue."

"Lord—I look to You and You alone!"

I want nothing more, and nothing less than Your blessing and Your mighty anointing, for me and for those I care for... *Oh*, how much I need YOU!

Jesus!

Psalm 4

Lord, why don't You answer me when I call on You? It seems like You never answer me when I call on You. Haven't I made you my God and my King? Is there more I can do? Aren't You a righteous God who loves Your children?

Lord—I need some help right now. Not tomorrow or next week, I need You to breathe Your precious Spirit over me and into me right now, or I'm losing it. I need Your Covenant Assistance—now.

As I look around, I'm surrounded by people pursuing their own selfish goals and treating You shamefully. The things they pursue are like gaudy advertisements that proclaim wonderful things, but their reality is so different, they are so unfulfilling—totally false. I'm surrounded by people chasing after these things and ignoring You and Your precious love and Your Presence. Even my own thoughts and desires are so easily seduced by their bright lights and easy promises—Aaaaah!

But Lord—I come back and remind myself of the destiny to which You've called me, and the wonderful plans and purposes You have for me—that You have called me for, that no-one else can do, to bring You Glory and Honour. Thank You, that You hear when I even just whisper Your precious name. "JESUS!"

And then as I toss and turn at night, I see how easily I could miss it altogether, like all the others—Aaaaaah!

So there in the dark, I grab hold of my thoughts and start to worship You again. *Oh,* that's so much sweeter, as I express my faith and my trust in You.

So while everyone else is whining and complaining about when they can start 'the good life', I turn my face to Yours, with a big 'Thank YOU', that gets even bigger as I sense afresh Your love and joy over me.

Thank You Jesus that the Joy and Grace You've put in my heart is so much greater, so much sweeter than the joy of winning that round of golf or the other equally stupid things people set such store by—though You may just need to remind me of that when they come in tomorrow celebrating something.

But tonight… Tonight, I'll rest with my heart fixed on You, celebrating the wonder of Your love and care for me. You're amazing, Lord. To think that You come and live in me—"me in you", and "you in me". Yeah God! Tonight I'm going to sleep like a baby, without a care in the world! Thank YOU so much!

Psalm 5

Lord—do You ever hear me, or listen to me? It really doesn't seem like You take any notice of what I'm thinking or saying to You... Do I have to remind You that I have made You my Lord and my King?—and I'm not just firing things around my head; in my imagination, I'm trying to address these issues to You.

Lord, You know that I start the day with You, looking to You and seeking Your direction and plans.

And I know that You really don't like the evil plans and purposes that so many dream up all around me, pursuing their own ends at any cost. Ugggh. Thank You that You are not party to that kind of thinking.

Lord, it's so easy to look around at arrogance, at malice, at hatred, at lies, *Oh,* this list could go on... but I know I'm only a step away from the same things myself, and these are such huge barriers to coming into Your loving Presence. Remind me, Papa, remind me of Your ways—to love my enemies, and give me the Grace to respond in patient love, like You do. Lord—I need Your help to do that, especially when they're slandering and dissing me out, while flattering me to my face.

I want to say "See they get what they deserve!" rather than "Father forgive!", but I know they're reaping precisely what they're sowing by ignoring You. I can see it happening.

But Lord... But Lord... But Lord—remind me to seek You and come to You in worship, encouraging everyone to join me, to fill up afresh on Your Spirit, on Your Joy. *Oh,* it's fun to shout Your praise—You're so worth it! You take such good care of Your children—Thank YOU! Come on, everyone, join me in a Holy Shout of praise to our Wonderful King Jesus... Hahahaha!

Thank You for blessing us so richly, and giving us such ready access to Your throne room, and surrounding us with Your Mighty Presence.

Psalm 6

Lord—please don't look at what I've done, or what I've not done… I really don't want Your pruning today. OK so I know You only prune and discipline those who You love, but I'm feeling far too fragile this morning.

Rather, Lord, I need Your Covenanted Assistance and help: I need Your healing—even my bones are aching.

Lord, whatever this is, it's serious. It seems like all of me, my heart and my spirit too, are screaming at me in pain. Heeeelp, Lord! Help! How much longer do I have to lie here in this agony?

Lord, haven't I often declared You as my healer and my deliverer? Come on, Lord, I need You to show up now.

Now, in Glory, I know everyone is praising You, and I look forward to joining them, but You won't get glory out of me dying—not right now, anyway. And it's not easy for me to encourage all of those here to worship and praise Your Wonderful name when all they've seen is You leaving me for dead, the very one who encourages them.

Lord, I'm absolutely exhausted—I'm shattered!

My bed is wringing wet from my sweating, my tears, and my worry…

This negativity is seriously getting me down—it's taking me under. It's got a hold of more than just my imagination…

You let go of me—you evil imaginings! Get out of my thoughts!

Lord it's in You who I trust—ahh that's better…

Lord it's in the Blood of Jesus I trust—the Covenant You cut with Jesus on our behalf… On *my* behalf! By His stripes I declare I'm healed, that I'm restored and made whole once more!

Jesus—I declare Your suffering wasn't in vain, but I receive Your healing and restoration! I receive it. I receive it right now!

You really don't get it, do you? You damnable demons! You're subject to the Mighty Name of Jesus! Git!

Wow!—Lord, that was closer than I care for. Thanks for saving me—I want to kick the head in of those horrible things! In Jesus' name I'll send 'em packing from all who come to me.

Psalm 7

Lord—It's me again… in trouble once more. I'm being hounded, and I need Your help again! HELP!

I just want to hide… and hide in You. I need an invisibility cloak…

I can hear the roaring of those lions getting forever louder and louder. They'll be on me in a moment and tear me limb from limb, slathering over me…

What have I done? We were getting on OK—I was helping them with their stuff—what's the problem now? What have I done to deserve this? Lord—if I've done anything to this bunch to deserve this, then OK—fair cop. But I haven't! Fair cop—then I'll just go and let them trample me. Aaaaaaah!

Lord—don't You ever get angry? I need You to get off Your butt and be angry for me. You may not care to protect my reputation, but everyone knows I go by Your name. So don't You care to protect *Your* reputation—Your reputation for righteousness and justice? I want You to gather and judge the nations and vindicate me in front of them. I know You judge the people with righteousness, so judge me in front of them all. I need You to stop their violent attacks on me, so give me Justice.

Lord, I give You full permission to expose my thoughts and the intents of my heart in this matter, because You are Righteous and Trustworthy. I trust in all that Jesus won for us—I plead the blood of Your Son. I declare that the scroll listing all my sins was nailed to the cross[1], and You have forgiven every one of them—not that I held anything against this bunch anyway!

---

[1] Colossians 2:14

Lord, I don't plead my righteousness in this, but Yours—take up my case!

I really don't want to be in the firing line of Your judgment—OUCH! Your sword is sharp[2] and Your fiery arrows always find their mark, just compounding the pain and misery of those who set themselves up against You. You see to it that their plotting finally falls from a great height, right on their heads.

Lord, I'm sorry for my attitude and self-righteousness a moment ago. I'm only counted as Righteous because of the amazing love and grace Your Son has shown to me. Thank You for Your wonderful forgiveness and for putting Your song of praise in my heart and on my lips. It's so, so good to sing Your praise! Jesus—You are so, so worth *all* my praise.

---

[2] Hebrews 4:12

Psalm 8

Lord—in coming to You I'm quite lost for words, and thoughts to express just how Awesome and Wonderful You are... My heart is just so full of Joy and Wonder at the magnitude and Glory of Your whole creation. And yet even babies and children as they shout and giggle with laughter declare how good You are! And there really is no answer to that.

When I look up at the night sky and see the amazing Hubble telescope pictures of galaxies so distant it hurts my brain to comprehend—I wonder at YOU! Did You throw them into space or set each of them in their place? If You planned the details of all of these billions of stars, how come You even spare a thought for each one of us?

And yet You gave us a remit to reign over the earth, to bring Your wonderful life, love, order and creativity into it. And even when we blew it and sinned You were still so intimately concerned that You came and became one of us, so You could give us back the baton we'd dropped... Absolutely amazing!

And You trust us as stewards to care for every aspect of this incredible world You put us in, whether it's the animals, the birds, the fish or the plants—You entrust Your unbelievable and intricate creation to us, whether it's the cities or those big open spaces, or the sky above or the deepest of the deep! *Oh,* help us to do a better job looking after it.

And yet after all that, You are so concerned as to the tiniest details of my life, my thoughts, my dreams and my longings. Lord—You are incomparable! I love You, my King and my God!

Psalm 9

Thank YOU Lord for Your amazing Love and Care—for ALL You do for me. Lord, from the very depth of my heart— "Thank YOU!"

This time I want to try and express all of those marvellous things You keep doing. *Oh*—this makes me so happy! I can't help but dance and shout and sing Your praise! Jesus, I lift Your name high—You are so worthy of all my praise and worship—Kings of Kings, and Lord of all Lords.

Many's the time it looked like I was done for, but somehow You always came through for me, and I know You always will. It never seemed to matter how small or big, or how self-inflicted, You've brought me through. Thank You that You never judge or condemn me, but even when I deserve it I find You are pleading my case and protecting me.

Thank You that, even when the nation's economy was taken down by greedy and unscrupulous bankers, they lost everything, and no-one will ever even remember who they were, but You still looked after my finances. It seems the same is equally true every which way I turn in every area of my life.

Oh, but YOU are King forever! You—King Jesus, Anointed One—thank You that Your throne is established forever, on the foundation of justice. Thank You that You never judged even the lady thrown at Your feet in adultery[1], and You're the same yesterday today and Forever[2].

Thank You that You have been such a refuge and help in the bad times, and through the truly diabolical times. *Oh*, what it is to whisper the name "Jesus!" and see You move. You are just so reliable.

---

[1] John 8:11
[2] Hebrews 13:8

Worthy, worthy are You, King Jesus—enthroned on the worship and praise of those who love You. You are never far away. *Oh*! it's so good to sing Your praise, and declare Your Goodness and Mercy to all; to tell everyone of Your loving care of me, delivering me, and providing for me. The foundation of Your throne is justice, and we can trust You that You will give it to us when we cry to You.

But Lord, I leave their case with You—I forgive them and refuse to hold their case against them, but at the same time I know You never forget...

Papa God, I worship You; I remind us both of the precious Covenant that Jesus cut with You on our behalf and I plead Your Covenant Assistance. Lord, I need Your assistance right now or I'm a goner, and I can't thrill Your people with the stories of the marvellous things You've done for me when I'm six foot under.

As I listen to the news and see the turmoil across the nations, it does look like they are falling into the very pits they have dug for themselves through their injustice—it's like I can see it happening in slow motion. I guess it's You showing this to me, 'cause others really can't see it. And it is so inevitable without You at the helm.

Thank You Lord that You never forget the needy; help me remember to do my bit for them, too, out of the richness of the care You have for me. Hope triumphs with You because You are the God-of-Hope[3].

As I look at the nations, Lord—stir Yourself! Please don't let those who don't know You triumph and rule. We need You to arise, Lord, and remind them of their mortality—that for all their efforts they are here only a moment, and can take nothing with them, while the increase of *Your* Kingdom never ends[4].

---

[3] Romans 15:13, 1 Timothy 1:1
[4] Isaiah 9:7

Psalm 10

Lord—where are YOU? Why is it that You always seem so far away, just at those times when I really need You?

Today it looks like I'm surrounded by arrogance and greed. *Oh*—it's *You* showing me the machinations of their thoughts and the evil they reap, as they hunt out those they can prey on—those who they can manipulate by their evil boastful scheming. And all the while they bless and big-up the greedy while turning their noses up at You.

Lord—I think I'd rather not see this—now You're showing me their prosperity, while all the time they totally reject You and Your ways. They even sneer and mock their enemies, while declaring nothing can reach them, or touch their fortune.

Lord—I really don't want to see this next scene—as they lie and threaten, bully and harass innocent people. What's this? An ambush, and murder—but the victim wasn't doing anything! Just in the wrong place at the wrong time. Now You're showing me a lion crouching in cover. *Oh* that this Lion was You, Lord—as the Lion of the Tribe of Judah—the Righteous Lion—King forever. But no—this one has evil intent waiting to catch the helpless. Hey—pick on someone your own size! Why do they always pick on the weak and helpless—I guess they don't fight back as hard. You cowards! How can you say, "God never sees or notices"?

OK, Lord—You've shown me that You *do* see. So what are *You* going to do about it?

Oh... You're asking *me* to...

But first, Lord, why do the wicked hate You so? How come they really think they'll get away with it and never be called to account? Lord, I don't get it.

You've shown me how You grieve over the weak and helpless and the mess they're in. Can I really help? Can I really make a difference? You really want *me* to comfort and help the victims—*Oh*, You've been showing me how *You* see them so I will pick up on Your heart and Your loving care. OK—so I need Your help and Your anointing for this, Lord, if I'm to lead them to You and introduce them to You, Holy Spirit, the Comforter[1], and to You, Papa God, so that they come to see they are orphans no longer, but ask to be adopted into Your family.

You what?! You also want me to shout abroad and blow open the wickedness and injustice that You've shown me, so that everyone sees and hears about it? They'll all be on *my* neck then, won't they? Ahhhh, but I have You at my back— Thanks—I'm going to need Your help if I'm to make any long term difference.

Oh… Thank You that You are King forever, at the back of all who look to You and trust in You. Thank You that You are such a Great Dad to all who come to You.

---

[1] John 14:16, John 14:26, John 16:7

Psalm 11

Lord—it's in YOU I trust. (Period!)

So all you thoughts telling me to go here or go there—you shut up!

I can see you plotting to manipulate me out of my current position, laying traps for me to walk right in. Even when I can't see you stretching your trip-wire in the dark, for those who love Jesus—*I* will not fear. You don't have to tell me that I'm not politically correct.

And don't give me that argument that there's nothing we can do 'cause the whole structure of our society is being destroyed by their crazy ungodly thinking'.

"Greater is He who is in me than he that is in the world"[1]. I declare that! Thank You Holy Spirit! Thank You that the *increase* of Your Kingdom shall never end.

I declare that You, Lord, still rule OK. You're still seated on Your wonderful throne in the heavenlies, and I too am Your holy temple[2], and You still live in me, and we have nowhere near finished the job You gave us to do, to make disciples of all the nations.

Thank You Lord that You still run to and fro across the whole earth[3] taking Your amazing care of those who love You. *Oh,* but what fearful judgment awaits those who violently set themselves against You and those You love, who reject Your amazing Mercy, Love and Forgiveness. Lord, I want to be out of the way when You bring the evil they've been sowing on

---

[1] 1 John 4:4
[2] 1 Corinthians 6:19
[3] 2 Chronicles 16:9

their own heads—the story of the destruction of Sodom and Gomorrah[4] is close enough for me.

So, Lord, I thank YOU that You are righteous, and that You love Righteousness. Thank You that Your Kingdom is a Kingdom of Righteousness built and established on a foundation of Justice[5]. I like that.

Thank You Lord that those who love You just have to turn their heart and spirit humbly up to You and they can sense the smile of love on Your face. Thank You so much that You've promised never to leave us or forsake us[6].

---

[4] Genesis 19:24
[5] Psalm 89:14
[6] Deuteronomy 31:6

Psalm 12

Help, Lord! I need Your Help. Are there any left who love You and Your ways? I'm having a job finding anyone who values Faith, Loyalty and Honesty. It seems I'm surrounded by people who despise these qualities, loving double-speak, exaggeration and flattery. *Oh* that You would shut them up, and spare me their boasting. They even boast how they can talk their way out of anything.

Oh Lord, go on. Please silence them. It's not just me; the poor and the needy have had more than enough of their boasting and exploitation. We look to You, knowing Your words aren't like that, but they are trustworthy and true, that "we can cast all our worries, our cares, and all that pains us onto You, because You care for us and watch over us with such loving tenderness."[1]

Thank You Lord that You watch over Your word to perform exactly what You promised[2]—and all You expect of us is that we remind You of Your promises. *Oh,* thank You Lord that Your word is true gold, refined, refined and refined—and not just Your word, but You Yourself are Trustworthy and True[3].

Thank You Jesus that You will give Your precious Shalom-Shalom—Your perfect peace—to those who keep their heart set on trusting You[4], saving them from all the grief of those who strut about, depending on sweet-talking their way through life.

---

[1] 1 Peter 5:7
[2] Jeremiah 1:12
[3] Revelation 3:14, Revelation 19:11
[4] Isaiah 26:3

Psalm 13

I'm still waiting, Lord—it seems like forever.

Lord—have You entirely forgotten me? Where are You? I'm so trying to find You—I've been searching everywhere. Where are You, Lord? How much longer do I have to contend with these crazy gloomy, self-destructive thoughts running forever round my head—will you never stop? Lord, they're gaining on me, and I'm sinking under their continual barrage.

Lord, I need You to come and find me and speak Your word afresh into my heart—Your word of Life and Light that dispels their impact in a moment. Just one word from You, that's all it takes. I'm losing it, Lord, I'm about to go under...

Now I don't mind Your people, Lord, dancing on my grave, when I've gone, in order to receive Your mantle of blessing on their lives as You've blessed mine in times past, but I can do without my enemies dancing and gloating that they've put me six foot under.

But Lord... But Lord—I trust in Your unfailing love, that Your mercies are new every morning[1], and Great and Mighty is Your faithfulness to Your word of life[2]—Your everlasting promises. Lord, I *choose* to rejoice that You have forgiven me and I can come boldly to Your wonderful throne of Grace to receive the help I need[3]. Thank You that You have made me a new creation[4]—that You've put Your heart and Your Spirit within me—so I can't help but do a Glory jig and sing and shout Your praise.

Oh, Thank YOU—JESUS!

---

[1] Lamentations 3:23
[2] Psalm 145:13
[3] Hebrews 4:16
[4] 2 Corinthians 5:17

Psalm 14

How stupid it is to say "There is no God." Now that really has to be dumb! It doesn't change for a moment the fact that He exists and that He loves outrageously—even someone as stupid as that! The trouble is that the person who says that goes on to a life devoid of the very things God likes and loves.

The Lord searched to find any who sought Him and His ways, and found none... People were so busy pursuing their own agendas, like pigs in muck pushing others aside in the muddy muddy to grasp their bit. They grab what they can from others and trample on them, never thinking of the Lord and what His agenda for them or those around them might look like.

But when You, my King Jesus, show up, then they will be genuinely terrified, and ashamed of their behaviour. Thank You that You are such a refuge for those few who do look to You in the middle of this pigpen.

Oh Come—King Jesus! Come, Holy Spirit! Restore the knowledge of You and of Your Precious Presence as we gather to worship You. For only then will the captive be set free from his bondage, only then will there be genuine rejoicing and laughter, carefree singing and dancing Your praise—Mighty King Jesus. You, and only You, know how to untie the heart and set the human heart truly free.

Psalm 15

Oh, My King Jesus, Anointed One, it's so good to dwell in, and spend time in Your precious presence, and to gather with others in worship and enjoying You and the wonder of Your lovingkindness.

Oh, how I love those who love You, who take the time and the care to do things right. Those whose inner world and inner voice matches the words of life that they speak. They cover for their friends' mistakes and take their rap to protect them. They don't look down their noses at those less fortunate than themselves, but bend over backwards to help lift them out of the chaos and mess they created.

They honour and respect those who know and love You—King Jesus.

They stick by their word and their promise even when that's seriously hard to do, and they don't change their minds, just because of the circumstances.

They don't lend money at extortionate interest rates, or take advantage of others, but rather seek how to bless; how to help and to raise the poor out of their poverty to a place of blessing and overflowing provision, so they in turn can go on and bless others.

Thank You that those who live life this way will always know Your blessing and favour on their lives, and on their families.

Psalm 16

Thank You Lord for all Your loving care.

Jesus, it's in You I trust.

You are my Lord, You are my God.

All the good in my heart, You've put there. Thank You so much.

All you His saints, you who love His Mighty name, I bless you and thank you for your encouragement—you are such a loyal bunch, full of faith in our King Jesus—I know our Papa God loves to delight in you and pour out His blessing on you all.

But you fearful ones who pursue your own selfish satisfaction—I take no part in what you get up to. Trouble is your middle name—it is chasing you down. Ugh—I don't even want your name on my lips.

But Jesus, You and You alone, are my Lord and my God, You are my inheritance, my royal provider, and You guard all that You have generously blessed me with. And then You go and give me this green and pleasant land flowing with milk and honey[1], as an inheritance as well and then promise that my lineage will rule for ever...[2] Lord, You're amazing!

Lord, I bless You for how You lead and guide me, and quicken my heart in You and Your ways in the night. Thank You that You are always with me, so I confidently say, "I will not be shaken," for You will never, ever leave me[3].

---

[1] Leviticus 20:24 et al.

[2] 2 Samuel 7:16

[3] Deuteronomy 4:31, Deuteronomy 31:6, Hebrews 13:5

So Lord, I rejoice and lift high Your wonderful name—JESUS! I'm secure in You whatever happens, so when they are dancin' around my grave I know I'll be in Glory dancing before Your heavenly throne, giving You the honour and worship that You so richly deserve. For Jesus, You are my Saviour, and Lord, and You live and reign Forever.

Thank You that You have revealed to me the path of life—the way of Joy in Your Presence, that simply continues on through all eternity.

Psalm 17

Are You there, Lord? Are You listening?

Lord, I need some vindication. I need some justice. Aren't You the God of Justice?

I'm not out to even the score, but I need it clear to all that You have vindicated me.

I need it clear to all that You have searched my heart, that You have cross-examined me in the night, and there is absolutely no case against me; that I haven't plotted or spoken anything that You would take issue with.

Lord—You've seen how people have tried to bribe me, violently confronting me and accusing me. But You've seen how I haven't retaliated with violence, though I sure came close a few times. Thank You for helping me not react their way—Your ways are so much sweeter.

So Lord, I call on You.

Oh remind me—remind me Lord, of the wonders of Your Grace and Your mighty Covenanted Assistance for those who seek You out, who love You and seek to live Your way, loving our enemies rather than claiming an eye for an eye[1]. *Oh,* protect me as the very apple of Your eye—Lord hide me! Hide me under the shadow of Your mighty pinions, Your powerful outstretched wings.

Lord, I'm surrounded, and these enemies have absolutely no compassion. They are so arrogant in their threats and lies about me. They keep looking for any and every chance to trip me up and flatten me. They're like hungry lions eager to tear me to pieces... *Oh,* thank You Lord for showing me that they're only like lion cubs, who are still learning how to stalk

---

[1] Matthew 5:38

properly in secret, but they crouch, pretending, right out in the open for me to see them—LOL!

Lord—how about You save them? How about You confront them with the unstoppable wonder of Your Love and Grace, so they are flat on their faces with their noses in the dirt before You? Thank You that Your sword divides even the thoughts and attitudes of the heart[2]. That would be neat, Lord. Then You can fill them with all their hearts' desire without them chasing jealously after me for it. And that way they will have enough left over for their children and their children's children too.

As for me, Lord—it's more of You that I want. I want to see more of Your loving heart, to know more of You, Holy Spirit, living in me. Jesus—just to know You more!

---

[2] Hebrews 4:12

Psalm 18

Oh, my King Jesus, Anointed One—You are my strength. Thank You that You have my back (and my front and my sides!). *Oh* what a rock You are to stand on—You never change; You are my fortress, and You always deliver me. You, Jesus, are my rock, the one in whom I trust, in whom I hide, in whom I take refuge.

Oh what a shield You are to me, my Saviour, hidden in You[1] is like being in a high tower, well out of reach of even my worst enemy.

Thank You Jesus that You always come to my help when I call—my enemies never get a chance, death and evil don't get even so much as a look-in—*Oh,* worthy, worthy are You my King, of all my praise. Death was tightening its grip on me as I was being bombarded by a torrent of ungodly abuse. I looked to be all in, done for, but I wasn't quite ready to give up—*Oh* why was I so slow to call on You, my King? The moment I cried out to You for help, everything changed! You heard my shout and came running... Your love for me was so fierce—it felt like the whole earth shook—the foundations of the mountains trembled at Your anger. I'm sure I would have seen smoke from Your nostrils—the smoke from the consuming anger that burns in Your heart, over me. Wow!

When the torrent was about to go over my head, You lifted me clear, and delivered me. Thank You Lord—they were so much stronger than I. They came when I was down already, but You, my King... Wow—You stood back of me—well more than enough! Thank You! And You brought me out into an open space where we could dance with delight—*Oh* how

---

[1] Colossians 3:3

You delight in me! *Oh,* thank You Jesus—*Oh,* You know how I delight in You.

Thank You that You don't reward us with judgment for our sin, but only with Your Mercy and forgiveness. Rather, You delight to reward our simple trust in You, and our simple boldness to tell others of the wonderful things You do for us. You so delight to honour our simple faith, in bringing Your Kingdom rule down to planet Earth. You know just how hard it can be to refuse all fear, and yet love, love and love again—to forgive even the most grievous hurt... and to keep trusting You, Papa God. Your rewards are really eye-opening when we finally catch them—how You reward love with more love, how those who generously forgive are themselves generously forgiven, those who show mercy at great cost, find Your great Mercy pouring into their laps.

Oh, thank You for showing me what it looks like on the other side of the fence. The liars find themselves being lied to. The thief's house is itself broken into, and the proud find themselves up against something a lot stronger than they are[2]— *Oh* Yes. Thank You Lord that You have Your ways of cutting them down to size!

Thank You Lord that You direct my path—that You floodlight it for me, and make me look like a super-hero! I single-handedly put an army to flight[3], and on Your springboard I can jump over anything! *Oh,* Papa God, Your ways are such fun! Can I really do that? *Oh* Jesus—Your word always works, for You show us just how. *Oh* what a shield and defence You are, if only we remember to call on You.

Oh my King Jesus—who is God but You? *Oh* what a rock You are, and You alone for me to stand on, so securely. And it's You, Lord, and You alone who gives me the strength to

---

[2] James 4:6, 1 Peter 5:5
[3] Deuteronomy 32:30, 1 Samuel 14:6-23

carry on, and carry on the way You want me to, keeping Your values of Truth and Love. *Oh,* You make my feet like those of a mountain goat—*Oh,* I love how they dance on the cliffs of Engedi springing from cliff edge to cliff edge. *Oh* that I may similarly jump and run in headlong abandon, trusting You my King, and being equally sure-footed through such perilous times and situations so that You can put me in high places—not just to admire the view, but to command Your Kingdom rule.

Oh, thank You Jesus for showing me how You would have me fight to tear down every argument, every proud logic that exalts itself against the knowledge of You[4]. And how to take my own thoughts captive to Your precious anointing[5]. You equip me with that wonderful shield of faith that blocks every fiery dart[6], so protecting my heart—that wonderful shield of faith in You, King Jesus, my Saviour. Thank You that You hold my right hand, and You don't let go[7], *Oh,* but You do it so gently.

Thank You for setting a clear path for my feet so that I can pursue and overtake every enemy—You even lengthen my stride and kept me from tripping… Yep, I need to keep going till I have blotted out every one of them—torn down, thrust through, and trampled under my feet… *Oh,* thank You for equipping me with all that I need for this battle, and that You have put under my feet every one of these arguments and pride that one time stared me in the face. *Oh,* they're now on the run, but You equip me to cut them down, every last one. They cried and argued, even quoting scripture, but no deal. Then I trampled on them, turned them to dust under my feet—that

---

[4] 2 Corinthians 10:5
[5] 2 Corinthians 10:5
[6] Ephesians 6:16
[7] Isaiah 41:13

blew away in the wind, 'naught but muck'.

Oh, thank You King Jesus for delivering me from strife—that's a killer. Rather, You have made me the head and not the tail. Many who need deliverance now look to me as their answer as their demons and fears cower and run at Your Mighty name, "King Jesus", on my lips. They truly run out of their victims, Yeaah!

Oh, my King Jesus—You reign—You are the King, all praise to You my Rock, my Saviour. For You are the one to clothe me with this anointing and subdue these under me—saving me from them all[8]. *Oh,* thank You, Thank You, Thank You King Jesus, for You have indeed been given all power, over the lot of them—all Praise to Your Wonderful name! *Oh* what songs of victory You give me to sing and dance to… Yeaaah!

Thank You, King Jesus, Son of David, that You are the great deliverer. *Oh,* thank You for the amazing lovingkindness and such incredible love and care You show to Your anointed ones who know and love You. Now and always, You're the same.

---

[8] Luke 10:19

Psalm 19

Thank You Lord for this amazing universe that You so carefully and wonderfully designed for us—every second of every day it declares Your wondrous Glory as stars radiate their light that streams out at some amazing speed, seemingly forever. Every facet that we explore, whether it's the sun in all its radiance or the night sky with its myriads of stars and galaxies, it all shouts of Your amazing handiwork! Every day it speaks to us of Your loving care and every night it speaks of Your Royal Grandeur as we delve into the weird and wonderful mysteries of the cosmos and try and comprehend its magnitude, its variety and complexity.

Though they don't use words, that doesn't mean they don't speak to us. All those looking up at the night sky, wherever they are, can't help but be in awe at Your magnificence, whether they're looking down their telescopes at the top of a mountain in Hawaii, or at the Amundsen-Scott base at the South Pole, or just gazing up at the sky from their street corner.

And it appears You set our sun in a very unimportant place, in a quiet corner of a very standard galaxy, and then set this world of ours spinning around it, so that every day, just like clockwork, the sun comes up in a blaze of colour and glory (like a bridegroom on his wedding day) and warms everything up just right as it traverses across the sky, and then descends in another amazing light show.

Thank You Lord that the universe isn't some random chaotic construction, but You planned and engineered it to work so beautifully for us, with simple physical laws undergirding the whole thing. And these laws aren't forever chopping and changing, but remain as You set them up at the outset. And then You even go on and share with us some of these amazing laws and principles so we can begin to comprehend not just our universe, but You and Your wonderful ways.

Thank You that Your law for us, too, doesn't forever change in the wind, but what was good yesterday is good today, and what was bad yesterday is bad today, too. Thank You for sharing with us Your wisdom in how to do life—without You showing us we really are so blind on that score.

And thank You that You are a God of Great Joy and that, as we understand You and Your laws and ways and choose to live that way ourselves, we can't help but become full of Your wonderful JOY. And with Your Holy Spirit's help we have clean hands and pure hearts, and start to comprehend just how wonderful life is when lived Your way—that Your law of love is just so true and right—and will always be so. *Oh,* thank You Lord!

Lord, it often doesn't look right or feel good in the moment, but Your law of forgiveness and mercy is simply the best. We have to acknowledge that Your law is right and true, and that knowing You and Your law really is so much more worthwhile, so much more valuable than a sack full of gold or a great meal. In simply living as You intend, You help us avoid making painful pitfalls, and we end up with those things that we really do value, after all. Lord, You're so amazing!

Thank You I haven't got to worry about all of those unintentional things that just happen, or worry about the faults I am completely oblivious to. Thank You that You judge the thoughts and intents of the heart, rather than the outward signs. So Lord where I really need Your help is in that inner world of arrogance and presumption.

Lord, the more I know and understand You, the more I want to snuggle up close to You—to clean up not just my 'act' but all that I am, so that I think Your thoughts, and see Life Your way, through Your eyes of Love. Lord, I know I can never earn or deserve Your love for a moment, but thank You so much that, as I trust in what Jesus has done, You count me Righteous and Blameless in Your sight—You count me as Your beloved one.

Oh! You are my Rock and my Redeemer—Wonderful One!

Psalm 20

Oh, thank You Lord that You always hear when I call to You. Thank You that there's power, wonder-working power in the Mighty name of Jesus, to which every knee has to bow, in heaven, on earth and things under the earth[1], and You have mandated us to use Your name[2].

Oh, thank You for how You stand back of Your Mighty Name, and You expect us to use it, and rely on You to come through for us. Thank You that You never fail.

Oh, King Jesus thank You for going through with the sacrifice of Yourself for me, as my sin offering, as Your love-offering on my behalf. Wow! & Wow!

All praise and Glory to Your mighty name!

And thank You Jesus for the desire of Your heart to bless me—to respond to the deepest longings and desires of my heart, with the amazing plans and purposes You have for me. *Oh,* You even tell us to ask Papa in Your name that our JOY may be full[3]. Help me to help You bring these things about and not sabotage them by my own failings, unbelief and sin.

Yeah! Yeah! & Yeah! Mighty King Jesus! I delight to shout the Wonders of Your Mighty name. You even ordained that my middle name should be Victory! *Oh,* I lift High the name of Jesus—for You are God—Lord of All! Thank You that Your banner over me is Love[4]—is Love, Love and yet more Love—from beginning to end, love.

Oh, thank You Jesus for giving us Your name—that You call us to know You and Your heart so that whatever we ask

---

[1] Philippians 2:10
[2] Matthew 28:18, John 14:13, John 15:16, John 16:23, John 16:26
[3] John 16:24
[4] Song of Solomon 2:4

You, we can consider it done[5]. That all Your promises are Yes, Yes & Yes, as we give You our Amen[6]. And thank You Papa that having given us Your Son to be our Saviour, You so freely want to give us everything we need to help bring Your Kingdom here to earth[7].

Thank You, thank You Lord that You and Your precious anointing wins *every* time![8] And You anoint us with the same Holy Spirit who raised Jesus from the grave[9]—Yeaaah!

---

[5] John 15:15-16

[6] 2 Corinthians 1:20

[7] Matthew 6:10, Luke 10:9, Luke 11:2, Luke 11:20, Romans 8:32

[8] Zechariah 4:6, 1 John 2:27,
   Acts 11:26 note "Christian" means 'little anointed one'

[9] Romans 8:11—Luke 24:49, Acts 2

Psalm 21

Thank You Lord for King David. Thank You for how You saved him and blessed him as an example for us of all that You so long to do for us too—and more, as Your New Covenant love slaves.

Thank You Lord that You crown me with so much more Joy than everyone else—haha! *Oh,* You are just so Good to me! Thank You for saving me and giving me a new heart and spirit—I can't praise and thank You enough!

Thank You that You know the deep longing of my heart without my saying anything, and delight to bless me with so much more than I would have dared to ask for. Yeaaaah!

Thank You Lord that the moment I turn my face to You, You meet me, and with such a loving and gracious smile—*Oh,* Thank You! And You crown me with a crown so much more precious than gold—with Your lovingkindness and tender mercy.[1]

Lord, You know how I love life—*Oh,* it's such fun, especially walking with You—and You've given me such a long and fulfilling life—it's been full of such good times— thank You Jesus! And then even when this is finished we have the rest of eternity to enjoy You—Wow!

As I glory in my weakness and Your saving Grace and Strength—Lord, You're amazing in how You honour me, and then make me look like You!

Can anyone be more blessed than I am? Is that possible? *Oh* Lord, there's such JOY in Your Presence[2].

Lord, I trust in You, that absolutely nothing can come

[1] Psalm 103:4
[2] Jude 24, 1 Peter 1:8

between us or move me from this joyful place of blessing and intimacy with You. Thank You that You take care of all the things that could spoil it, way before I would know, and You just deal with them. They just get burned up by the fiery jealousy of Your love for me. Absolutely nothing will come from them—they really don't have a chance to take root before they disappear in flames.

Thank You Lord that what was meant for evil against me has just vaporised in Your precious Presence—it had no chance! Rather—their arrows pieced their own hearts.

Oh! Be exalted, Mighty King Jesus! All Praise and Glory to Your wonderful name!

Psalm 22

Lord, this next Psalm ties my heart up in knots. I take my shoes off—this is Holy Ground—before You—that You should steady Your thoughts, while hanging there on the cross for me, for my sin, by reciting this Psalm. So, out of what experience did David pen this? Or did You place this prophetically on his spirit? Whatever—Lord—these words describe Your situation even more graphically than Isaiah, and yet no-one, even those hearing You, seemed to make that connection.

Oh God, My God, why, why, why have You left me now— right when I really need You? Why are You so far away? Can't You hear my painful groaning, I really don't know how much of this I can take.

But Papa, forgive them—they have no idea what they are actually doing—they don't know who I am, I'm just another one they've been told to crucify.

Oh my God, I cry out, I cry out to You—and I sense You are just so far away, and totally deaf to my cry...

So this is what sin and shame does, it cuts the person off from any sense of Your Presence, even of Your reality. I know You haven't left me, Papa—though it sure feels like You have, but I know You said "I will never leave You or forsake you."[1] I just don't feel You answer, and even now as the sky darkens like night time, I still feel nothing.

But You, Papa, You are still the Mighty Holy One, the God and Covenant Partner of Israel. It was in You the Patriarchs

---

[1] Deuteronomy 31:6

trusted, and it was You who came to their rescue and blessed them so. They cried out to You and You didn't disappoint. You never disappointed.

Papa—I'm crying out to You now—and I too am trusting that You won't disappoint me. There's too much hanging on this.

Oh, but We, the Trinity, planned this before We even started to create this universe. Did I really volunteer for *this*? Why on earth did I volunteer to leave the two of You and come to this orphan planet...? Yes—it was love, love, love calling out to them. And, Yes, they are so, so worth it. Yeah... they needed an example to see just how loving and good You are Papa... I can see now just how one of the effects of sin and shame, is it makes that so impossible to see.

I'm reduced now to a worm, it feels like I've been stripped even of what it was to have been a man. All around, they scorn me and mock me. The mockery shows as they jeer and shake their heads and wag their fingers at me:

Papa—it's in You I trust—I see this playing out to the letter.

"He trusted in the Lord—let Him rescue him now; if He loves him like he always boasted, then let Him come and rescue him now, in front of us."

Wow—that's a tough side-swipe, Papa. I'm hanging in there.

For You prepared this body for me, implanting it in a very special and wonderful Mum. And timed everything so perfectly. And from that moment on, even when I was just a baby suckling at my mother's breast, we had to depend so heavily on Your care and protection.

42

Oh Mary are you here watching this? Thanks for everything. John—is that you there? Is that you there with my Mom? Thanks! Thank you so much—will you take her in and look after her for me? Mary—this is your son, now. John—she is your mother, from now on[2].

Oh Lord, please keep close—for trouble is all around me, and there is no-one to help. Many fierce bulls have surrounded me—encircling me. Their snorting and taunting are like roaring lions squabbling over their kill.

You've lost it now... see even all your disciples have deserted you. We've got you now. Who do you think you are? You'll be forgotten in a moment. You don't really think anyone will remember you do you? Get real.

I refuse to listen to you demons. Your time will come.

My very life is just draining away like water; it feels like all my bones are dislocated. My heart is just a fire inside melting away like wax, while my throat is just so dry, like on old broken bit of pot; my tongue is stuck to my mouth; it can't be long now.

It's OK, Papa—we still on track. Thanks for the reminder with the details, yes my shoulders are well and truly dislocated, and what happened in Gethsemane to my heart— something just broke there, but it'll last long enough.

I'm surrounded by baying dogs; this pack of evil is closing in on me. They rammed their nails through my hands and my feet, and it feels in my nakedness that all of my bones are on display—I could count them all.

We've got you now... trapped and as good as dead— Hahaha. Right where we want you... Hell next, but we'll

---

[2] John 19:26,27

enjoy making the journey as painful as we can for you. There's no hope for you now.

You demons—you can bay and yelp all you want…

Thanks, Papa—thank You that these here can't see it, and realise what's going on. Please forgive them—they have no idea that this is for them.

They stare gloatingly at me; they share my clothing among themselves casting lots for my one garment.

It's almost like we're ticking off the details… thanks, Papa—it is reassuring to see the details being played out.

But Papa—I love You—please don't leave me now. I trust that even now, even when I can't feel Your precious Presence, that You are indeed faithful, and "You will never leave me or forsake me—ever!" And as my strength ebbs away, You are the strength of my life… please come quickly to help me.

Thank You Papa—not much longer now…

Please deliver me from the cutting edge of their attacks on me and deliver my life from the grip of these evil demons. I'm looking to You Papa to save me from being ripped to pieces by these lions and my very life gored and skewered on the horns of these wild bulls…

Papa—I've only ever known Your precious presence. I daren't think of the horrors and terrors ahead, but I'll carry it this one time for the sake of all these brothers and sisters You've given me, however black it gets, they are so worth it.

Then I will Praise You my Lord and my God in front of all my brothers and sisters! In the mighty throne room of heaven I will praise and lift You high, Papa God, before that crowd too numerous to count. You who know and fear the Lord—give Him honour and praise… Give Him the reverence He deserves. You mighty crowd of witnesses lift high your praise, for He hasn't really spurned or scorned my suffering, and even though it looked like it, He didn't hide His face from me. Thank You Papa that You listened to the cries of my heart through this. And before Your mighty throne I'll praise You with that countless host; and I will fulfil absolutely and completely the promises we made together on their behalf.

Thank You Papa for this reminder of our Heavenly home—and the Joy that awaits.

Those who love You will then eat their fill of Your loving-kindness and goodness, and those who seek You and hunger to know You more, will be filled to overflowing and praise You—rejoicing in Your life and love through all eternity!

Thank You Holy Spirit for impressing this on David. Thank you David for setting down this Psalm, and thank you for including this last stanza.

And thank you Mama for teaching me this precious Psalm while I was just a child on your knee—long before I would have any idea of what it would mean to me.

Even the ends of the earth will one day learn of You and Your ways, and turn to give You honour and worship; and the nations of the earth will become like families, loving, providing, and caring for each other, and will Rejoice in their worship and love of You.

For You, Papa, are the only true King of all the earth, over all the nations. And all who have gone before will also kneel and bow in loving adoration of their High King.

As for me—I will love You forever, and my descendants also. And their generations too will learn of You and tell everyone of the deliverance; the redemption that You have engineered and implemented, for all generations.

Thank you David—One day… One day even the ends of the earth will come to know You, Papa, and Your wondrous love. All those who have already died will have the choice to bow before You, Papa, in worship, and for generation after generation down the ages will come to know You.

But for now—no person or demon will take my life from me, I choose to lay it down when I choose.

I freely lay it down, Papa, and I trust You that in due time, I may take it back.[3] No-one takes it from me.[4]

Continued in Psalm 31:

Papa, it's in You I'm trusting. I bear this sin and this shame as a free-will, love-sacrifice to You, that all those You give Me may know Your deliverance from them and all their effects. Thank You that You know the whisper of my heart and that You will be delivering me soon enough. Oh, thank You that You are such a strong and solid rock for my heart to stand on, even now, and Your Word stands forever for me to rest on and trust in.

May I represent You well, Papa, even here.

Thank You, that You will pluck me out of this net, in due time. It's in You and You alone who I trust.

Papa, it's into Your Mighty hand I commit My Spirit![5]

---

[3] John 10:17
[4] John 10:18
[5] Luke 23:46

Psalm 23

Today Jesus, I look to You. What a privilege to have You as my shepherd. You're the best; You know each one of us by name as You call us out. *Oh,* what a shepherd You are! Thank You that today and tomorrow I will lack no good thing, but rather You are going to lead me today by still water, where I can drink in Your Love and Your Presence—Your Joy and loving care, that restores Your Joy and Peace afresh in my soul, my inner man. Thank You that today You will lead us to green pastures where I can eat my fill of your words of LIFE to my spirit, my soul and my body.

And when tomorrow's route looks rough—down a path of deep hopelessness, grief and despair—a darkness such that I can't see the way ahead, I will set my hope and my trust that You will be the same then as You are today, leading me, protecting me and providing for me. I will listen for the tap, tap of Your shepherd's crook on the rocks in front of me, that will reassure me. I know You are always on the lookout for what would take me out, and that You use that crook so skilfully to guard, and defend me and keep me close to Yourself.

You so love to prepare a wonderful feast for me; a feast fit for a king, with the table laden with all of the things You know I find just so delicious, while my enemies can do nothing about it, but look on with their drooling tongues hanging out and their bellies rumbling with hunger.

And having feasted, You've then booked me an appointment in your massage parlour where You anoint me with Your Mighty Overcoming Spirit, while I drink in Your love and truth that overflows my emotions and my understanding. Ahhh—too Good!

You so transform the jagged raw places of my heart and life that with Your anointing overflowing, I leave behind me a trail of Your Goodness and Mercy—Your Healing, Your Forgiveness and Grace—Thank You so much!

Then one day I get to spend the rest of eternity with all the others who love You like I do—where we can worship You, Wonderful Jesus—King of Kings, forever. Hey—but don't bring that on too quickly, I want to make the most of all of this that You so richly lavish on me here in the land-of-the-living. I want others to see what You love to do for those little lambs who look to You.

Psalm 24

All power and authority over the earth has rightfully been given to You my King Jesus. Worthy are You, the Lamb that was slain. For by Your sacrifice You redeemed this orphan planet and all who would ever live on it.

After all, it was You who made it and set it in its place in the cosmos in the first place.

So who may walk directly into Your Holy of Holies, where You live, and not be bowled over by the awesome nature of Your incredible presence, but rather be able to stand and commune directly with You? This is what my heart longs for, Lord.

I hear You saying, "Those who have clean hands and a pure heart—they can come right in. They are always welcome. But my Presence will put a spotlight on all the impurities of the heart; it will expose all the things people put their trust in rather than Me. My Presence will expose all the selfish actions of those hands stretched out to Me.

"But come to Me and be blessed. I expose things only so You can be forgiven and made whole, in body mind and spirit. If you are prepared for that, then come right in and seek My face. Come and spend time with me like Jacob did, when he wouldn't let me go unless I blessed him[1]."

So, will you people hearing and reading this open the doors of your hearts that the King of Glory—our Wonderful King Jesus—may come in? He so longs to come in and help

---

[1] Genesis 32:22-30

you, bless you, love on you and make all things new for you[2]. Will you open up for Him to enter? You wonder what He's like?—well—He's the only one strong enough to break the chains of your sin and addiction, and set you free. So, will you open up and let this King of Glory come in[3]?

He's the All-Mighty one—He's big hearted enough not to break down the door of your heart, but wait for you to invite him in.

He's knocking, but you have to open your door to Him.

---

[2] Revelation 21:5
[3] Revelation 3:20

Psalm 25

Thank You Jesus that You are just so trustworthy—it's in You I put *all* my trust.

I trust that you will see I am never ashamed, and that my enemies—both within and without—will never triumph.

Thank You Jesus that shame is no part of Your world, but that of those dead set against You; that it's a facet and result of sin, of those who lie and deceive just because they want to.

Oh Jesus—rather—show me Your higher ways, lead me and teach me Your heart, Your paths—for You are my Lord, my God the very God of Hope. So, Lord, I remind You that Your tender Mercy and Lovingkindness have always been Your hallmarks—so I ask that You choose to never remember the craziness and sin of the life I led before I knew You, but choose now to remember me by the yardstick of Your amazing and wonderful love that You demonstrated in giving us Your Son, to be made sin for us, at Calvary.

Thank You so much that You love us to come and spend time with You in Your magnificent presence, where You share Your heart, Your mind, Your ways with us, and teach them to us. Lord, You are amazing! You're just so full of love, and You're so faithful to the Covenant that Jesus cut with You on our behalf. He said, "All of you drink this cup, the cup of the New Covenant in My blood shed for you and for many for the forgiveness of sin,[1]" And Lord, as I trust solely in the blood of Jesus, I too am 'one of the many', so I come boldly into Your Mighty Presence[2] as one whose sin is totally forgiven and wiped out[3]. Thank You Lord that You so love to instruct those

---

[1] Luke 22:20
[2] Hebrews 4:16
[3] Jeremiah 33:3, Colossians 2:14

of us who choose You this way.

Lord, Your ways are truly incredible that You take complete losers and show them how to live prosperous lives that bless all around them. And You even show them how to bless their many descendants, who then also learn how to inherit all the same wonderful blessings and pass them on down the generations.

Thank You so much that You confide in those who come and spend time with You—You show them things no-one else has ever seen or thought of[4]—You show us Your hidden covenant promises that we can depend on so firmly. Lord, I so love these times, for it's in these times You show me the way out of the mess I was in—and it's only as You show me the way out that I realize just what a mess I had got myself into.

Lord, will You put Your arm around me and give me a hug, and draw me real close to You? I'm lonely. With all of the troubles I was in, for a moment, leaving behind, and all of the issues of my heart chasing me down too… just take a glimpse at them, Lord—see the glint in their eyes, how they hate me! *Oh* Lord, will You show me the way to leave them behind, healing my heart and speaking Your Shalom to my thoughts.

Lord—will You please guard me from them, look—there seem even more than before—Help, Lord! Please keep me from shame—yes I know that's all I deserve, but it's in You I trust. It's You who I cling to; to Your integrity, and the integrity of Your word and Your Covenant promises to us.

Jesus—I look to You as my Redeemer—You and You alone.

---

[4] 1 Corinthians 2:9

Psalm 26

Help, Lord! I'm in trouble again—Help! *Oh,* thank You for reminding me I'm seated with You, Lord Jesus, high in Heavenly places. Thank You for reminding me, Lord, I choose to look up and Praise Your Wonderful name in the middle of this trouble—that You are still King of Kings, You are my Redeemer and You are already redeeming this crazy situation and turning it to my good—that's just who You are. It's just what You do—*Oh,* Thank You Jesus! Yeaaaah!

Thank You that You know my heart is to snuggle up to You and see You move.

Oh Lord, thank You for Your wonderful salvation—Lord, we rejoice, we dance, we shout, we sing in honour of Your wonderful name and All that You have done in and for us. Jesus—these banners we wave in worship are in honour of You: You have truly given us far more than we dared to ask You for.

Thank You for showing us so unequivocally that You do so much more than just save our souls, but You redeem every part of who and what we are, and then fill us to overflowing with Your Holy Spirit. Thank You that You hear and respond to the deep cries of our hearts and rescue us, whatever the situation we've got ourselves in.

Some trust in their bank account, credit rating or flashy car; Lord, we Praise and magnify the name of Your wonderful Son, King Jesus!

Thank You Lord. You always hear us, even when we're in so deep it's all we can do to whisper Your precious name…

Jesus!

Psalm 27

Lord—You are always and forever my Saviour and the fire that burns within. So I *will* not fear. I will not fear anything— for You, Jesus, Anointed One, are the Lord and foundation of all that I am.

When I see men coming to make mincemeat out of me, then I know my adversary and his cohorts have no chance. When I see I'm totally surrounded with no way of escape, my pulse may rise a tad, but I *will* not fear. I've learned better than that. When it looks like WWIII is about to break out all because of me—*really*! Get real! I'm naught but a little love slave of the Mighty King Jesus.

Lord—there's just this one thing I ask. In the end it all boils down to only one thing—that I may live in Your Glorious Presence all my days. Wherever You are—that's where I want to be, so I can get to know You and Your wondrous heart of love. That I can look and keep looking deep into Your wonderful loving eyes—*Oh* so full of love! It's going to take all my life and eternity too, to plumb the depths of Your heart—You're so amazing, my King Jesus!

When things get rough, thank You that I will be safe with You. Thank You that I'll be completely safe in Your wonderful Presence, even if that means You've set me high on a rock for all to see. I'll just rejoice and praise Your wonderful name that You have chosen to set me high above all that would come against me. I will gladly sing and dance and worship You Jesus, You're so worth it! But Lord please come when I call out for You—I need You so much! When my heart reminds me I need to come back into Your precious Presence, then Lord, I *will* come. But please then don't hide Yourself or slam the door in my face. It's in You and You alone who I trust, 'cause You have always been the one who helped me through. Please don't make it difficult for me, 'cause You are my Lord, my Saviour and my God.

Thank You, thank YOU Jesus that You will never leave me or forsake me. When it looks like everyone else has—even my own mother and father—thank You that You never will. *Oh,* teach me Your wonderful ways, and keep me on Your straight and narrow path, Lord. It seems I so easily get led astray. And Lord, keep me from those bullies and those voices that shout off against me on the inside as much as those around who delight to slag me off and say 'it's all my fault.'

Lord—I would have given up completely a long time ago if it wasn't that I knew I was going to experience Your abundance and blessing here on planet Earth. *Oh* Lord—bring it on—I'm waiting.

Now listen up! Take heart—believe your beliefs and doubt those doubts and trust the Lord to fulfil His Word to you. He won't delay any longer than He has to[1]—He's just as hungry and eager to bless you, as you are to receive.

---

[1] Hebrews 10:37

Psalm 28

Help, Lord—My rock and my Redeemer! All hope is just draining away... Help, Lord! If You don't, I may as well be dead and buried.

Please hear me Lord when I come to You—when I come with my hands outstretched high to You in worship.

Thank You Lord that there's nothing You would put in my way to come between us. Thank You for keeping me from people with the kind of twisted thinking that speaks sweetly to their neighbour while all the time plotting how to get one over on them. As like as not that would twist my thoughts too.

Lord may they reap exactly what they sow in their disregard of You and Your ways, and the justice You always bring.

But Lord... But Lord, I bless—I lift high the wonderful name of Jesus. Thank You that You always hear my call— You are always there when I turn to You.

Thank You Jesus—You are my strength and my shield— all the way around, and back again. My heart trusts in YOU and Your unfailing love—You help me so much! *Oh* my heart rejoices in You so that I can't help but sing Your praise.

Lord—You are my strength—and You Holy Spirit are a mighty fortress in me and all around me, too.

Lord—how much we all need Your help and blessing: Be a shepherd to each one of us—Lord—forever, and always.

Psalm 29

Come on, all you His saints—get real in your praise and worship of our wonderful King Jesus! Ascribe to Him Glory and Strength.

Ascribe to Him the Glory His name deserves!

Come and put on those garments of Praise. Slip on those dancin' shoes and join me in worship of our Mighty Glorious King.

Lord, I think of the sound of Your voice—those huge waves crashing on the shore in a big storm, or the crashing claps of mighty thunder—they've got nothing on Your voice! Your voice is so powerful, and full of majesty.

Your voice breaks wide open those people who resist You like the giant cedars of Lebanon. All the other things they worship instead of You, You just break into tiny pieces. There's no stopping Your voice as those echoes gallop across the mountaintops.

It was Your voice that split the heavens when You anointed Your Son Jesus at His Baptism. It was Your voice that split the heavens again and brought precious Holy Spirit flames of fire to Your people on the day of Pentecost. Lord, do it again—we need the fire of Your precious anointing.

Lord, Your voice shakes not just those who know You, but in Your majesty, You call those round about to bow Joyfully before You. And in the throne room in heaven there is the roar of mighty waters as the whole host of heaven, men, angels and archangels shout their praise of You our King, "Glory, Glory, Glory. All Glory, Honour, Power and Majesty to our King

Jesus!"[1]

Just like You ushered in a whole new era after the flood, so now You reign till all things are put under Your feet[2].

Holy Spirit, You are so awesome. Your Fire is so awesome to empower the spirit of man, to usher in across the whole earth, Your Mighty Shalom Shalom—the reign of our Wonderful, Mighty Servant King Jesus.

Thank You Lord that You reign; Your Kingdom is forever increasing[3]. Your Peace is forever gaining momentum.

---

[1] Revelation 5 and elsewhere
[2] 1 Corinthians 15:25
[3] Isaiah 9:7

Psalm 30

All Glory to You Lord—You're so special! I bless and praise Your Mighty and Wonderful name.

Thank You Jesus for lifting me up and making sure my enemies never got the better of me when I was so ill—when I cried out Your name "Jesus!" Thank You so much for healing me. That was a close shave—too close, I really thought I was done for this time.

Come on, everyone—all you who love Him like I do, join me in singing His praise and lifting high His Mighty name in thanks to Him. He does get angry with a fierce jealous anger, but only for a moment. But His favour... *Oh,* His favour is somethin' else! His favour lasts forever—it's truly amazing. He sees you weeping and sobbing through the night, but that's quite enough—He comes sweeping in with His Joy, come the morning. Trust me on this!

Very foolishly I was boasting one time of the Lord's favour on my life, saying "I'm the Lord's favourite—absolutely nothing can shake my world." *Oh* dear—He just turned His precious face away and that was more than enough to send me into a tail-spin. *Oh,* it's a fearful thing to fall into the hands of the living God[1]. "Help, Lord!" I cried, "Lord—Mercy! No-one gains if You let me die now—the dust from which You made me won't thank You. It won't sing Your praise and tell everyone of Your faithfulness. Help—Lord—MERCY!"

Oh, but Lord—You're so, so GOOD! Thank YOU!

---

[1] Hebrews 10:31

All those horrible thoughts of death and dying You swept away in a moment, with Your Life and Love afresh—*Oh, Thank You Lord.* You gave me back my dancin' feet, clothing my heart with Your Joy and Gladness, once more. *Oh,* thank You that You are truly the God of JOY and Gladness. How could I ever stop praising You my King Jesus—You are so, so worth it. Thank You Lord that when that time does finally come, I will simply step into an eternity of giving You the Honour and Glory Your precious name so richly deserves:

JESUS!

Psalm 31

Help, Lord! Where are You? I just want to come and hide in You; shame is so horrible, thank You that You never shame us. Please keep me from ever being put to shame, especially for my love and trust in You. Thank You for bearing my sin and my shame on the cross, for me. You are the altogether lovely and altogether righteous one, and it's in You who I trust to always deliver me.

Can't You hear, Lord? Please rescue me, and quickly, Lord. Be Your usual Big, Unassailable-rock for me to stand on, I need a strong and safe castle where I can relax and feel safe in You and Your love, once more.

For You and You alone are the Rock of my Salvation, and a mighty stronghold. Lord, I'm marked by Your name, so for the honour of Your name, please direct my path, so I don't mess up and discredit You in the process. Lord, I'm beginning to see I've been trapped and hemmed in on every side; will You extricate me? Please show me a way out—it's in You who I trust—You are so safe. Lord, I commit myself to You and Your ways, I commit my very spirit to You—that's the least I can do, to You who gave Your all to redeem me. *Oh Lord, what a God You are—You're so Faithful!*

I look around and see people clinging to such worthless things—crazy priorities that never fulfil the inner man. Thanks for showing me that faith and trust in Your unfailing love—in knowing You, and being known by You, is what really matters. I trust in You, for You always bring such peace and deep joy to my heart and spirit, I can't help but have a praise party, and tell everyone of the wonderful, amazing love You have for me. Thank You so much that You saw me beat up and overwhelmed and didn't leave me there to be yet further crushed, but You came and rescued me and put me instead in Your large royal palace.

I'm just remembering... I was so distraught, I'd lost all hope—that's never a good moment. Those voices of gloom, of sorrow, sighing and death were pressing in on me, squeezing the life out of me. My body felt like it was starting to shut down as I just got weaker and weaker. With so many rejoicing to see me brought so low, even those who I thought were my friends became contemptuous of me. As for my true friends, they were concerned it was catching and did their best to keep their distance.

So I was left all alone once more—like I was completely broken and left for dead—just like a broken pot about to be swept up and thrown in the trash.

And then I caught snippets of the slander and lies about me, just to add to the terror in my heart... the plotting of those surrounding me, but keeping their distance, conspiring how to finish me off...

But somehow I turned to You Lord and whispered once more—I love You Jesus! You and You alone are my Lord and my God. My times are in Your hands, Lord—it's in You who I trust. Please deliver me from this gang—from all of these pursuing me so forcibly.

Please show me Your love afresh—remember, I'm just Your little love-slave. It was You who taught me that Love never fails[1]. Help, Lord! Please, please save me from being put to shame. Dish that out on those who I heard plotting against me—give them what they were planning for me—the silence of the grave.

Lord—please shut them up. Those lies... Such pride and

---

[1] 1 Corinthians 13:8

contempt spills out of their arrogance, particularly targeted at those who love You.

Thank You Lord for all the loving care You have for those who look to You—abundance everywhere. Thank You that You are El Shaddai, the God of more-than-enough—that this is Your name, and this is Your nature. Thank You that You delight to show off to those who love You, sharing openly with them such wonderful things—things that really satisfy, and no-one can take away—things across every area of life, emotionally, relationally, financially, spiritually—*Oh,* thank You, Lord.

Oh, Your Presence, Lord... Thank You—thank You so much—*Oh,* it's so good to hide in Your Presence where all of those voices of contention, backbiting, slander and the like are silenced.

Thank You that when sickness totally debilitated me, You rescued me and healed me through Your wonderful help and assistance. I was far too hasty to say I was past even Your help—*Oh,* thank You so much for hearing my pitiful cry.

Set your heart on the Lord afresh, you who say you love Him. He takes precious and wonderful care of those who genuinely and humbly trust in Him. But you proud—watch out for His payback, you really don't want to go there. You who hope in the Lord, stick to your guns, He will see You are never put to shame—be strong!

Psalm 32

Oh Lord, it feels so, so good to know that You have forgiven *all* my sins, and that they are not just covered over, but absolutely and totally forgiven, and that You've promised to never remember them ever again. *Oh* that I could do the same. It's amazing to know that that list You had against me, that Jesus has Himself wiped it absolutely clean, nailing it to the cross[1], and taking my sin and shame upon Himself, taking my place. Thank You that You wiped out deceit from its place in my spirit too.

While I kept it all in and pretended, even fooling myself, I just got worse and worse—inside I was disintegrating… falling apart, groaning under it all.

But You never let up for a moment, wooing me with Your wonderful heavy, thick Love, even as my spirit caved in like it was blasted with the full heat of the blazing desert sun, You kept up with the pressure of Your Love for me.

Finally I gave up trying to cover it all up and hide it from You. Thank You that nothing I could ever tell You could ever shock You; You saw it and know it all anyway. I said, Lord, I acknowledge my sin, I've hidden lies, deceit, rebellion, *Oh,* the list goes on—Lord I've hidden these things in my heart— Lord—please forgive me, and cleanse me of these horrible things. Please—please, Lord, put Your new and right spirit inside me—and that's exactly what You did!—far more than just forgiving me my sin, huge though that was.

So listen all of you, and hard though it may be, follow my example—it's so worth it. Seek the Lord who forgives all who

---

[1] Colossians 2:14

come to Him. Seek Him while He may be found[2], 'cause it's a whole lot harder when you're up to your neck in it and you desperately need His help. And He longs to do so much more than just forgive you—He wants to keep you from getting anywhere even close to those crazy perilous situations—He wants to make you one of the family—one of *His* family.

Oh, thank You Lord that I can come and hide in You—under Your mighty pinions, where You keep me from trouble. And just when I sense that trouble is really getting too close for comfort, I catch the sounds of that multitude too numerous to mention worshipping You King Jesus in Your throne room—*Oh* that I could press in closer... Aaaaah!

So please listen up and let me teach you the little I've learned. It's so simple I can put it all into one sentence! Look to Jesus, and let Him teach you His ways. You take a horse or a mule and you have to put a bit, a bridle, and a harness on them to get them to do what you want. You don't really want God to do that to you, do you? So get to know Him. Take time out to spend time, just with Him, getting to know Him and His ways, and inviting Him to get to know you too—that's just as important—maybe more so![3]

Those who never learn to come and trust in Jesus and get to know Him are guaranteed a life of sorrows, problems, and difficulties. But for those who know Him and look to Him—now that's a different story—He takes their sorrows and turns them into Joy and Gladness, into reasons to rejoice and give Him Glory, 'cause He knows best and will change things somehow to our good[4]. He always does!

---

[2] Isaiah 55:6
[3] Matthew 7:23
[4] Romans 8:28

He surrounds us with His love, His care, His Oh-so-tender Mercy. And can I let you into a secret? He does so much more than that—He comes right inside, if You'll ask Him—He can reach those aching places of the heart that nothin' else can—His middle name is 'Comforter'.

So you who know Him—may I give you some strong encouragement—be glad in Him—*Oh,* be glad in Him—he's our God-of-Joy! He's outrageous fun to be with—put a smile on your face and let Him do the rest—LOL! Take your boots off and put on those dancin' shoes...

Will you join me with a shout of Praise to our King Jesus—He's just so, so worth it—Yeaaah!

Hallelujah!

Psalm 33

Have you got a song that really expresses the JOY the Lord has put in your heart? Sing it out—it doesn't matter how good your karaoke is, how tuneful, or in tune you are, it's the Joy, joy, joy there down in your heart that He's listening for! It's just what His children should bring to Him—often! What instruments have you got? A pair of hands and some vocal chords to start with, add in a guitar or two—yeah! give Him a new song, with some good loud choruses—we've got lots to sing and shout about, lots to thank Him for, haven't we!

Oh, thank You Jesus, Anointed One, that You are always, always, always true to Your word—You are just so faithful to us Your children—yeaaah—Thank YOU Jesus! Thank You that You love good things like Righteousness and Justice— that Your throne, Your Kingdom—is Righteousness established on that foundation of Justice, and on that basis Your Kingdom is love, love, love—a love that never fails.

You spoke and the creation exploded into being. You breathed and the stars lit up—wow! And then You created this little spinning ball especially for us—giving us mountains, and valleys, dry land, wet land, seas and mighty oceans, all ordered and beautiful, and full of all the things we need for life—they are giant storehouses, can't you see it, everyone—it all shouts of His loving care for you and me. Isn't He awesome? He spoke and it jumped to it, just as He commanded...'cause His word is like that. Probably took a little while, as we measure time, though...

Nations plan such crazy stuff—and He delights in seeing they never come to fruition, but don't you try and stop *His* plans and His purposes—now that would be really stupid.

Rather like the creation, He's not in a hurry, and once He's decided, once He's made up His mind, then that's it, through all generations... all down the ages...

You want to make sure your nation is one He's chosen and set on blessing, that have made Him their Lord, and their God, because He's looking on—He sees it all. You don't seriously think He's not going to see you, do you? He sees everyone—no problem—their good, their bad and their ugly—but He sees their heart too. So it really doesn't matter how big a country's war machine is, or their nuclear arsenal—He's very specifically on the lookout for those who love Him and His ways—His Covenant partners, those who have chosen to get to know Him intimately, and who know, know, know that His love never fails[1]. He's scouring the earth to find them to bless them right in front of their tormentors, especially with His bread of Life.

We, and they, wait on You, Lord. We hope in You and Your unfailing love; for we look to You alone for help, to You and You alone to be our defence. And while we wait, we'll praise You Jesus, our Mighty and Wonderful King, the one who cut Covenant with Father God on our behalf, and we'll bless and praise Your precious name.

So Lord we remind You of that precious Covenant sealed by the body and blood of Your Son. Our Hope and our Trust is in You, and Your Covenant Assistance.

---

[1] 1 Corinthians 13:8

Psalm 34

ALL praise to YOU, LORD! I bless and I lift high Your Mighty and Wonderful name, "JESUS"! *Oh,* may I never stop giving You praise! You're so Good, my King Jesus, Anointed One, You're so Faithful, and True, You're so Loving and Kind to all who come to You.

Those who've bowed the knee to our King Jesus, listen to my testimony and join me in giving Him praise, 'cause what He did for me, is just the precursor of what He longs to do for you too, if you ask Him. Remember He's no respecter of persons[1].

Jesus, we exalt Your wonderful and mighty name, worthy King of all Kings, Mighty God, Prince of Peace...

Now the moment I sought You, You came, and You delivered me from all fear, every last trace. My whole trust is in You. *Oh,* thank YOU Jesus—You are just so, so trustworthy! You are just so Gooooood!

All those who set themselves to look full in Jesus' wonderful face can't help but reflect His Glory and Grace. *Oh,* stay in His Precious Presence and get Him to fill You with His Holy Spirit too—then You will glow from the inside with His love in a way that no-one can deny.

I cried out to Jesus, and He heard me and came running and saved me so wonderfully. Did you know He commands angel camps to be set up all around those who love and honour Him? Now they provide amazing protection!

---

[1] Acts 10:34, Romans 2:11, Ephesians 6:9, Colossians 3:25

Now the Lord doesn't come in trial size, you can't try a little bit and see if it works, but if you'll jump in wholeheartedly putting *all* your hope and your trust in Him, you'll very quickly find out just how Awesomely Good He is. He so longs to bless all who look to Him, with Faith and Love, and provide a true Father's loving care, protection and provision for them.

You look around and see others, just like the animals, even powerful ones like lions, have times when things are short, and they go hungry. But not so for those that love Him; famine, pain, heartache and the like are in short supply, but not the good things of life—you'll find they are never short of those things that really matter, and make life truly fulfilling.

Listen carefully now and I will teach you…

What do you really want in life, what is really fulfilling for you? While we're all so crazily different and unique, when it comes down to it we all want much the same; we want to experience the richness and fullness of LIFE! And if you're like me you want to make that a good long life, too. Right?

And you want to know how to do it? I could easily give you a great list of instructions, such as mind what you say, mind what you hear, and mind what you see, but while true enough, they are superficial things. Rather—mind what you store in your heart, and mind what that heart of yours chews on… Set yourself to pursue Jesus, Prince of Peace, Lord of Lords, to know Him and to know His ways, and to open yourself to Him, so He knows you too. If you do that, then only good stuff will come out of your mouth, because "out of the abundance of the heart, the mouth speaks"[2]. You do that and you'll find His favour on you whichever way you turn, and He's always listening, for even the faintest whisper of a cry for help, which He so delights to bring.

---

[2] Matthew 12:34

But it's truly a different story for those who set themselves against Him with evil intent; you really don't want to go there. There really is no place to hide from Him, and such people are quickly forgotten forever.

Oh, give me the story of those who love our King Jesus, tell me one more time, tell me *your* story—you cried and He came running—yeaah! He never promised that you wouldn't go through tough times[3], but He did promise to be there with you and in you, and see you through, and see to it that those things that are really important to you, come through too— Yes, He's that good! You know—He's especially close to those whose hearts are broken, and are humbly trying to put their lives back together again. He promises never to break a bruised read or snuff out a barely smoking flax[4]. Rather, one of His key mandates is to bind up the broken-hearted[5]—He said that of Himself—and nothing gets close to His balm, to heal and to redeem.

Those who set themselves against the Lord and His ways find their own evil descending on them—they don't need Him to take them out! Those who hate you because of your love for Jesus—don't worry about them. They are left desolate because they never win, so they die a horrible death, only to face eternal condemnation.

No-one who loves Him faces that—*Oh*—give me a shout of praise for our King Jesus! We all get to join the saints and go marching into Glory on that great day. Don't you want to be in that number?

---

[3] John 15:20
[4] Isaiah 42:3 Matthew 12.20
[5] Isaiah 61:1 Luke 4:18

Psalm 35

Help, Lord! Help! I need You to come and fight for me. I don't know what I've done this time, but boyo, do I need some help! Lord, I'm doing my best with my sword and shield—please grab Yours and give me a hand. Pick up a spear while You're coming[1] and bar the way of that gang chasing after me. I need to hear Your voice once again, Lord, I need to hear You've got my back. *Oh*, remind me that You indeed are my Saviour!

The disgrace and ruin they are planning for me, bring on them instead Lord, and show them just how shameful they are. And as it all descends around their ears, bring the lot down on them, so they see the only thing that can't be shaken is You—that You are the only one worth trusting. Then if they really won't turn to You, that'll make them really miserable.

Holy Spirit, blow Your mighty breath over them—Your breath that strips away the chaff to reveal the genuine grain inside—if there is any. May Your mighty wind just blow that chaff away, down into dark and slippery places.

You can see how they've dug a pit for me, carefully setting their net to trap me for absolutely no reason, Lord. *Oh* that they would fall into just such a trap themselves, caught in just the way they had intended for me—and fall headlong, into it.

But Lord... But Lord—You make me so glad. You give me so much to thank You for! *Oh*, thank You Jesus, Yeshuah, Saviour—I rejoice and bless Your wonderful and precious name. Who is anything like You? Who can in any way be compared to You? You are so amazing how You deliver the

---

[1] They don't like it up 'em, you know, they don't like it up 'em.

poor and the weak from the strong, and the poor and the needy from the thief. I love it!

Lord, You've seen those lying accusers, accusing me of all sorts that I know nothing about, and not content with that, they then go on and pile up their evil muck and blame me for it... Ugh!

And aren't they the very ones who I prayed for and brought before You Lord, when they were sick? Didn't I fast and have deep compassion for them, as I prayed to You for them? And just as I was going around feeling sad for them, like they were one of my family, they all had a good laugh at my expense, and then came and laughed in my face. They really had no idea when to stop. Lord, that's really *not* nice.

And Lord they mock and belittle You too, as they get really heated about my love for You, and my trust in You. Just how long are You going to allow this to go on? Please rescue me—these lions, they're getting far too close for comfort.

But I look to You, Lord. In that great and wonderful crowd of those who love and worship You, I will take great delight in leading everyone in rejoicing and giving thanks to You; I will lead them all in our praise to You, my King Jesus!

But those who are so set against me, may they have nothing to gloat over, or catch in my behaviour to shame me, for they are of such evil intent—and it's not just towards me—but everyone just going quietly about their business. They shout out their baseless accusations, "We've seen you, we've seen you." Thank You Jesus that You've seen them, and You have seen through them. Keep close to me Lord, and *do* something. Stir Yourself, I need some justice, Lord. I need You, the God of Righteousness, to judge my case. Please don't let those accusers rejoice over me—I can hear them already rejoicing and saying, "We got him, we won, we won, we were right all the time!"

But Lord... But Lord—will You shine the light of Your

Truth, and Your Love on these accusers. That'll cause no end of confusion for them. Lord show up the shameful things they've done; highlight their disgrace.

May those who love to see Your Righteousness prevail, see Your light of vindication of me and join me in singing Your praise. And I will sing and shout Your praise all day long... Yeaaaaah Yeshuah—my Saviour!

Psalm 36

Lord, I look with bewilderment at those who don't know You, and then when I look back at You, I'm so thankful You saved me from their lifestyle and their way of thinking. They have absolutely no fear of You—now is that foolish or what! They flatter themselves that they can get away with murder and no-one will ever know. Their language is full of cussin', boasting, exaggeration and lies, so before they know it they have completely lost any comprehension of what is good, bad or downright ugly, let alone lift a finger to help anyone else.

They lie awake at night plotting their next big break without a thought for the cost to others, or even themselves—now is that stupid, or silly?

Oh, thank You Lord that You aren't like that! Thank You so much that Your Lovingkindness stretches from sunrise to sunset, and back again; Your Faithfulness is like the clouds that bring rain on the just and the unjust alike, watering the ground to bring forth its fruit in due season. Your Righteousness is like a great mountain range, like the Himalayas, high above all, and Your thoughts are as deep as a Pacific Ocean trench—scarcely comprehended or explored by anyone. You take so much care over Your wonderful creation, over every aspect of it—You're amazing, Lord! Whether they realise it or not, all of humanity live every day under the shadow Your wonderful mighty wings. Ultimately, You're the one who provides for us, and not just food for our bellies, but all that makes life fun and worthwhile so uniquely, for each one of us. *Oh,* how much we need Your special bread-of-life daily for our spirits, too.

Thank you Lord, that You are a veritable Fountain of Life and Love and all that we really need, to truly enjoy this precious life that You give to us so richly and freely. Lord, it's You and Your love that's the top of the list—that so precious privilege of knowing You and searching Your heart—Your amazing heart of love. *Oh* Lord, don't ever stop sharing Your heart with those who long for more of You—*Oh,* how much we need *You*!

Don't ever let those who snub and mock You put one over on me—Ugh! I know once they're down, they're out, but I really don't want them to take me down too. I don't even want to look and see what happened to them.

Oh, thank *You* Lord for Your such wonderful love and care.

Psalm 37

Oh, Thank You Jesus for the wonderful plans and dreams You have for our lives. Thank You that You really don't want us fretting and worrying about a thing, but rather, looking to You and trusting You. And thank You that envy doesn't feature, either, even when it does look like evil, or those pursuing evil, appear to get all they dream of. Thank You that You remind me it is but for a moment and it will all disappear like grass in summer heat and drought, whereas Your favour lasts a lifetime.

Oh, my King Jesus I feast on You and on Your Faithfulness—on Your Faithfulness to me and my family—Faithfulness that I have personally experienced and can give testimony to—Thank You! Papa God—I delight myself in You! Holy Spirit, I delight myself in You—for not only are You Faithful and True, but You are such a God of Joy and Love—I draw close to You and it rubs off... *Oh,* the Joy you fill my heart with, when I dance and sing Your High Praises—when I party with You. I love it! I love You! I may have started downcast, but I sure finished with a big smile on my face and right across my heart—*Oh,* Thank You Papa! *Oh,* I delight in You for who You are, and all You are to me, and then I catch You bringing my dreams to pass—*Oh* Papa—You're so amazing—thank You.

Lord—the plan, the direction for my life—it's Yours. I give You every step, with all my heart—thank You that You know that. I would say I'm Your little love-slave, but You don't do slaves—Lord, I'm learning to be Your child, one of the family—I'm learning Your heart and the things You dream about—*Oh,* what a privilege that You should choose to open Your heart to me. I know the things You have planned for me.

You will bring about in Your special and wonderful way.

You ascribe Your righteousness to me, and then light me up like a spotlight! Those times I've struggled to follow You and do the right thing—You spread wide for all to see—*Oh* Lord... I rest in You. Thank You that You gave us an example of rest on the seventh day of creating when "You rested[1]!" That's not doing nothing, or having a lie-in, but 'resting'; delighting in You and Your Love, delighting in the largesse You've poured into my life with my wife and family... delighting in Your open heart to me—the dreams and the longings You stir and cause to rise to the surface. Lord, I gladly wait in Your sweet and Oh-so-precious Presence, drinking in all that You are, all that You mean to me. *Oh, thank YOU!*

Thank You that in the atmosphere of Your Presence there's no place for worry, envy or competition at others doing well and being blessed, 'cause I know just how rich Your hand of blessing is on me[2]. And when it looks like it is ill-gotten gain, Lord I give that to You, rather than getting angry myself over it—as that helps no-one.

Thank You Lord that You never want us to worry about anything as it always leads to bad stuff—either bad stuff filling our imagination, our hearts and then our mouths, or worse still it actually happening—ouch! Thank You Lord for the wonderful gift of our imaginations to dream and dream big; to worry our worrier with dreams of the things we could do with You—especially those things we could do together to bring Glory and Honour to King Jesus.

Oh, thank You Lord that Your dreams for those who take the time to soak in Your Presence long enough to pick up on them, is for them to inherit a Promised Land, flowing with

---

[1] Genesis 2:2-3
[2] Proverbs 10:22

milk and honey—their own land of Promise that flows with all the things they so uniquely love and appreciate. And the pictures of what that looks like are different for each of us, LOL! *Oh,* You are so Good!

We turn round, and the worrier, and the mischief maker has totally vanished! Even if we go searching… Wow—what a contrast, to those who look to You, who so enjoy You, and the abundance of Your Shalom, stepping into their inheritance.

Looking at it the other way around, the picture gets even funnier. When the worrier and envious see the riches of the saints—they plot and gnash their teeth and You laugh at them, for You see the end of their sorry story! Now that is funny! Their 'wisdom' is so flawed—they pull out their choicest weapons and then trample over the poor and needy—as if that's going to make them either rich or happy! To set to on those who love You is a sure way of coming seriously unstuck—those weapons have a horrible backfire in those circumstances.

Oh, thank You Lord for reminding me to stay thankful hearted at what You've given me, rather than to start down the road of envy. Thank You that You've already disarmed the powers set against us; the seeds of envy, greed, lust, and their like, have no place to germinate in a heart full of thanks to You. *Oh,* how You take care of us!

Thank You that You know all our days, and know the inheritance we leave for generations coming lasts forever. Thank You that no shame will ever stick, even when the times get really murky, and You always provide, even when it looks like there's absolutely nothing to be had.

But it is not so for those set against You—they look good for a moment, like a lush meadow full of colourful wild flowers—but come the drought it's up in smoke in seconds.

They borrow, but never pay back, whereas by contrast, Your people give readily to those in need, not even thinking to ask for any return. These are the ones who inherit the land—the others are literally cut off.

Oh, thank You King Jesus for how You direct my path through life, in spite of all my failings. *Oh,* how I delight in You. I long ago gave up counting the times I fell—*Oh,* I'm so slow to understand, so selfish and self-orientated; I miss it so often—and yet You rescue; You never let me go, but keep hold of my right hand and lift me back up again. *Oh,* Thank YOU!

Through all my years, and I've seen a few, I have never seen those who love You left dangling and cut off from You and Your loving care and provision, begging for bread and shelter. Somehow You see to it that they are still able to be gracious and generous to others, and their children blessed and thriving through it. *Oh* Papa—Your provision—Your Love— is so special, so caring—*Oh* what a Dad You are!

Will you, dear reader, give evil a wide berth and seek to know Jesus and His ways? If you want to leave a legacy that lasts, then that's the way to do it. King Jesus loves justice, but He knows that mercy triumphs over justice every time, and He never ever forgets those who love Him. But the others? Cut off—you really don't want to go there.

That inheritance lasts forever; you are creating the place for your descendants to come after you. That's where those who love King Jesus learn His wisdom, His ways of Justice and Truth coming from hearts that have chosen His law of Love. They don't stumble around in the darkness.

Thank You my King that when the others stake out those who love You, in order to steal kill and destroy[3], You always have Your ways of vindicating Your chosen. It's good to wait on You, Jesus, and keep to Your ways of Life—in due time[4] You will raise us up to bless and be a blessing, and even see the others cut off in front of our very eyes.

I remember one time, a boastful, arrogant character suddenly grew rich, powerful and influential, only to turn round and everything had gone pear-shaped—his fortune, his reputation, his marriage—all gone. I went looking to see what had happened—not a trace.

But thank You Lord for the stark contrast You demonstrate to me of those I know, who love You, and put You first—the Joy in their homes and families—always Your Shalom. But the others? No future, no hope, no Shalom.

Oh, thank You King Jesus that You are forever the Saviour for *all* who turn to You. You are always such a stronghold when things get really tough—how You help and rescue all who turn to You. No matter what the evil, no matter what the problem—You are able to save to the uttermost those who come to You[5], my God and my Redeemer.

---

[3] John 10:10
[4] 1 Peter 5:6
[5] Hebrews 7:25

Psalm 38

No, Lord! No, No, No... I can't take Your anger—please... spare me Your correction, well at least while it feels like You're this angry with me.

Your arrows don't miss, they stick fast, and then You crush me. It feels like my whole body is shutting down, and caving in, my bones too, and I'm beginning to see it was all my fault—it was my sin. My guilt is crushing me—Lord, I can't carry this. My wounds (sores) just get worse and worse—Ugh, they're horrible enough already. Why was I so stupid?

How much lower can I go? All day long, it seems that death hangs close and morbid thoughts are never far away. My belly is on fire—something clearly is badly wrong. Now I'm losing it altogether, I'm starting to panic. Lord, You know my heart's desire, and You know all my sighing and groaning. My heart is really pounding now, while I just get weaker and weaker, and my eyes dimmer and dimmer.

Now even my friends and family are keeping their distance, seriously thinking it's catching and my neighbours are keeping well away,

As for my enemies and those keen to see the end of me, they are busy with their plans, saying wicked things while plotting my demise. Perhaps it was just as well my hearing has pretty well failed, and my voice given up. (One way of hearing no evil, and speaking no evil, but really not to be recommended.)

Inside, I'm saying "Lord, it's in You who I trust, and put my hope, surely You, my Lord and my God, are going to hear me. Surely, Lord, You aren't going to let them rejoice at my collapse, and gloat over my sliding into oblivion. It's increasingly looking like I'm done for, and my guilt is staring me in the face, for which I am truly sorry.

Oh, but You haven't seen the enemies I've made over the years, cunning and strong, who hate me totally without cause. They take great delight in paying back mischief for blessing, and the one thing that sticks in their craw is that I pursue all things Good, especially You, Lord.

Help, Lord! You promise never to leave me or forsake me[1]—I need You real close right now.

Oh, Come quick, Lord—my Jesus, my Saviour, my Lord and my God! *Oh,* thank You so much!

---

[1] Hebrews 13:5

Psalm 39

I shook myself down—I vowed I would take hold of my tongue and put a stop to the junk that I oh so readily let it spew out. I thought, "Yes I need to bridle my tongue, especially when I'm with others who know nothing of You my King Jesus, of You and Your ways."

So I tried it and said absolutely nothing—not even what would have been good. I just started to boil inside. Thoughts were running round my head until I had to leave the party and finally let it boil over.

Oh, my King Jesus, please remind me—show me afresh just how brief my time is here on planet earth—just how quickly it's all over. My lifespan is scarcely a hand-span—and in Your scheme of things, in Your timescales, a blink and I've missed it. In that frame, every man's best looks very pointless. Aaaah!

All our work and effort is a moment's show, that in reality achieves absolutely nothing. We try and store up this world's riches[1], but have no control over what happens to them when we're gone.

So Lord, I'm silent once again—only this time, before You. Will You show me what's really of eternal value and significance—Lord, my Hope is in You, my King and my Redeemer.

Clearly my vowing to say nothing doesn't cut it. *Oh* Lord, will You deliver me from these things that weigh me down and trip me up[2]. They really do make me look so foolish.

---

[1] Matthew 6:19
[2] Hebrews 12:1

I kept my mouth shut because I sensed Your hand on me, that You had a purpose in mind. Well, thanks for showing me, Lord, but I'm left struggling. You make it look like all that I was working so hard for, is in reality, moth-eaten junk. Aaaaah!

Lord, that's really tough without showing me the other side of the picture. In the middle of all my tears will You hear me and show me. Lord I'm only too aware that this is not my real home, that I'm an alien and foreigner here, as all those who love You are, in reality.

But, Lord... Will You give me Your perspective in this. Will You show me what is of real lasting value in the light of my true home[3].

---

[3] Matthew 6:19-20

Psalm 40

Help, Lord, Help! Asking how I got here in this slime pit probably isn't helpful, but if it was my mistake, I really don't want to do that again.

Oh, thank You for hearing me, as You always do, and rescuing me from that disgusting hole I was digging for myself. *Oh,* thank You for setting me back on solid ground, on You, my King Jesus, my rock and the foundation of all that I am. You've given me a new song of praise to sing—my rescuer, my Saviour, King Jesus, my Lord!

I know I'm really not that special, so if You'll rescue even me, then You'll rescue any and every one. And You've given me a new song of praise to sing—my rescuer, my Saviour, King Jesus my Lord! Yeaah Lord!

Turn to Jesus, everyone—make Him your rock.
Call on Him for rescue and He will.
For He is Good, Good, Good
– far better than you dare imagine.
With Him is no guilt or shame,
But Hope and Love and Love again.

Oh, thank You Jesus—You're Good
Thank You Jesus You're the always the same.
No matter what the problem
– we can put our hope in You again.

I praise You Papa God,
Oh, I praise You my Lord, my King
For giving me Your son
To rescue me again.

Your love endures, Your love's the same
Yesterday, today and Forever
– *Oh,* Amen! And Amen! Yeaaah! Amen!

Oh, how You bless those who trust You—what a privilege! The arrogant, the puffed up liars who care nothing for You, have no idea what they're missing out on. When I stop and remind myself for a moment of the wonderful things You've done for me, let alone those recorded in Your book, that's humbling. Your loving care is so awesome; who can compare to You? I certainly can't write down here a fraction of what You've done for me, or even think to number Your thoughts for me…

Thank You for opening my understanding to appreciate that animal sacrifice is really not what You're about, but rather, the sacrifice of a heart wide open and hungry for You and to follow Your ways. Now, Lord, that's me—thank You that You know the delight I have in You and doing things Your way—You know that Your law of love is written all through my heart. Thank You for the example of Your Son who opened the scrolls and found Himself on every page, how He delighted in You and in Your ways, with all His heart— *Oh,* Thank You Jesus!

And thank You Jesus, Anointed One, that You preached and demonstrated what right living looks like—healing the sick, cleansing the leper and raising the dead. Lord, I've hidden this well in my heart, but it's a fire inside me that wants out—I have to tell everyone how Faithful and True You always are—I have to tell them that You, King Jesus, paid for their sin, so they can know Your special and precious forgiveness. Lord, I can't hide Your Lovingkindness and Truth!

Oh, Jesus, how I need Your Mercy, Your Covenant

Assistance; Lord, I need Your Lovingkindness and Truth to watch over me. With the evil that's surrounding me—Lord, I need Your Lovingkindness and Truth! *Oh,* my sin, my failure, and my mistakes keep haunting me—I'm so ashamed—I not going bald yet, and my mistakes are more than the many hairs on my head. My heart is quite overwhelmed—*Oh,* remind me Jesus of Your precious forgiveness, that You paid such a price for. Thank You that You promised to never remember my sin ever again[1], so I shouldn't either, now, should I?

Shame on you who would remind me—trying to pull me back into shame and confusion and take me out. You be exposed for the lying demon that you are, as you try and point the finger at me. I've been forgiven, and my sin has been washed away and blotted out.

Oh, Jesus, thank You for the wonderful Joy of knowing I'm forgiven—of knowing I'm made new—a new creation[2]—*Oh,* that makes me glad, and happy. Now all of you who know you have been forgiven, rejoice with me—hey let's sing of just how Great our King Jesus, our Saviour, is. Thank You Lord.

Lord, while I thank You for all You are to me, I'm hungry for so much more. You are my Help, my Healer, my Comforter, my Saviour, my Provider, but Lord... *Oh,* but Lord—I want more of You—Holy Spirit, flood me afresh with Your life, Your Love, Your compassion and Your Miracle-working-power to demonstrate the Lordship and Redeeming Love of King Jesus to the sick and the broken-hearted. Lord I open my arms wide and high in worship to You—Fill me, now Lord, now!

Oh, Thank You, thank You, Thank You Lord.

---

[1] Jeremiah 31:34, Hebrews 8:12, Hebrews 10:17
[2] 2 Corinthians 5:17

Psalm 41

Oh, thank You Lord that You are so concerned over the weak and the poor—those with no voice—they do need someone to speak up for them. Thank You that You take special care of those who do speak for them, and for those who care for them. Thank You that You protect and look after these—so that Your blessing on them stands out to all. Their enemies don't get a chance, and on those rare occasions when they do get sick, You quickly restore them to even greater health and vigour. Thank You Lord that You know my heart on this...

Lord, I realised how I had missed by miles the mark of the high calling[1] You had intended for me when I called out to You for Mercy—please show me Your Grace once more, and restore my spirit. That taunting voice is never far away, that when I die, there will be no fruit left of my life, no legacy, no inheritance to pass on to the next generation—that it is all stubble[2]. It forever feels like all my failings are broadcast to the world for everyone to see, tirade and condemn me, rubbing salt into my wounds. As for that whispering campaign—they don't speak Your healing and life over me, but rather gossip that I'm on my death bed.

And what's happened even to my close friends—those I trusted with my life? Right now, it feels like they too have deserted me. It sounds like they too are thrusting their knives into my reputation.

But Lord... But Lord, it is in You who I trust—please remember our Covenant—sealed with the body and blood of Your Son, Jesus. Raise me back up that I may be a walking

---

[1] Romans 3:23, Philippians 3:14

[2] 1 Peter 1:7

demonstration to them, and to all, of Your Love and Grace. Lord, when I see them struggling for anything to gloat at, then I will know afresh just how You delight in me. Thank You so much for helping me not to take justice into my own hands, but helping me to keep my mouth shut and trust in You and Your unfailing Love. You do these things so much better than I ever could. Thank You that You are always smiling on me.

All Praise and Honour to You Mighty King Jesus—Lord of all. For all eternity, Your name be lifted high—for You and You alone are Worthy of all praise…

Amen and Amen!

Psalm 42

Lord—my whole internal world is screaming out for more of You! My spirit is shouting for more of you! I'm so thirsty for more of You—to know You more, to have You know more of me. I'm hoarse and gasping for more of You, Holy Spirit, to renew my spirit with Your Life and Love. I feel like a deer desperate for drink in the heat of the day. *Oh,* where can I go to meet with You and spend time with You? I seem to have been round all the usual places and Your Precious anointing and Presence feels like You've moved on.

I can't live by bread alone[1], I need Your precious 'bread of life' and all I've had to drink are my own tears, because people keep asking me, and mocking me with "Now—where's your God?"

I remember I used to so enjoy coming to You, giving You worship and shouts of praise, dancing with all my brothers and sisters in Your House and worshipping at Your feet, under the covering of Your mighty pinions[2].

Oh—it does me good to remember those times! So why am I so downcast and put out—Jesus the All-Conquering-Lion-of-the-Tribe-of-Judah is my King and my hope is in You, Jesus, my Saviour—that You will get me back there somehow, so I can praise Your wonderful name plenty more times.

So why am I so downcast?—I can still remember those precious times when I first knew You and came as a fresh new believer into Your wonderful Kingdom. I can remember the heights You took us to—wow—they were Glorious! All Praise to You, King Jesus!

But now, as deep calls to deep, it seem like I'm being

---

[1] Matthew 4:4, Luke 4:4
[2] Psalm 91:4

sucked down under a waterfall. It's like being a surfer one minute curling along inside a huge wave, exhilarated, and the next being munched, over and over, over and over—smashed on the bottom with the wave pounding and pounding. Ugh!

Oh, but by day You are still my Rock above the storm, and at night Your song of love to my heart—the one that only You know how to sing to me—reaches through the darkness in such a way I can't help but respond in love to You:

Yes, You are my Rock[3], King Jesus. Why is it I feel like You've so completely forgotten all about me? Why is it that all of those fears and taunts are shouting at me through the thick black of night, squeezing out the very life that You put within me. It feels like that wave is munching more than just my body—"Where are You, Lord? Help!"

Hold on a minute—why are you listening to those fears and taunts? No wonder you're being munched! Put hope back on your lips.

Lord—it's You who I worship—it's You in whom I trust—Lion-of-the-tribe-of-Judah, King of Kings, and Lord of Lords—my King Jesus, the Anointed One. And worthy are You of all my love, all my praise, because You overcame All principalities and powers, every demon and every evil authority, and You lead them bound in chains in Your triumphal procession.[4] I love You Jesus!

---

[3] Psalm 27:5
[4] Colossians 2:15

Psalm 43

Oh, thank You Lord, that You are the God of Justice and Righteousness. Lord, I look to You for justice—You plead my case—You be my advocate[1] right in the middle of this nation that despises You and Your ways. Lord, will You please deliver me from deceitful men and their warped and twisted thinking.

Lord—I look to You, Holy Spirit, for life and strength—it feels so like You've rejected me, and that makes me weak in the knees, morbid in thought, and paranoid in spirit.

Lord, I so need Your flashlight lighting the path ahead for me, reminding me of Your amazing and wonderful loving care for me—*Oh,* I so need You to guide me afresh. And will You bring me back to Mount Zion, that special place of Yours where all those who love You are found giving You praise, honour and adoration. I just so want to join them, right at the front where I can lead them with my guitar—that brings me such Joy deep inside, to praise You and lead everyone singing about just how amazing and wonderful You are. Lord—You sure are the most wonderful God there ever could be.

So why on earth am I so depressed? Why on earth do I feel so cut-up inside?

Hey, you soul of mine, "quit it!" Put your hope back in King Jesus—now get back to giving Him the Praise due to His Mighty name. You will soon have a raft of new things to thank Him for.

---

[1] 1 John 2:1

Psalm 44

Lord, we know the stories that have been passed down the generations of what You did centuries ago. We can flip back the pages and read how You drove out the nations in front of Your people as they came into their Promised Land. We can read how You planted them and blessed them and helped them. That it wasn't their military prowess or the sharpness of their swords that meant they won every time, but rather how it was You and Your strength, Your favour that did it—all 'cause You loved them so much.

Thank You that You are still just the same—You are *my* King, and *my* God—King Jesus! Thank You that Your mandate is still just the same, that it's through You and You alone that we push back the powers of darkness and in Your Mighty name we trample all over them[1]. Lord—I don't trust in my ability or in my strength—You are my Saviour.

Oh, thank YOU that You are *the* Saviour, and that You save us from everything that can come against us; that those that hate us, turn and run in shame, as we proclaim Your mighty name—Jesus! Lord it's in You we delight to boast all day long. *Oh,* we'll lift You high with our praise and thanksgiving through all eternity—Yeaaah!

So what's wrong, Lord? It looks very like You've thrown us out, so we've fallen flat on our faces, and You left us to try and fend for ourselves. It seems like we're grub for our enemies, like sheep for the slaughterhouse. We're scattered among the nations, being sold as slaves, and for not-a-lot at that, too.

And I don't think they got much out the deal either. We're a reproach to our neighbours—they scoff and laugh at us to

[1] Luke 10:19

their friends. Lord—did You really mean to make us a byword among the nations that we would be pointed to as the scum of the earth? It doesn't stop Lord, it's day in, day out, and my face burns with shame and embarrassment while they cuss and swear at You and us.

All this, Lord, but we haven't forgotten You or our Covenant with You. At no point have our hearts or our feet turned back from following You. You really have brought us low, making us people to be avoided—it's like You covered us with thick, tangibly thick, darkness.

Now if we had forgotten Your name, Lord, or gone off worshipping anything other than You, then of course You'd know all about it, because You know the secrets of our hearts, and we would well deserve this mess. But Lord... it looks like it's for Your sake we're counted as sheep for the slaughter, and that's not nice.

Lord—Wake up! Are You going to leave us like this forever? Why have You allowed this to happen and not helped us—it really looks like You've forgotten all about us and are completely oblivious to our situation.

Lord—we're well and truly in the dirt on this—please come and help us. You are our Redeemer, Lord. Remember Your very nature—remember Your Lovingkindness.

Note by the author—this evidently wasn't written by David, as there is no mention of calling for Covenant Assistance (Mercy) in this Psalm. The one thing that separated them from their enemies was their Covenant with the Lord. Similarly with us—if we want His help, don't plead your righteousness—which is a filthy rags—or even God's good nature—His Lovingkindness. We have a Covenant with Him signed and sealed by the body and blood of His Son—King Jesus.

It is one thing to remember the Covenant and quite another to claim the help and assistance you need on the basis of that Covenant.

Psalm 45

I'm cookin' today! I'm bubbling over with some amazing ideas for a new song of praise to our wonderful King Jesus:

Lord, You are so so Gooood—Jesus, You are so much more special than anyone else. Your words are True—*Oh,* they are so anointed with Love and Grace and Wisdom. You have so much of Papa God's favour and blessing on You—forever...

Oh, dress Yourself in all Your royal splendour, with Your mighty two-edged sword at Your side, and head up Your mighty army to display Your victory in Truth, Meekness and Righteousness—the awesome deeds of Your right hand. Thank You that Your sharp arrows are full of love to pierce even the hardest of Your enemies' hearts. *Oh,* may the nations bow in awe and wonder at Your feet, King Jesus.

Not just Your Kingdom, but the *increase* of Your Kingdom will last for ever, for all eternity. And the sceptre of Your rule is the sceptre of Righteousness[1]. *Oh,* thank You that You love Righteousness, and hate all that is evil: no wonder then that Papa God has anointed You with such a special anointing, the anointing of JOY, above everyone else. You so deserve that, Jesus!

Jesus—You are so clothed with such wonderful garments that smell of humility, and lovingkindness, grace and mercy, though some will say they smell deliciously fragrant, like myrrh, aloes and cassia. I hear the worship accompanied on the guitars coming from the throne room; it puts a smile on my face, and my heart leaps with Joy—Jesus—You're so worth it!

---

[1] Hebrews 1:8

I'm catching glimpses of a wondrous occasion—such Joy!

Waited on by Your Princesses, Your Queen stands at Your right hand, clothed in garments interwoven with purest gold. I hear someone addressing her, "Listen up, *Oh* Queen, listen very carefully. Has Your love for Him so ravished your heart that you have all but forgotten your own people and where you came from? For He is Lord of all—will you reverence, and bow low before Him, for your King is enthralled by your beauty?"

Even the daughter of an alien land comes with a wedding gift; while their rich beg Your favour. Now all are looking on in glorious wonder at this happy moment. The heart of the Queen too, is clothed with Glory to match her outward garments embroidered with gold as she is led to You with her beautiful bridesmaids coming up behind. *Oh,* and there's such Joy and Gladness as they enter the throne room, such anticipation for this wondrous moment!

And now it's the Bridegroom's turn to say, "My Father shall be your Father[2], but you will make your sons princes in the earth. Throughout the generations people will remember your name and praise you forever."

---

[2] I'm reminded of Ruth's classic vow to Naomi, Where you go, I will go, I will go, and where you stay, I will stay. Your people will be my people, your God my God. Ruth 1:16. And this is the heart of the preceding paragraph.

Psalm 46

Oh, Papa God, thank You that You are such an amazing strong shelter for us, always ready whenever we need You.

I will *not* fear, regardless of the changes I see all around me, even when I see great mountains shaken and disappear under the waves and experience the roar of the resulting tsunamis. Yeaaaah!

I will not fear, for I know of another reality where there's a river of Joy that flows from a very special place.

Thank You Papa for that wonderful river flowing from Your throne room—such a river of Joy to all who love You. For You are there in the middle, and You aren't about to be moved or shaken. Rather, You are there always to help everyone, really quickly—*Oh,* that's such good news!

What a crazy contrast to the physical world staring me in the face: Nation raging against nation all they want, but it ain't goin' to move You. The reality is that You whisper, and the raging melts away in a moment. *Oh,* thank You Lord!

Thank You that we have You with us, the commander of heaven's mighty host, and that You, Jesus, our Redeemer[1], are our Refuge, our Fallout-shelter[2]… Yeaaah!

Oh, come and see what He has done to those who set themselves against Him—not a pretty sight!

He just put a stop to all war, destroying all their crazy weapons at a stroke.

But for you and me, stop and listen and enjoy the peace. Appreciate that our Papa God is still God—and He has appointed our King Jesus to be far above every principality,

---

[1] Psalm 94:22
[2] Psalm 91

every republic, every kingdom, every ruling authority, both the known and seen and those in the unseen realm, far above every name that is named, not only in this age, but also in that which is to come[3].

Oh, thank You Papa that You have put *all* things under the feet of Your Son, and gave Him to be head over everything[4]. He is so worthy of that honour!

Oh, that settles the fear in my heart, once and for all.

Worthy, worthy are You Mighty King Jesus; thank You that You have promised in so many places in so many ways that You will never, never, never ever leave us[5]; that You are forever our strong refuge. Yeaaaah!

---

[3] Ephesians 1:21
[4] Ephesians 1:22
[5] 1 Kings 8:57, Isaiah 42:16, Hebrews 13:5

Psalm 47

Oh, Come and clap your hands everyone—give our Mighty King Jesus a truly triumphant shout of praise! And again; give Him another one—He's so worth it!

For our Wonderful High King is truly awesome— awesome in His Might and Power, and awesome in His Servanthood.

Worthy are You our King Jesus to have been given ALL Authority in heaven and earth. And then You go and give that authority to us[1], to trample on all the works of the enemy, and to subdue and rule the nations with Your loving servant heart. What an inheritance You have chosen for us—all the Glory that You purposed for Your special chosen one Israel and his descendants—Wow! & Wow!

What a roar of Praise and Rejoicing greeted You as You returned triumphantly to take Your seat in heaven's throne room—King of Kings, and Lord of Lords—*Oh,* hear the shofars ringing out! And as that praise party in the heavenlies continues You then give us the precious privilege of joining them—singing out our praise of You—King Jesus.

Oh, sing out your heart's cry of love to Him, sing His praise, for Jesus *is* King over all the earth. And as You praise Him in the language of heaven, put your thinking cap on and praise Him in your earthly language too—give Him a new song, expressing all of the wonderful reasons why you love Him so! He has sat down at Papa's right hand in the heavenlies, and He reigns over the nations, over all the earth, through each of us as we are gathered and adopted into His wonderful family.

---

[1] Matthew 28:18

Thank You that You are the Covenant-keeping God of Abraham, Isaac and Jacob, and that all authority on the earth is Yours. Worthy, worthy are You, our Wonderful High King to be highly exalted, far above all!

Psalm 48

You are so great, our Wonderful Papa God! You are so worthy of our praise, whether that's in Your Holy City—the one where You chose to set Your name[1], or in the middle of Your redeemed people as they gather to worship You, or in the middle of the New Jerusalem—that place where we will all gather before Your magnificent throne to give You honour and glory through all eternity.

"Mount Zion" is such a beautiful portrayal of all three— the Joy of all who have come to know You and Your wonderful Lovingkindness—the city where You dwell, where Praise and Worship are the mighty defence around this glorious stronghold.

Kings came with their armies, but had no weapons to fight this fight. They bow in honour of our King, or they flee in terror, shrieking like a woman in labour! You turn their plans and their might to matchwood like a fleet of ships smashed on a lee shore in a gale.

Oh, we have heard and seen such wonderful testimonies of Your awesome Lovingkindness, Papa—in the midst of Your people—Your people for *all* eternity—Yeaaaah!

As we listen in the midst of such a beautiful gathering, we can't help but be deeply moved, Papa, by these incredible stories and declare Your name is indeed the High King of Righteousness, which our Praise and Worship declares to the very ends of the earth.

Oh, may Mount Zion be glad, and the daughters of praise rejoice with dancing—Your ways are so True, and so amazing. Explore this wonderful place, and take good notes of Papa's

---

[1] 2 Chronicles 6:6

ways as shown by these testimonies. Mark them well; count the towers and the memorable places, so you can share their significance and what they speak of Him to the next generation. Because this is just what He is like, now and forever and through all eternity. This is how crucial it is then that we let these testimonies guide our walk in life.

Psalm 49

Listen up everyone—listen very carefully—all of you. Yes the rich and the poor—you all need to hear and take note of the wisdom I'm about to share, including me. May your heart respond with understanding as you think about it.

I will start my song quietly:

Why should I be full of fear just because the days are evil, and evil people press me on every side? There're many who trust in their wealth and boast of their bank balance, but absolutely no-one can redeem himself from God's judgment of him, or redeem anyone else. For we have all fallen so short of the glory that we were designed and created for, we don't have any of the right currency. A life is so costly—it's a life for a life[1]—so is way beyond anyone's ability to pay the necessary ransom to keep himself from the eternal consequences of his sin, so he can live forever. But thank You our King Jesus that You did just that for each one of us—Yeaaaaah. You first lived life in the full Glory that Papa gave You as His beloved Son, and then You gave Your life as a ransom for many[2]!

As for man—we don't have to look far to see that even the wise die one day, just the same as the foolish and stupid—leaving all of their riches to others. In their dreams they imagine their descendants carrying on their family line forever, carrying on the family name and title. But they all die, regardless, just like the animals.

Most people trust themselves, if they ever stop to think about it long enough, just as those who follow them do, but they all end up shepherded like a flock of sheep to the grave,

[1] Numbers 35:31
[2] Matthew 20:28, Mark 10:45

where they rot. But for the godly, death has lost its sting[3]...
They know that by His death Jesus broke the power of death[4],
and as Jesus said of Himself "that all who believe in Me will
never die",[5] because the law of the Holy Spirit of Life in
Jesus' Wonderful anointing has made me free from the law of
sin and death[6]...

So fear can't threaten me with death—I just get to join the
multitude in Mount Zion praising and worshipping our Lord-
of-Life, King Jesus, and all because Jesus is my Redeemer—
from death and hell and sin. Yeaaah!

So don't worry if you find yourself rich and famous, just
remember it's only for a season, and you can't take it with
you. But your fame—whether for good or for bad—will live
on. You can choose to bless yourself and have a good time,
and that's a sure way of making flattering fleeting friendships,
or you can look out to bless others while you're at it, and make
friends who remember you and honour you long after you've
gone.

So it doesn't matter how honourable, influential or
wealthy a man is, if he hasn't understood that it is Jesus who
has the keys to death and hell, then he really is no different to
the animals.

---

[3] 1 Corinthians 15:55, 56
[4] Hebrews 2:14
[5] John 11:26
[6] Romans 8:2

Psalm 50

God of all Gods—Lord of all Lords, Mighty are You over all this earth of ours from sunrise to sunset—You see it all. Your radiant Glory shouts "Perfection!" as it shines out from Your throne room. Come, Lord, come, and rend the heavens once more with Your devouring fire[1], Your jealous love that stops at nothing to care for those who love You.

Call out Your judgments and Your ways, to the heavenly host and to the gathering of Your people here, that Your judgments would be good and clear for everyone to see and follow…

Come, You people, those who've cut covenant with the Lord, draw close and see the heavens declare His Righteousness, that the Lord Himself is the judge—Yeaaaah!

Listen up—listen for His voice, everyone, and He will explain His judgment—The Lord—the one who you say is your Lord—listen and He will explain what He sees as good and bad.

I have no problem with your worship sacrifices and the sacrifices of your heart—which I see very clearly—but do you really think these are the things that matter to Me? In the days of animal sacrifices, bullocks and he-goats really weren't what I was looking for—these were but outward symbols. Don't you see that I know all the birds on the mountains, and the wild animals in the plains and savannahs, and if I was hungry I

---

[1] Exodus 24:17, Deuteronomy 4:24, Isaiah 29:6, Isaiah 30:30

really wouldn't need to come to you for a bite to eat, now, would I? The whole world is Mine and everything in it. Do you really think I eat beef and mutton?

What I am asking is that you offer Me a sacrifice of praise and thanksgiving—and not just when things are good and going well, but just as much, or more so, when things are really tough—as your expression of your faith and trust that I will come through for you. Will you still honour your promises to Me when it's really difficult, and call for My Covenanted Assistance to see you through? This is what I call a sacrifice. Your testimony of how I helped you brings Me much Glory.

Now those of you who delight to say your prayers, and ever so correctly recite your liturgy, taking the words of My Covenant with man just so religiously, but never acting on it in believing Me to heal, set people free from their demonic bondages and give new birth—forget it! I see how the reality of your hearts is very different—you hate being shown what really matters to Me, and treat My words with contempt. When you saw a thief you encouraged him, or someone in an adulterous relationship you helped them. As to the filth that spills out of your mouth—Ugh! I see all the lies that just trip off your tongue...

You laze around and slander even your own family and think I don't see it, because I never said, or appeared to do, anything about it. *Oh,* how wrong you are! Your thinking is so twisted you even think that I'm like that. But shortly things will look very different, and you will see My judgment with your own eyes and there will be no escape.

So consider it well, all of you who outwardly go through the motions, jumping appropriately through all the religious hoops, thinking this is what really matters, but at heart don't care a fig about Me, or consider what I am looking for. I might just come and tear you limb from limb, and you will have absolutely no-one to come to your help.

But those who have learned to offer Me their sacrifice of praise and thanksgiving through the same tough time, will find this becomes a sweet smelling sacrifice that brings Me Glory. It is to these who I will show My real name and character—Yeshua—Saviour,   Healer   and Deliverer.

Psalm 51

This Psalm of David, he wrote after Nathan the prophet confronted him over his adultery with Bathsheba.

We all need to learn the same lessons, for all of us have sinned and fallen way short of the wondrous glory that Papa God intended for us. To a greater or lesser degree we have all been there and more importantly we need to learn the way out.

Lord, I deserve nothing but punishment, but I come to You because You have shown me that Your nature is to be full of Mercy and Lovingkindness. So according to Your nature, and the sacrifice of Your Son, I ask that You blot out the record of my sin. Please, please wash me clean from this that got a hold of me, and scrub it well and truly out of my heart. I don't have any way of washing my heart clean—these things stare back at me.

For it was against You and only You that I did this, which was just so, so wrong in Your sight—I too can see it now. Your judgment against me is absolutely right and proper.

Like all mankind except You, Jesus, I was conceived a sinner, and needed to know You and Your redeeming love even as I grew as a baby in my mother's womb. *Oh,* thank You for teaching me so much of Your wisdom and Your ways, even there. *Oh,* how much I need to know You!

But Lord, if You wash me, You can make my heart clean again—whiter than snow. *Oh,* thank You that You have made a way by the washing of the word[1]. *Oh* that I could once again feel Your Joy and Gladness, instead of You crushing the very life out of me. Will You indeed cast my sin as far away from

---

[1] Ephesians 5:26

me as the East is from the West[2] so that it doesn't stare You or me in the face any longer—*Oh,* please blot out the very record against me of what I did[3].

Lord, please create a pure heart within me, and Holy Spirit fill my spirit once more with Your life, Your Grace, and Your Strength. *Oh* please, please don't shut me out from Your Precious Presence, or take Your Holy Spirit away—*Oh,* I so need You, Holy Spirit. Please restore the Joy You gave me when I first came to know You, and life started over, all fresh. And will You please put a willing spirit inside me, that I may run to follow You and Your ways. That will be such a source of inner strength—thank You, Holy Spirit.

Then I can start to teach others of Your ways, so that those tempted just as I was can learn to live differently—in right relationship with You.

Guilt, Lord, is a powerful brake on us continuing down a path of murder and evil, but please will You deliver me from it? *Oh,* my God—Yeshua—Jesus my Saviour, may I hear You say to me it is forgiven and the guilt of it taken away. Thank You Jesus for being that once-and-for-all sacrifice for my sin that takes it away[4], and declares me perfect once more[5] as I come afresh to worship You. Only then can I sing of Your righteousness and shout my love, my worship, my praise of You that You so richly deserve.

I know that animal sacrifices don't cut it with You or I would have rushed off to do it. Lord, I bring what You've shown me means something to You—my broken spirit, and my broken heart, horrified at what I have done, combined with a deep-hearted willingness to change.

---

[2] Psalm 103:12
[3] Colossians 2:14
[4] John 1:29
[5] Hebrews 10:1-2

May You find joy in blessing Your people, Lord, in giving them new songs and revealing Yourself, Your heart, to them in new ways. Then they, in turn, can offer themselves more wholly to You in love, in sacrifice and worship You delight in.

Psalm 52

The man about whom this Psalm was written took delight in slaughtering 85 of the Lord's priests[1].

You evil braggart—why do you boast of your evil? Why on earth would you want to boast about it all day long? While thinking yourself to be a mighty hero, really you are a truly evil disgrace before the Lord. Your tongue is like a sharpened razor, sharp in devising treachery and deceit. It demonstrates how you love evil rather than good—Ugggh! Your deceitful tongue illustrates your love for destruction of all kinds.

You may think yourself to be a mighty hero of the moment, but God Himself will destroy you in a moment, for all eternity. He will break you, tearing you from all that you love, even life itself—Yeaaah!

Those who love the Lord will see your demise with fear; as it unravels, this will turn to mocking laughter, "Just look— this is the man who trusted in his great wealth and despised the Lord, growing strong at the expense of others."

As for me—I am a green olive tree in the house of the Lord—the one whose never ending Lovingkindness I trust in, absolutely.

Again and again, You have done absolutely amazing and wonderful things for me, for which I take great delight in praising and thanking You, with all those who equally love You, Lord.

Lord, it's in You I have set my hope upon, for Your name is truly the God of Hope[2].

---

[1] 1 Samuel 21:1-9, 1 Samuel 22:9-23
[2] Romans 15:13, Jeremiah 14:8

Psalm 53

Only a fool says "There is no God." And they demonstrate it all too much with their corrupt and disgusting ways. Such thinking spreads all too easily—it becomes very hard to find any who do good. But the Lord looks down from heaven on everyone, looking to see if there are any who understand or are looking for Him. Has everyone really gone down that route—is there really no-one left?

Is everyone this evil—are they all this corrupt? It certainly looks like it, seeing the way they devour the Lord's people at every turn, and never think for a moment of calling on God.

But then, even the Lord's people have forgotten to call on Him in their day of trouble, and are overtaken with fear when there was absolutely nothing to be frightened of! He really put them to shame, 'cause He scattered their attackers all over the place as He despised this gang even more than His own people.

Oh that You, Jesus, our Wonderful Saviour, would once again be honoured and glorified by Your people. When they finally get free once more, then they will sing and dance and celebrate You as You so richly deserve—with great Joy and Gladness.

Come Holy Spirit and revive that Joy in Your people once more.

Psalm 54

Oh, King Jesus I look to You to save me, my Saviour King. Listen up, Lord; please listen to me.

Some seriously violent people are after me. Lord, they clearly have no regard for You, and I haven't a clue as to even where they've come from. Yeaaah !

But Lord... But Lord I'm looking to You—for You are my helper: You, the Lord of Heaven's armies, are the one who I am trusting. Thank You Jesus that those who come against me end up paying for their trouble many times over; cut them off—even as You are Faithful and True.

Lord, I bring You my sacrifice of praise. I praise and lift Your name High, Mighty Jesus, Faithful, Anointed One and True. *Oh* Your name is so Good! I'm trusting You my deliverer, that You will deliver me, and in due time I will look triumphantly on those who have come against me. Lord, I count it as a done deal, because my trust is in You. Thank You so much! All praise to You, Mighty King Jesus!

Psalm 55

Are You listening, Lord? Do You hear these things that are being said about me? They're winding me up something shocking. Help, Lord—please don't ignore me—please do something—well at least…

Lord, the anxiety is getting to me because of what I hear all the time—all these aspersions they're casting on me. Lord, surely You see their anger—Yes they are getting seriously angry at me. It's getting to my heart now. I feel palpitations starting, together with a multitude of morbid thoughts, and now I'm shaking with fear—*Oh,* what next?

Oh that I was a dove and could simply fly away. I'd go and hide in the wilderness, Yeaaah! That would be a lot pleasanter than here—a nice shelter from the storm and the wind… Nice thought, but…

Lord, I need You to intervene and do something—I've seen all too close up just what these get up to—it's not pretty—their violence and strife. Day and night, night and day, surrounding me with their mischief, their oppression and their cunning plans. Now if it was a long standing enemy of mine, then I could perhaps understand it, or someone puffed up with his hatred of me—envy and jealousy do strange things. Against these I could just go and hide, but these aren't like that. These are my friends—well I thought they were. We used to discuss things together, we'd worship You together…

Lord, will You shut their mouths and send them back to the pit where they came from. Evil and wicked is all they are.

Oh my King Jesus, I call on You, my Lord and my God. Lord, You are my Saviour—*Oh,* thank You that You will rescue me. Evening and morning, morning and evening, I call on You. Thank You that You do hear me. *Oh,* thank You that

You are my Redeemer, and You have redeemed me from all of these voices, every last one. *Oh,* thank You for Your peace, Your Shalom that You promise will guard my thoughts and my heart[1], as I bring my worries and fears to You with a thankful heart and spirit, and leave them with You. *Oh,* thank You that Your Shalom is a garrison against any amount of evil—You silence the lot of them—'cause You don't change—You are King forever, Yeaaah!

Oh Lord, I'm so easily seduced, and drawn in by their smooth talk, but it's all lies out to get my shield down for their sword attack... Ugh, I'm so ashamed when I finally see it.

Oh, Thank You Lord that I can cast every care on You, every worry, every fear, knowing that You care so much for me[2]. Thank You that You have set my feet on such a firm foundation[3], on Your Rock—Jesus—my Saviour.

Thank You Lord that You have a place assigned for all of those who haunt me, and that those who listen to them won't live out half of their days. As for me—Lord it's in You I trust—in You and You alone.

---

[1] Philippians 4:7
[2] 1 Peter 5:7
[3] Matthew 16:18, 1 Corinthians 3:11, 1 Timothy 6:19, 2 Timothy 2:19

Psalm 56

A Psalm of David written about his time in Gath, the key citadel of the Philistines, who trapped him there[1]. It was a bad move he made to run there in his flight from King Saul, who was after his life. Many of us can readily identify with David's thoughts and prayer, even if our circumstances aren't quite so dramatic.

Mercy, Lord! I plead Your Covenanted Assistance—my Covenant Partner. Lord, I seem surrounded by men after my blood, pursuing me and pressing home their attacks. Lord, it seems like my adversaries want to trample me underfoot all day long.

But Lord—when I am afraid—that worst of enemies—rises up inside, then I put my trust in You and in Your Word, Lord—my Saviour and my God. It's Your word that I stand on and praise and lift high. *Oh,* thank You Lord that as I do so, fear loses its grip, and my trust in You rises till I can say, "I'm an anointed child of King Jesus, I will *not* fear—what can man do to me?!?"

All day long they twist my words while their thoughts are of evil intent against me. They gather and hide, marking my every movement, as they plot for my very life. Surely, Lord, You are as angry with them as I am, and aren't going to let them get away with their evil plans.

But Lord... You number my footsteps. I know You count every one, just as you put my tears in Your bottle, recording every one in Your book of my life. So Lord, right now I call on You as my Saviour, for I know that You are for me, not

---

[1] 1 Samuel 21:10-14

against me, and I will therefore see these enemies of mine stopped in their tracks.

I praise You Lord for Your precious word—it's Your promise to me that I trust in. Jesus—I lift Your Mighty and Glorious name high—for You are so worthy of my praise and honour. Lord, it's in You who I trust—*I will not fear*! What can man do to me?!

Thank You Lord for all those many wonderful and special promises for my future here, that You have given me. Thank You Lord, You've promised me such amazing things. Thank You Lord that time after time You have delivered me from certain death, and time after time, You have delivered me from going headlong into things I shouldn't; that would have killed my relationship with You. *Oh,* thank You so much! It is truly a very precious privilege to walk through life as Your child, knowing Your protection and favour.

Psalm 57

A Psalm of David when he fled from Saul into a cave[1].

Mercy, Lord! Mercy! Help! Lord—I'm trusting in You and Your word to me—that You and You alone are my refuge. Lord, I'm snuggling up into You under the shadow of those mighty wings of Yours[2]. Lord, I'm going to stay right here just as long as I need to. Lord—the Most High—I'm trusting Your promises to me. I've seen You fulfil them before, in the most unlikely of circumstances, and I trust You again right now.

Thank You that somehow You are going to save me once more—even when he who would eat me alive is so close on my heels. Yeaaaah, God—I trust that once again You will come through for me.

Once again I am surrounded by lions and I never quite know which side they are on, or how much I can trust them... their hearts are on fire, and not too godly a fire most-times. You don't want them to get their teeth into you—their teeth are like spears and arrows, and as for their tongues—they are sharp swords.

But Lord... But Lord—I lift You high in the middle of them—right now is exactly when I choose to worship You— *Oh,* may Your Glory be known over all the earth.

They have spread a net wide to catch me, it seems close to hemming in my very spirit. *Oh,* but thank You Jesus, my Saviour—I see them digging a pit for me, and they've gone and fallen into it themselves! Yeaaaah!

My heart, my mind and my spirit are fixed on You, Lord;

---

[1] 1 Samuel 24
[2] Psalm 91

locked on. I will sing, *Oh* Lord, I will sing Your praise—*Oh,* You are so good to me.

Wake up spirit, wake up tongue, switch on the PA, the electric guitars, mikes and drum kits... we've got some praising to do—and don't tell me it's too early in the morning... We've got some thanks to give to the Lord... Come on everyone—join me, we need to get this streaming too, so all the nations can hear and join in our praise with us.

Lord—Your Lovingkindness is just so, so good—it's like it stretches to the heavens... and Your Faithfulness to Your promises stretches to the vivid morning sky.

Oh, Mighty King Jesus, we lift You high—high above the heavens—we lift You high in our hearts. May Your Glory be known over all the earth.

Psalm 58

You demonic principalities and powers—do you ever speak about justice or judge people fairly? No way! You are forever devising injustice and how to stir up violence—this people group against that one, this nation against that one... You infect people from birth, from the womb, with your lies—just like a deaf cobra—wicked venom, but no snake charmer's going to charm you.

Oh, Thank You Jesus that You have disarmed *all* principalities and powers[1], making an open show of them, triumphing over every one. Thank You that You have smashed their teeth in and ripped out their fangs—so it's all bravado with no substance. They run away at a whisper of Your Mighty name, "Jesus!". They get me in their sights, but their arrows always fall short—LOL! All their slimy plans are still-born—*Oh*, thank You Jesus! They are like brambles that are swept away before they even grow their thorns.

Oh, how You rejoiced when Your disciples learned to trample on all the powers of darkness—*Oh*, that made You so happy[2]! Thank You Jesus that Your blood still avails today, and that we overcome by Your precious blood[3]. So we too can rejoice today that You, King Jesus, still rule—indeed Your rule is forever increasing, and always will do[4]—Your rule of Justice, of Love and of Peace.

---

[1] Colossians 2:15
[2] Luke 10:17-21
[3] Revelation 12:11
[4] Isaiah 9:7

Psalm 59

Help, Lord! Lord, You are my deliverer I need you on my case again. Will You protect me from this bunch set to kill me. Lord—these are evil, bloodthirsty men lying in wait to take me out. Maybe I could understand it if it was for something I've done to annoy or hurt them, but I haven't. I know they are running round preparing traps for me—I need You to wake up and see what they're up to, Lord. Mighty God, the Lord of Heaven's armies, my Covenant-Keeping God, I call on You to come and visit the nations, especially this one, and bring some justice. Your continued mercy to the wicked ain't working— they really aren't getting the message. Yeaaah!

They come around at sunset stalking round the city like a pack of dogs, but I know it's me they're really after. The knives are out, but from their words they would be after Your blood, Lord, as much as they are after mine, as they boast that You can't hear.

Remind me again Lord that You're laughing at them, and that You're laughing at all the nations that think that way. Lord, You are my Strength, and my Fortress, so I will listen carefully to You. Thank You for Your Presence—and for Your amazing Lovingkindness towards me. Thank You that You give me the privilege of seeing that what *I* choose is precisely what happens to them. Now, don't kill them, Lord—no way— or everyone will forget and before I know it, we'll be back round the same loop all over again. But Lord, my shield, try this one with them: see to it that they row with each other, and distrust each other so they are scattered, and then one by one, You bring them down. For their cussin' and the rest of the junk that spews from their mouths, You deal with them, Lord; You consume them, Lord, till every one of them has been completely dealt with. And Lord, do it in such a way that they know that Jesus rules—to the ends of the earth, to the end of time—Yeaaah!

Then as evening comes I will listen for their mournful, pitiful, hungry howling as they wander up and down, famished, looking for scraps, while I feast at Your table[1].

As for me, Lord, I'm going to enjoy singing Your praise every morning, declaring to everyone Your great Power and Lovingkindness. For You are my high tower, for You are my fortress when I really need You. Lord, You are my strength and it's Your praise I sing, for You are my fortress, for You are the God of Mercy, the God of Covenant.

---

[1] Psalm 23:5

Psalm 60

Lord, have You really forgotten us altogether? It certainly looks like it! Everywhere Your people are scattered and losing it. Lord, please help us and bring us back to You. The earth itself has been shaken and cracked open, and is in desperate need of You to heal and restore it. Your people are similarly broken and in desperate need, Lord. They are reeling and staggering like drunkards, bewildered at their circumstance.

Aaaah, I see You have set up a banner for those who worship You Lord, and they are rallying to it in the face of any and all arrows levelled at them. Yeaaah!

Lord, You see those who are still worshipping You gathered to Your banner; please hear us and save us with Your right hand of love and of power. Lord, You are Holy—I exult and worship You as the God of Holiness, and true to Your Covenant, You divided and assigned the Promised Land to Your people from East to West, North to South, places for each of the twelve tribes, from the small tribes like Manasseh, to Ephraim, that champion of champions; all different, but each given the land and the space they needed.

And of the surrounding nations, You promised to make Moab nothing more than a dirty bowl for the dirt from Your people's feet, and similarly Edom—nothing more than the one who cleans their sandals. As to Philistia, You give Your people a shout of triumph over them. Lord, this was exactly what You had promised them.

Now who is going to lead me straight into the heart of those strongholds that those who don't know you, trust in—surely You will, Lord—my Covenant-Keeping Holy God. I'm not surprised at Your not helping people that presume on You, or rely on human assistance. But Lord we thank You that with

Your help we will have total victory and trample these who defy You, our Covenant-Keeping, Living God. Thank You that You appoint us to trample on every demon and tear down every demonic stronghold that raises itself against the knowledge of our Saviour King, Jesus.

Psalm 61

Lord, please hear my shout to You from wherever I am, even the ends of the earth. So please take note even of that faint whisper—when totally overwhelmed, it's all I can do to whisper Your wonderful and precious name—"Jesus"! *Oh,* lead me to You, my Rock[1] and my Redeemer—just so much higher and more secure and safer than I am. For You my Lord are a refuge and a mighty tower of strength from every enemy.

Lord, I so look forward to that day when I will come and live in Your wonderful throne room, through all eternity giving You Glory and Praise. But as I praise You and take refuge in the shadow of Your wonderful, mighty wings, I realise I'm part of that great company already. Yeaaaah!

For You, Wonderful Saviour, have heard me, and given me the Precious inheritance You so love to give to all who know and love You[2], Your Holy Spirit—the very same who raised Your body back to life again from that tomb and seated You in Heavenly places far above all[3].

Lord, may I live long here, as Your child, my King, and see many generations of my descendants. May I know Your precious Presence as I regularly take my place in worship in that heavenly company, knowing Your Love and Faithfulness protect my every step.

And I will forever and always sing Your praise, King Jesus, and lift High Your Mighty and Wonderful name—day by day fulfilling my heart's cry of love to You.

---

[1] Psalm 62:2, Psalm 62:6
[2] Ephesians 1:14
[3] Ephesians 1:17-22 Ephesians 2:6-7

Psalm 62

Oh Lord, it's so good to wait, quietly meditating on You, for You are such a Wonderful Saviour, my Rock[1], my Jesus. What a Fortress, what a Refuge You are! In You, I will not be shaken.

Just how long are you going to keep pressing in on a man who is already bowed and bent over like a rickety fence? It looks like you have gathered with but one objective, to pull me down from my Rock. To that end you delight in lies; with words of blessing, but in reality cursing under your breath... Uuuugh!

But Lord, I meditate on Your Faithfulness, for my hope is in You, and You alone: You are such a Wonderful Saviour, my Rock, my Jesus. What a fortress, what a refuge You are! In You, I will not be shaken. Jesus—You are my Saviour and it is in You whom I am trusting as I pour out my heart, my helplessness, my brokenness to You *Oh* Lord—my Refuge. Yeaaaah!

The servant or the king, and all in between—they all amount to nothing of value without You, Lord. Tyrants oppress while servants steal to boost their egos and their bank balances—but neither truly satisfies.

Check back in God's word and He has said it loud and clear that power belongs to Him, the power to rule[2], and the power to get wealth[3]. So trust Him for it.

---

[1] Psalm 61:2
[2] 1 Chronicles 29:12
[3] Deuteronomy 8:18

Thank You Lord that You see that everyone eventually reaps the reward for what they have sown. But above all of that, *Oh,* thank You Lord that one of Your greatest attributes is Your Lovingkindness—to us—*Oh,* thank You—thank You that when we come to You, You forgive us and make us new, saving us from reaping the result of all of our sin—so that in You we get to start over. Thank You so much Lord for Your Forgiveness and Grace.

Psalm 63

Oh Lord—Jeshua, Jesus, Saviour—You are my God, and I so long for more of You. I'm so thirsty for more of You; All that I am longs for You, like I'm in the middle of the Sahara—dry, dusty and barren. Lord, I've been hugely privileged to come close to You and tangibly feel Your Presence in times of worship with Your people. I've seen Your power changing hearts, restoring lives and healing bodies—I've seen Your Glory cloud show up[1], and gold dust fall on people.

Your Lovingkindness is just so, so sweet. You are better than life itself—I can't help but praise You, Wonderful Papa God. While I have breath left in me, I will praise and magnify Your wonderful name—"JESUS"—and lift my hands high in honour and worship to You. Inside I am deeply full of Your love—I'm satiated… I can't help but put love-songs to You on my lips. When I lie down at night, my thoughts inevitably turn to You and the so precious and intimate love You show me.

For You and You alone have been my help, the very source of my life, and my protection. In the shadow of those mighty wings of Yours I rejoice; my spirit soars, and my dreams take flight. My heart so longs for You, to hug You real close: *Oh,* thank You that You hold me by Your right hand[2], and You will never let me go.

Thank You that those who seek my life don't need me to take them out, they'll do that for themselves—for those that live by the sword will die by it too. Will anyone finally bury them, or will they be left to feed the foxes?

---

[1] I personally happened to be at Bethel Redding in the Autumn of 2013 when a Glory Cloud of the Lord did indeed appear in the sanctuary area, for all to see.

[2] Psalm 73:23

As for me Lord, I bless and praise Your wonderful name; Jesus, I rejoice in You while You delight in shutting the mouths of those who, for whatever reason, set themselves against You.

Thank You that You so delight to bless all who declare their love and trust in You.

Psalm 64

Are You listening, Lord? Please help me: fear is overwhelming me, big time. Can I snuggle up and hide myself in You once more? Please protect me from the plotting and planning against me, and from that rabble who hate You. I catch glints of them sharpening their tongues like swords as they practice which bitter words will pierce the deepest. Then they watch for their perfect moment to let fly at the innocent when they least expect it, without a care in the world. Rather, they encourage each other, vying with each other as to who can be the most vindictive. And all the while saying (and thinking) that no-one will see, or spot what they're up to. Their devious plots merely illustrate the depth and depravity the human mind and spirit can sink to.

But Lord… thank You that Your arrows are much sharper and You know just when and where to hit. Thank You Lord that You will see they reap the ruin their own words have sown so that everyone will shake their heads at them, and think a lot more respectfully of You and Your ways.

But Lord… *Oh,* I thank You that Your children are safe in You… that You provide us with a real safe and secure shield from all the fiery darts of our enemies[1], especially fear[2]. Thank You that above all, You really don't want us afraid of anything[3]… and that You give all who love You so much to praise and thank You for!

---

[1] Ephesians 6:16
[2] 2 Timothy 1:7, Hebrews 13:6
[3] 1 John 4:18

Psalm 65

Oh, Papa God, Wonderful Lord—You are so worthy of our praise in the gathering of Your people—in Your Mount Zion. Our hearts thrill to express their love to You—You, who draw near when we turn our hearts to You and worship You… You, who hear us and answer us when we call on You. One day everyone will bow the knee to You—Your love is just so amazing.

When we are overwhelmed and totally enslaved to our sin, to our dysfunction, to our habits and our addictions, You choose to love us so much that You aren't content to merely forgive us, but You made a way for us to be cleansed from all this junk and set free from its hold over us. *Oh,* Lord, You bless us so wonderfully, choosing us to have such free and ready access to You and Your special Presence. Lord, we are full—full of all the good things You have for us in Your Presence, in Your house, in Your throne room. Thank You Lord that You know exactly those things that just hit the spot for each one of us.

And then You go and lavish them so richly on us—*Oh,* You are so awesome and everything You do is so right and true. *Oh,* what a Saviour You are! All the earth—even the islanders in the farthest atolls of the Pacific—long and hope for just such an intimate experience of You that You share so freely with us, while the very ground beneath us groans for us to enter into the blessing that You have appointed to Your people to bring.

How on earth can we even begin to comprehend Your power that You make so freely available to us? You formed the mountains, You still the roaring of the ocean waves, and you quiet the turmoil of the nations. If we stop for a moment we are filled with awe and wonder at the beauty you create at dawn and at sunset—both the sky and our hearts sing our Joy to You.

What care You have for this creation! You made it so carefully for us so that Your rain waters the ground for growing things for us to eat. You drench the fields and furrows, and send gentle showers to keep things nice and moist so that the new growth sprouts perfectly—then You crown the year with Your bounty and blessing so that we have more-than-enough, because that's just who You are—El Shaddai—the God of more-than-enough.

Even the wilderness and the hills are clothed with Your Joy, the fields are ripe and full for the harvest, while the meadows are full of flocks and herds of cattle. Listen out and you'll hear them baaing and mooing for joy, just as we are. Thank You Lord, for Your amazing abundance[1], especially on those who know and love Your name.

---

[1] Matthew 5:45

Psalm 66

Hey, come everyone and give our wonderful Papa God a joyful shout of praise! He's so worth it! Sing out the Glory of His precious name—Jesus! Lift Him high over all with glorious High Praise. *Oh,* tell Him, tell the whole creation, how all the things He does are truly wonderful and awesome.

Oh, thank You that Your mighty and wondrous love is such that one day all will bow the knee to You, our King Jesus, and all will worship You. They will all lift high Your Wonderful name in song... Jesus!

Yeaaaah!

Listen once more to the things He did in times of old for His Covenant partners—just remember He's still the same yesterday, today and forever... When the Israelites were leaving Egypt and trapped by the Red Sea, He didn't just part the water, but He sent a wind to dry the sea floor so they all walked over on dry land[1]. *Oh,* they didn't half celebrate that one[2]!

If you really object to Jesus' rule of love, then I should keep quiet about it. Jesus' love rules OK, for ever and ever—just watch Him watching over the nations—the increase of His government shall never stop. Yeaaah!

Oh, Praise the Lord everyone—give Him a joyful and loud praise offering! He's the one who holds us and everything together[3], He's the bread-of-life to our spirits[4], He's the one

---

[1] Exodus 14:22
[2] Exodus 15:1-21
[3] Colossians 1:17
[4] Matthew 4:4, Luke 4:4

who guards us from all harm!

Praise You Lord! You took us through tough times to see just what we were made of, just like silver is refined, You put us through the process… You didn't leave us there, but brought us through every possible kind of debasement, steamrollered and trampled over by the nations, our hearts stretched to the limits and beyond, through fire and water… until finally You brought us through. Finally You brought us through into a place of wealth and abundance—You couldn't leave us any place else, because this is who You are.

Oh, Papa God, I come with great Joy to You and to Your house to offer You my sacrifice of Praise—the Love and the thanks of my heart for what You have brought me into. And Lord, here's what I promised in those tough, tough times—the promises I made to You. Freely I give back to You of the richness that You have lavished on me. Lord—I promised You a mighty Praise Party to give You the very best of what I came into—wonderful Papa. I bring these to You now with a truly thankful heart. Blessed be Your Mighty and Matchless name—Jesus! Yeaaaah!

Listen everyone to my testimony—all of you who love the Lord, come and hear just what the Lord did for me. I cried my "Help!" to Him. In the middle of being taken as low as it was possible to go, I chose to still worship Him and tell Him how special and wonderful He is, and that I still trusted in His ability and love to raise me back up.

Now if I harbour doubt, unbelief, despair and the like in my heart, that ain't going to get me very far, and the Lord isn't going to put Himself out to help me with quite the same alacrity. But He did hear and He is the one who so completely changed my situation and circumstances.

Oh, thank YOU Jesus! Thank You so much for hearing my pitiful cry for help and not leaving me there, but rescuing me with Your precious Lovingkindness. *Oh* You are so, so Good to me. Thank You Lord so much!

Psalm 67

Lord, thank You so much for the wonder of Your Grace that You lavish on us so freely—all the riches that Jesus won for us, and paid such a high price for—our forgiveness, our healing, our cleansing, our being declared righteous, our being seated in heavenly places with You. *Oh,* may we drink deep of Your unending Grace that we really don't deserve, but You choose to bless us with anyway. May we drink so deep that our lives glow with Your Glory, the glory of Your throne room, of Your Presence. Yeaaaah!

Lord, may others see this and know it's from You and want it too, that Your way of Salvation may be known and understood by everyone—by every people-group, every language and every nation[1]. May all the people praise You, Lord. May all the peoples lift high the name of Jesus our Saviour, and may they rejoice and be glad and sing for Joy. *Oh,* thank You that You are our God, full of Joy and it delights Your heart so much to see us, too, filled with Your Joy.

Oh, may all the nations be glad, rejoice and sing and shout for JOY! For You, our King Jesus, are the one who will judge the people and the nations fairly and govern the nations of the earth. Yeaaaah!

Oh, may all the peoples praise You, King Jesus—You so deserve it! May all the peoples praise You and lift Your name High—for then Your wonderful blessing will flood our lands, fill our bellies, and overwhelm our hearts.

Oh Lord, we ask for Your precious blessing, so that all, even to the ends of the earth, will see and recognise that this is so much more than good luck, or man's best, but has to come

---

[1] Revelation 5:9, Revelation 7:9

from You, and You alone. May they come and seek to know You too, and honour Your Wonderful, Mighty and Matchless name... Jesus!

Psalm 68

Oh Lord, will You rise up once more and invade this earth doing the things we heard about long ago. Lord we need You to scatter those who hate and despise You—Lord send 'em packing! Blow them away like smoke—may their hearts run molten like wax in a fire—in the fire of Your mighty Love, Mercy and Grace…

But Lord… those who love You have so much to celebrate and party over—thank You Lord that You are our God overflowing with Joy, Laughter and Fun—*Oh,* thank You for Your Joy.

Lord, we sing to You—King Jesus, we praise Your Wonderful name, and with our praise we build You a highway from the clouds of heaven through to the desert places here in need of Your transformation—a multilane freeway for Your delivery trucks full of Heaven's best—for You, El Shaddai, the God of More-than-enough, You who demonstrated Your love, and Your provision for Your redeemed ones, by giving us Your Son, our King Jesus, will You not also freely and graciously give us all that we need[1]?

For You are a Father to the orphan, a Judge for the widow and You set the lonely in families, and set the prisoner free into a place of prosperity and wealth. These are Heaven's best indeed! Lord, with our praise to You we call these blessings into this desert[2], that this place may blossom like a rose[3].

Thank You Lord that You so love to bless Your people as we praise and worship You, while those who refuse to honour You remain stuck in that sun-blasted desert.

---

[1] Romans 8:32, Matthew 6:11, Luke 11:3
[2] Matthew 6:10, Luke 11:2
[3] Isaiah 35:1

Lord, we remember the stories of when You went ahead of Your people tramping through the wilderness. Yeaaah!

The earth under their feet shook while Your Presence brought sweet rain, and when they arrived at Sinai the whole mountain shook with Your Presence—the Holy One of Israel—Jesus! *Oh,* that was delightful rain You brought them; plentiful rain that restored Your people, confirming Your love for them, and all the time they were there You provided so richly for all of them.

And there You came and brought them Your Word—the ten commandments spelling out the basics of how to do life Your way, healthy, wealthy and wise, and You showed Moses all of the details for the tent of meeting, the sacrifices and the ark of the covenant where You met them, which all spoke so prophetically and intimately of You our King Jesus and Your once and for all sacrifice of Yourself for us.

Oh, and it was the women who caught it and understood. They were the ones who rose up a mighty army to tell the world of You and Your ways—an army of lady evangelists and worship leaders... *Oh* thank You King Jesus that in Your fight, it's the stay-at-home mums who win Your battle every time, who divide the spoils—the wonderful blessing and Shalom from You filling every member of the family and strengthening families and family ties with Your powerful Love. Their work may look menial, but this is where the real battle is won, and kings run a mile from it (LOL!)—cleaning, cleaning and more cleaning, babies' bottoms, floors and pots and pans... but they are the ones who evangelise the next generation[4]. They are the ones who carry Holy Spirit comfort to those in need, they are the ones who provide the silver lining to every situation. They are like gold. And that silver lining reflects Your Glory, Lord, like a blanket of snow on a

---

[4] Psalm 78

mountain glistening in the sunshine—it covers everything—
every circumstance of life.

And you rugged, tall and majestic mountains—why do
you have issues with the mountain the Lord has chosen—
Mount Zion where He will reign for ever and all eternity? He
doesn't judge and value by the highest or most rugged. He
uses a different yardstick[5].

Oh, King Jesus, what a lot changed when You inaugurated
that New Covenant on our behalf, when You moved Your
royal court from Mount Sinai to Mount Zion[6]. No longer a
mountain of fire and smoke, of fear and trembling, but to the
City of the Living God, to the church of the firstborn—Mighty
King Jesus—where thousands upon thousands of angels and
the redeemed give You Praise, Honour and Glory[7].

For You took captivity captive[8], and led the redeemed in
Your triumphal procession to Glory; all the rebellious, the
scoffers, the unbelievers who You redeemed and captivated
with Your love. *Oh,* what gifts of Praise and Honour we lift
high to You our Wonderful King.

All Praise and Blessing to You King Jesus, Anointed One
for all the blessings You pour out on Your children every day.
Oh, what a Saviour You are—Yeaaah! Thank You that You
don't just save us from death by giving us eternal life, but You
load us with wonderful blessing and Joy here and now;
blessing and life that those who refuse to come to You never
experience.

Oh, what a procession is streaming into view, coming to
Mount Zion! A people from every tribe, little tribes and big

---

[5] Isaiah 11:3
[6] Hebrews 12:18
[7] Hebrews 12:22-23
[8] Ephesians 4:8

tribes, every tongue and nation, washed in the Blood of the Lamb[9]. A people from every age from the depths of time, they come streaming to Your throne. *Oh,* what a holy procession, what passion, what Joy! The singers lead the way followed by those playing all the instruments. And then there's the ladies with their tambourines, twirling and dancing—*Oh,* bless and praise our Saviour King—"JESUS!" the Lord, the God of Abraham, Isaac and Jacob. See the tribes coming in glorious array—it's a bit like the procession at the start of the Olympic Games... tribe by tribe, nation by nation—flags lifted high—in celebration of Our King Jesus.

They come bearing their gifts to the temple throne room at the very heart of Mount Zion, their kingly gifts for the King of Kings. In demonstration of the King's power given to His saints, the adversary is humbled throughout the nations. Stripped, his riches are brought in homage to the King, while the nations who still delight in war are scattered.

Princes come, while others stretch high their hands in worship, as the kingdoms of the earth sing their songs of worship and triumph to the King. Yeaaaah! Ascribe greatness and power to the King who is King over the highest heaven, by whose mighty voice the whole creation came into being, whose Royal Throne is over the whole family of Israel—the children by birth, and those by adoption. Awesome in power and love, our wonderful King Jesus, what power and anointing You give to Your people.

Blessed be You, our Mighty, Awesome, King Jesus, who created all things, and by whom all things were created[10].

---

[9] Revelation 7:14

[10] John 1:3

Psalm 69

Help, Lord, Help! This mess is way over my head—it's eating into my soul, and I'm sinking deeper and deeper... I'm way out of my depth in this one, Lord, and those rollers are still piling in, munching me. I'm worn out with my crying, my throat is parched and my eyes are stinging with my tears... Lord, I'm waiting on You 'cause no-one else is going to help me but You, and I know You never fail.

There are so many who hate me—all for no reason—there are more of them than the hairs on my head! And they have their hatchets out for my blood. I'm down to giving away stuff like I stole it, but I never...

Oh Lord—You... You know my stupidity, my weaknesses and my sin. Thank You that I can be real with You 'cause You know it all anyway.

Above all, Lord, may those who love You and are waiting on You to move, may they not be put to shame by what happens to me. That just reflects back on You then, Lord. I have done my best to cover for them, Lord, and ended up with shame on my face as a result. It's got to the point now that my own family have disowned me and cast me out; even my own brothers and sisters are treating me like a foreigner.

I am consumed inside by my zeal for You Lord, and for Your house. The insults and cussin' against You are falling on me and my heart, and when I'm in tears for my love for You, I wear my aching heart on my sleeve as I fast and seek You. All the while the people mock me and scorn me, and make fun of me. I'm now the butt of the song they're singing in the pubs and the bars.

But Lord... But Lord It's You who I seek, and I thank

You that today is the day You save[1]. Jesus—in Your great love, come and save me. Lord, please rescue me before I sink any lower, if that really is possible! *Oh,* deliver me from those after my blood—from these deep, deep waters. Lord they are overwhelming me, overwhelming my heart as they flood over me. Please don't let everything close in over me.

Lord I need answers, I need help; all the while I'm trusting in Your Loving Kindness, in Your Mercy, Lord. Please may I sense Your smile on me once again; and quickly Lord, 'cause I'm seriously losin' it. *Oh,* come close, Lord, my Redeemer. Thank You for paying the full price to ransom me from my slavery to sin and the evil one. Thank You that You know my history; You know all my sin and shame, my weakness and disgrace—You know all my enemies and yet You still paid my ransom and set me free, to have a whole fresh start. I was heart-broken and sick as a pig, looking in vain for sympathy and comfort. Rather, they fed me bitterness to eat and vinegar to drink[2].

If they were human it would be hard not to curse them— sometimes people do seem to take on the very embodiment of evil, and loving them while hating their sin does get very difficult. *Oh,* may their table be for them a snare, so that as they gorge themselves at ease with their world, they find themselves trapped in a dark world where they can't see properly and their guts go on fire with the runs that won't stop, as they get more and more dehydrated and delirious. *Oh* that they would sense Your anger and judgment steamrollering over them, Lord. May they have no descendants and their houses left desolate and derelict.

---

[1] 2 Corinthians 6:2

[2] Matthew 27:48, Mark 15:36, Luke 23:36, John 19:19, John 19:30

For they rejoiced and laughed with mockery at the wounds You bore for me, Lord Jesus. They made fun of the anguish and pain that You carried that I may know Your peace and forgiveness. Compounding their sin and shame I want to cry "may they never be forgiven—may they never." But rather, may they be blotted out of Your Book of Life, and never counted as one of Yours, Lord.

And yet You said, "Father, forgive them—they haven't a clue what they are doing[3]." And to be fair they didn't—they had no idea that You were God's precious Son—potentially their Saviour. *Oh* yes, the demons egging them on did—that's a different story. But *Oh* how quickly I forget—it was only a moment ago I too was one of them, mocking You, and poking fun at Your suffering—*Oh* Jesus, forgive me too, please.

But now Lord, I see my own poverty, poverty of heart, of love, of thought, of spirit, quite apart from my bank balance. Lord what a mess, I am so sorry. Jesus—I take You as my Saviour and Lord—please deliver me, and set me afresh on Your solid rock.

Jesus, I praise and bless Your precious name—I honour Your name and lift You high in my songs of worship and thanks to You. I've come to see how much more You appreciate my sacrifice of praise and thanks, than animal sacrifices or gaudy public financial gestures. Those who You've raised up like me, see and rejoice and join my praise party—*Oh,* You are Good, my Jesus—You are so Good. Thank You that You always hear those at the end of themselves, who have finally turned to You—and You never turn Your back, but pick them up, dust them down and give them a new start and a new life.

---

[3] Luke 23:34

Oh, that all of heaven and earth would praise You my King. May the sound of the waves be a hymn of praise to You and everything that moves be a dance in praise of Your Glory, and the Life You so freely give.

Thank You that You are building a new temple of living stones—a family of brothers and sisters, a people of praise and thanksgiving to You. Thank You that You are building again the cities of Praise—the communities of believers who rejoice to sing Your praise, King Jesus. Thank You that from them comes hope, and life and the knowledge of You and Your ways, so they build on a firm foundation that lasts through the generations as their inheritance. Thank You that my children, and my children's children, will love You and worship Your precious name—King Jesus!

Psalm 70

A Psalm of David

Help, Lord, Quick! Help!

Lord, my life is on the line this time. Lord, You don't bring shame on anyone, but this lot—that's what they deserve… Confuse them and bring all that they're planning for me on themselves. And quickly too, please Lord, before they start their chanting "Ah, Ah, I told you so…!" in trying to dishonour me.

But those who seek You and Love You, King Jesus, *Oh,* give them good reasons to rejoice and be glad in You. May those who long for more of You always have good reason to shout "The Lord is Great—He's so Good!"

As for me, Lord… I'm poor, and I need You so much… *Oh,* my King Jesus, my Saviour, my Deliverer—*Oh,* please come quick!

Psalm 71

Lord, it's in You, my King Jesus, Anointed One, who I trust—my Saviour, My Lord! Thank You that You never shame me, and You guard me from shame like no other. Deliver me again, please Lord, my Rescuer, my Saviour. For You are my Rock, the foundation of all that I am, and it's me in You, and You in me[1] that I live for all the time. *Oh*, thank You Lord for Your wonderful and amazing promises of protection. What a solid rock and fortress You are!

Deliver me, Lord, once more, from the grasp of evil and out of the machinations of godless cruel men, for my hope is, as always, set on You, King Jesus, my God-of-Hope. From birth I have depended on You and from before that—You took care of me and saw me through. All Praise to Your wonderful name—Jesus!

And now I'm a sign that many look to, and watch to see just how You deliver—*Oh* Jesus, You are my strong, strong refuge, and my mouth can't help but shout Your praise, declaring Your Glory all day long.

Now just as You looked after me when I was being born, please don't leave me when I get old and my strength starts to fail. I catch my enemies conspiring again to do me in. I overheard them muttering "God has left him this time, now's our chance—let's get him for now there's no-one to rescue him."

Oh, don't be far away, Lord; *Oh*, come quick, Lord. Help!

Shame on you, you demonic accusers—you who know no shame. May your plans to bring me down be brought low by

---

[1] John 15:4, John 15:5, John 15:7

your own machinations, with the dishonour intended for me crashing around your ears.

Lord, my hope, as always, rests in You, so I will praise and worship You more and more, deeper and deeper, higher and higher. I will take great Joy in telling how right and good You are, and of how You love to save to the uttermost all who come to You—there's no counting them all.

You came, King Jesus, with signs and wonders demonstrating Your Father's love to heal, to bind up the broken-hearted and restore—*Oh,* You did all things well! You really are so Good, Jesus, for You never change. You love to do the same today through us too. You taught me from childhood of Your Lovingkiness and I take great Joy in sharing those stories of Your wonderful deeds. Lord, please don't leave me when I get old and grey-headed—I need You to give me the strength and the anointing to share with the next generation the wonders I have experienced, that my ceiling can be their floor.

Oh, what great and wonderful things You have done, my King Jesus; who can get close to the things You've done?

I know sometimes the way You have led me has been down in the valley of trouble and difficulty, but You always brought me through. So now, this time Lord, I'm asking that You lead me out one more time; that You comfort me, and increase Your favour on me.

Oh, how I long to praise You, King Jesus, and celebrate Your Truth, in song, with all of the instruments. I will shout for Joy in my songs, as I tell of how You delivered me. All day long I will tell of just how right and true You always are. I will take particular joy in shaming and exposing those who wanted to take me down.

Psalm 72

Thank You Papa God for Your most wonderful Son, King Jesus—Your royal prince—who forever and always shares Your heart for Justice and Righteousness.

Oh, thank You Jesus that You judge everyone in righteousness and bring justice for the poor.

Thank You that You give wisdom, vision and anointing for prosperity on the mountains of influence, that Your life and Your prosperity is released to flow, bringing righteousness in its wake. Thank You that You defend the poor, the broken and the orphan, breaking oppression.

Oh, may You rule as long as there's morning and evening—for all generations. May Your Grace and Love come down like rain showers watering the ground hungry for more. For with You in charge, the righteous flourish and everyone prospers till the moon is no more.

Oh, may You rule from sea to shining sea, from the Euphrates to the very ends of the earth. May the Arab tribes and nations bow the knee to You King Jesus, while those who refuse, eat the dust.

May the kings of trade and of commerce join with the kings and presidents of the nations in giving You their gifts, while the queens and patrons of art and culture come with their offerings to give You Glory.[1] May all the kings of the earth bow to You, King Jesus, and all the nations look to Your Lordship.

For You deliver the weak the needy, the poor and the broken who cry to You, who have no-one else to help them. You take pity on them and Redeem them; rescuing them from

---

[1] Revelation 21:24

oppression and violence, because they are precious to You—our Redeemer King.

Gold and wealth from the nations will be given to You King Jesus—may You rule forever, as people pray to You and bless Your wonderful name all day, every day.

Abundance shall flow from the mountains of influence, grain from the prairies and fruit from the orchards, so everyone has more-than-enough and the cities shall flourish like the grass of the earth.

Your name, King Jesus, shall endure forever—it will outlast the sun. And all the nations of the earth will lift You high in blessing, in worship, in their adoration of You. All praise to You Lord, the Mighty God of Israel, who alone does such wonderful things. All praise to Your glorious name forever; may the whole earth be filled with Your Glory, King Jesus! Amen and Amen!

Psalm 73

Oh Papa God, You are so, so good to Your children, to those who've given their hearts to Your precious Son. Just when I had so very nearly lost it, I had come so close; I was just about to slip into envying the arrogant, and the prosperity of those who totally disregard You and Your ways, when You caught me.

They are strong in life and don't give a hoot about death. They conveniently avoid the 9-5 rat-race, and aren't burdened by mortgages and all the normal humdrum stuff of life. Rather—

They wear their pride like a chain necklace as something to be proud of—Ugh—while clothed with aggro. Their greed knows no limits, with no limit to how they get themselves their next 'must-have'.

They spout off with malice and arrogant threats, and as You well know, not even You Lord are exempt from their boasting as they lay out their claim for everything that glitters. So people follow the glitterati, hooked on following their every fad, envious to be just like them. They boast of how You don't see them—that surely You don't know *everything*! This is what the wicked look like—carefree, foot-loose and fancy-free, as they carry on grabbing any and everything that catches their eye.

So what's the point? I've struggled so hard to do right and in all innocence keep my conscience clear. All day, every day, I have struggled physically and mentally to make ends meet, with each new day bringing more than its fair share of pain and grief. And if I had spoken out like them, I would have been slagging off Your very children, Papa.

I don't get it, Lord, I really don't get it.

Well—that was until I came back into Your so Precious Presence again, and drew close to You once more, and You started to show me... You showed me where their lifestyle leads... that their path is hugely more slippery than I had realized—that in a moment their fame and fortune vanishes in a puff of smoke, leaving them absolutely desolate and terrified.

Their reality is like a fantasy—a dream, the moment You come on the scene, Lord.

Oh Lord, how that envying of them grieved You—such bitterness of spirit... I was being really stupid wasn't I? Just like a senseless animal.

I live with You forever; You hold my right hand. You lead me and guide me every single day of my life, and when I finally step over that threshold into eternity, I have eternity with You in glory. And who or what even vaguely compares with You and the wonder of knowing You more each and every day? *Oh,* there's nothing compares with You my Lord, My King Jesus.

When my strength in this life finally gives out, then You, You my King Jesus, are my Lord and my strength for eternity—forever and always.

Oh, but what happens to those who live out their days far from You... they die and are forgotten, like they had never been.

But me—*Oh* Papa God, how close can I get to You, my refuge? I love to tell everyone of the wonderful things You do and the wonderful things You show me. Thank You Papa, thank You so much!

Psalm 74

Oh Lord, are You keeping Your distance from us forever? It sure seems like that. I sense Your anger is still smouldering against us—the few of us left from the earlier moves You made across our nation. Please remember the saints of old who You won to Yourself—aren't they in that throng around Your throne, pleading that You move once again on their tribe, on their descendants. Will You visit us and see for Yourself the ruins of what was once a thriving number of congregations who worshipped You? It's all been torn down and trampled over; You can see how few of us are left, and the sorry state we're now in.

Those religious demons and legalists shouted off in the very places where we used to meet with You, lifting high their dogmas, their laws, and their demands for decency and order. They axed their way through Your promises of forgiveness and love, smashing and tearing down the beauty of Your Presence, of knowing You, of time spent in abandoned, joy-filled praise and worship to You, my King Jesus. Their set liturgies and hymn sandwiches crushed and burned the last vestiges of relating meaningfully to You. It's got to the point now where Your name is mocked as a byword for being irrelevant and out of touch with reality.

They planned to crush us altogether and destroy every one of those places of worship where there's any life left—and Lord, You see just how close to that they're getting. Signs and wonders, conversions and healing stopped so long ago, no-one remembers any more, and the few who call themselves prophets only add their condemnation to the misery, and that surely isn't from You, our loving, forgiving, Papa God, who gave us Your Son to Redeem this world—*Oh* Lord, how much longer?

How much longer, Lord, will You allow the enemy to mock You like this; they aren't going to change? Lord, why do You do nothing to change this situation? It feels like even You have Your hand folded up behind Your back. Lord, get it out and sweep them away.

Oh my High King, my Papa God, You always wanted to save everyone. Thanks for reminding me, that You gave us Jesus to be our Saviour... OK, Jesus, You said You didn't come into the world to condemn it but bring life, and life more abundantly.

Oh, thank You Papa God that in a moment You did indeed rend the heavens and come down, and declare how pleased You were with Your Son, King Jesus, and how You anointed Him with Holy Spirit. And thank You Jesus that having won Your rule over this earth, at Calvary, You have judged every demonic ruler and principality, breaking their power, their rule and their authority.

Thank You Jesus, that You rule, that You are the one who holds this creation together, and it is by You, our Wonderful Creator, that sun and moon stay on their course, and You determine the rain and the flood, summer time and winter, the deserts and the rivers and their courses.

Lord, remember how the adversary mocks You, and causes foolish people to join them. But Lord... But Lord, please watch over, and guard those who know and love You, those filled with You, Holy Spirit—it even looks like their lives are held in the balance, forgotten and cast aside by You.

King Jesus, will You remember Your Covenant once more; violence, and lawlessness look to be taking over as this land descends back into chaos. Lord, please don't let the poor, the needy and the oppressed back up any further—remind them that You are still King. *Oh* that they would remember and praise and lift high Your wonderful name "JESUS!" Remind them that it is they You have appointed to bring in Your Kingdom Rule and Reign—that You have anointed them for just such a purpose[1], for 'just such a time as this'[2]. Give them great boldness once more[3].

Oh! Come Lord! Come and fight Your corner; back up their words with signs and wonders that demonstrate the Kingship, and Lordship of Your Son Jesus. Remember those who mock and trample on Your precious name, "Jesus." And while You're at it, don't forget that array of politically correct voices raised against You, that's pushed in front of our noses, all the time. Lord, anoint my words to shut their mouths even as You command even me to trample on these things[4].

---

[1] Isaiah 61:1-4, Matthew 28:19,20
[2] Esther 4:14
[3] Acts 4:31, Acts 16:26
[4] Luke 10:19

Psalm 75

All Praise to You our King Jesus—Praise to Your Mighty and Matchless name! It's such fun to tell people of the wonderful things You've done, and we all shout Your Glory!

Thank You that You are the one who sets the time for judgment and will judge with Righteousness and Fairness. Thank You that when earthquakes and tsunamis hit, this is not Your judgment, because through it all You still hold everything together—Yeaaaah!

Thank You that Your judgment will be hugely more awesome than this.

Thank You Lord, that through these things You remind the arrogant to cut their boasting, and the wicked to watch their step. That as they defy You so boastfully, You can bring them down in a moment. Thank You that while they seek many ways to promote themselves, You are the Judge and You raise one up and cast another down.

Thank You that in Your hand is a cup of wine. For those who love You, a cup of Covenant and of Promise. But for those who set themselves against You and Your ways this same cup is a cup of opportunity that they drink down, dregs and all, and in doing so reveal their true natures.

I praise You King Jesus—all Praise to You forever and always. Thank You that You break the strength of those who are against You, but increase the strength of those who love You and delight in Your wonderful and precious name.

Psalm 76

Thank You Jesus, Anointed One, for that privilege of knowing You, that as we come to You in praise and in worship You make Yourself known to us. *Oh,* thank You that You build Your throne in the midst of our praise as You dwell in Mount Zion, that building and temple made of living stones[1].

Oh, thank You that You dismantle aggression and the weapons of war… Yeaaaaah!

Thank You that Your ways are Glorious and Majestic, so much higher than the ways of those who steal, kill and destroy[2]. Now it's their turn, they are plundered and sleep their last sleep, and can't lift a finger. At a whisper from You, their weapons are matchwood.

Oh it's You and You alone, we love and honour, for who can stand before You? *Oh,* thank You that You are so slow to anger and so quick to bless[3]. That You declared Your judgment from heaven and gave us Your Son to seek and to save everyone[4]…

Yeaaaaaah!

The very wrath of man was poured out on You, King Jesus, and yet You didn't retaliate but stayed the course, like a lamb led to the slaughter[5]. *Oh,* So worthy are You of our praise, that Your blood speaks "Father Forgive"[6] so that the judgment we deserve is restrained.

---

[1] 1 Peter 2:5
[2] John 10:10
[3] Exodus 34:6, Numbers 14:18
[4] Luke 19:10
[5] Isaiah 53:7
[6] Luke 23:34

Make Jesus Your King. Give Him your heart and bring Him your love offerings, for there is no fear in love[7]. For He will break the spirits of those who don't acknowledge His Lordship while raising up and empowering all those who love Him.

---

[7] 1 John 4:18

Psalm 77

Help, Lord, HELP!   Help me!

Lord—I need You so bad… Where have You gone?

Even though my hands are lifted high in praise and worship to You, my spirit is as blind to Your presence as my eyes are in this thick dark night.

Lord I need You!

I remember that precious quickening You brought—it seems like months ago now, when You seemed so close—so reassuring… But where are You now?—You seem like miles away. My spirit is about to give up altogether. Aaaaah!

But now, even with my eyes closed, the turmoil in my heart is such that I don't even know where to start. I catch a glimpse of a memory from long ago; the love song I used to sing to You in the night. Where did that come from? I haven't sung that in years!

And then more questions flash across my mind—no answers—just more questions:

'Does the Lord turn His back forever?'

'Have I lost His favour forever?'

'Has His unfailing love failed?'

'Does He no longer stay true to His Covenant promises?'

'Has He forgotten His Covenant Assistance?'

'Has He got so angry that He's forgotten His caring, loving nature?' Aaaaah!

Then I think, 'I will set myself to recount the Covenant Assistance our All-Mighty covenant partner gave us year in, year out, stretching out His hand of blessing over us, His Covenant people.'

Lord—I will remember what You did—those marvellous miracles that have come down the generations from long ago. I will remember them, and meditate on them, and all that they will tell me of You and Your nature.

Lord—Your ways and ALL that You do shout of Your Holy nature. You demolished all of the Gods of Egypt, one by one, from the least to the greatest[1]... There's none like You! You love to do miracles for those who look to you with faith and love, and to display Your mighty power to save and redeem a people for Your own possession. And You're in the same business today in redeeming us as the bride for your Son Jesus[2] as you were in redeeming the descendants of Jacob and Joseph from their slavery in Egypt. Yeaaaah!

Just what did those miracles look like, Lord? I picture You coming to the Red Sea and the water just running away, churning, convulsing—no wonder it rose up in a wall on either side. And before that there was that crazy thunderstorm when the thunder just echoed back and forth, shaking the ground, while the lightning was so continuous the night became almost like daytime. And the rain!—yeah—the heavens opened! Indeed they did![3]

That was a path, indeed, through the midst of the sea that You prepared for them. Fancy even drying it up for them.[4] I think if I look hard enough I'll see Your footprints checking whether it's dry enough for them to cross.

And through it all You led Your people like a flock of sheep led by a couple of ordinary shepherds, Moses and Aaron.

Oh Lord—do it again! That's all I ask. Do it again!

---

[1] Each of the plagues was God's judgment against one of Egypt's gods.
[2] Revelation 21:2, 21:9 & 22:17
[3] Exodus 9:23
[4] Exodus 14:21-22

Psalm 78

Come everyone and listen *very* carefully. I've got a parable to tell you that you will find really helpful, if you will but 'hear' it. These are truths that have been hidden for centuries, but passed down, generation to generation, to those who had the understanding to hear them. And each generation promised to pass them on to the next—the key is the amazing and wonderful things the Lord did for us in times past.

He made the Patriarchs promise to keep this key and established it as a law in Israel that each generation was commanded to pass on to the next, so that the next would know. In this way each succeeding generation, even those not yet even a twinkle in their parents' eyes, would in due time pass them on to their children. In this way, each generation would put their trust in the Lord and His glorious acts, and thereby learn to trust Him and walk in His ways. By doing this, they would then not be like their ancestors who, in their rebellion, walked in a very different direction, refusing to put their faith and trust in Him.

You see, the menfolk from the tribe of Ephraim[1] one of the most powerful of the twelve tribes, came all armed with their bows and arrows one time, and were all ready to fight, but they had forgotten the key. They had forgotten to pass down the generations the wonderful things that the Lord had done for them. Now because they had forgotten what He had done, they also forgot His Covenant and Covenant promises, and the part they had to play in those promises. So when the crunch came, they ran away, rather than stand and fight.

---

[1] Ephraim was the younger of Joseph's two sons, but carried the greater blessing from his Grandfather Jacob than Manasseh who was the elder.   Genesis 48:13-20

Their ancestors saw the Lord do amazing miracles that resulted in their being set free from Egypt. On leaving, He divided the Red Sea and dried up the ground so that they all walked across without even getting their feet wet, with the water rearing up on either side. That must have looked awesome! Then every day He guided them with the cloud of His Presence during the day and the light from His Fire all night. When they were thirsty He split the rock so they had water in abundance for themselves and all their livestock—the water just poured directly out of solid rock!

They still never learned His ways and His loving and caring heart for them, but chose to whine and complain out of their rebellious hearts. They quite deliberately put God to the test saying, "OK, so can God really feed us properly here in the desert? He gave us water when Moses struck that rock, but there's no way He can give us meat and bread. We're sick of manna, manna, and more manna!" Now that made the Lord pretty mad that after all that, they still had no appreciation of either His loving care, or His power to provide for His people. His fire flashing out was not a pretty sight. But yet He commanded the sky to yield her fruit and it rained—not cats and dogs but birds, birds and more birds, everywhere—both in and all around the camp. In the middle of the desert there were so many birds they were like the sand on the seashore—in the tents, around the tents—everywhere. Cook these with some manna and you had a delicacy fit for the angels! Ahhh so good! They stuffed themselves. Well, wouldn't you, if you hadn't had some solid meat for a month? And this was exactly what they had asked for, and had said He could never provide for them.

But while they were still stuffing their faces, God's anger burst out and killed many—even the strongest and toughest, the young and the old—He was quite indiscriminate. And the people still didn't get it, and ended up dying in the desert—terrified rather than knowing His love. When death got a bit too close they pretended—they pretended very well, and remembered that God was the one who had redeemed them from their slavery in Egypt. They said all the right words, but never got it inside where it really matters, that He is a Covenant-Keeping God, and all they had to do was call on His Covenant Assistance. Thanks largely to Moses interceding for them time and again, God forgave them and didn't wipe them out when He got angry at their lack of trust in Him. He remembered they were only human, and their lives were just like a puff of wind—gone in a moment, leaving no trace.

Oh, how often they lost it in the wilderness, grieving the Lord so much when He wanted to be like a loving Father to them. They kept putting Him to the test rather than simply trusting Him—that He was (and is) the Holy One of Israel—the ALL-MIGHTY creator God, for whom nothing is impossible. They forgot His power and the signs and wonders that He did to see them redeemed from their slavery back in Egypt. He turned the Nile into a river of blood so that no-one could drink any water. He sent horrible swarms of flies, and mosquitoes that bit them, and then a plague of frogs that just spread everywhere. As if that wasn't enough, He sent grasshoppers and locust swarms that devoured their crops, and hail and sleet to demolish their vines and sycamore-figs. Then came the thunderstorms—with huge hailstones and tremendous lightening to destroy the cattle.

Finally He couldn't contain His hot anger and fury any longer, and released a band of destroying demons. He opened the way for them to vent His anger, and didn't spare those hard-hearted Egyptians, but struck all the firstborn dead with a plague—just overnight.

But Israel—His chosen people—He led like a flock of sheep through the wilderness. His cloud by day and protecting fire by night guided them so they didn't need to have any worries or fears. But rather, He let them see what happened to their old slave drivers as the water of the Red Sea crashed in on them as they tried to follow. Their chariot wheels stuck and so did they[2]. So even if they returned to Egypt their old slave owners wouldn't be there anymore.[3]

And when they got to the Promised Land He drove out the nations gradually, so they could walk in and take over houses and cities, fields and vineyards. He allotted their land, tribe by tribe, family by family, as their inheritance forever—homes for all of them.

But even then they put God to the test with their rebellion against the simple laws He had given to them through Moses. Just like their predecessors, they were disloyal and faithless, as useless as a crooked bow and arrow. They set up idol worship that they picked up from the surrounding nations in their key religious sites, their 'High Places'. That got God mad with jealousy so He rejected them altogether, abandoning their special tabernacle at Shiloh where the 'ark-of-the-covenant' was kept. So when they put the ark in the middle of the battle as their idol to give them victory—it was taken by the Philistines, and the people were thoroughly routed. God was furious! Fire once again flashed out and killed their young men, so the girls had no weddings—no celebrations, just funerals. Even the priests were slaughtered in such a way that their widows shed no tears over them.

So just when it had seemed like the Lord was fast asleep, He woke up like a mighty warrior after a night on the town. He wasn't content just to beat to pulp those who had mocked Him,

---

[2] Exodus 14:25
[3] Exodus 14:28

He put them to eternal shame. He rejected Joseph's descendants and the others, but just chose the tribe of Judah— the tribe of Praise—on which to lavish His affection. And there in the midst of the Praise of His people He built His temple, and placed there His Name, His eyes and His heart, FOREVER[4] where the cries and praise of His people can rise to His throne in the heavenlies.

He chose David as His servant from looking after the sheep and lambs to caring for His people to shepherd them back into the faith and ways of the patriarchs. And David did a good job with integrity and skill.

---

[4] 2 Chronicles 7:16

Psalm 79

Oh God, what have they done?

The nations have invaded Jerusalem and reduced it to rubble, demolishing and defiling Your beautiful temple. They have left dead lying everywhere as vulture food—the people called, nominally at least, by Your name, for wild beast fodder. Blood has flowed like water everywhere so there's no-one left to bury the dead. Our neighbours look on incredulous, scornful and mocking.

Oh Lord, how long are You going to stay angry? For how long does Your jealousy burn? Why pour Your wrath out on us rather than on these nations that don't acknowledge You, on the kingdoms that would never think to call on Your name? Look, Lord, they stripped the place—devastation everywhere.

Lord, please don't have us pay for all the sins of our forebears; Lord, we need Your Mercy, Your Covenant Assistance, and quickly; we're desperate for You. Help, Lord! Jesus—Saviour—for Your name's sake forgive us and help us.

Why should the nations look on, mocking us with "Where's this God of theirs?" Show 'em Lord. Show 'em… avenge the blood of those who loved You who they slaughtered. Do You hear the groaning of the prisoners of war, and those they've determined to kill off? Lord, show 'em that You are Mighty to Save. And while You're at it, Lord, how's about repaying to our neighbours sevenfold for the contempt they threw at You.

But Lord, we are Your people, and we thank You for Your love and care for us—forever—generation after generation—we'll thank You and Praise Your Wonderful name—Jesus—Saviour!

Psalm 80

Thank You Jesus that You're the Good Shepherd—You're the Best! Thank You for the tender and loving way You lead Your flock of the redeemed. For You are the Great Redeemer, as You are the one who has earned the right to sit on the Mercy seat between the Cherubim, with those mighty angels at either side of You. Will You come and seek and save those who have wandered away, like the tribes of Ephraim, Benjamin and Manasseh that separated from Judah and their Lord?

Oh Lord, will You come and draw us back once more with the warmth of Your precious Presence, and save us? *Oh* Lord of Heaven's armies, how long will You be angry with those prayerfully seeking You? All they seem to have experienced is tears, tears and more tears—tears to eat and tears to drink. Our neighbours laugh and our enemies mock us.

Turn us again, *Oh* Lord of Heaven's armies, that we may once more know the radiance of Your favour, blessing, and above all, Your Presence. Remember how You brought us like a vine from Egypt and drove the nations from the land here, as You planted us? You made room here for us so we could take root and fill the land, and we spread out so our shadow and influence covered the mountains, and our branches swayed like the branches of mighty cedars; we stretched from the Mediterranean right across to the Euphrates.

But look at us now; our walls are broken down so anyone passing through can come and help themselves. Wild boar dig and ravage the roots, while other wild animals feed on the rest. But turn us again, *Oh* Lord of Heaven's armies, come and take a look and see. We need You to come and visit us with Your mighty army, come and visit this vine once more—this that You planted so carefully, and with Your careful husbandry grew so strong and fruitful.

169

See it now—see us now—cut down and burned. One look from You and we're dead and done for. *Oh,* but bring Your favour, Your Grace, Your strength of character and strength of anointing in You, Holy Spirit, on King Jesus, 'The Son of Man' who will show us the meaning of Your name and draw us once more back to You—then we will never again turn back from following You, and from calling on Your mighty and wonderful name—Jesus!

Turn us back to You, Lord—King of Heaven's armies, mighty Saviour, that we may once more know the wonder, the blessing the Joy—*Oh,* the fruit—of Your sweet Presence.

Psalm 81

(For the feast of tabernacles, 'Sukkot' when the people slept outside in shelters to remind them of their time in the desert. This feast is at full moon)

Come everyone and join me in a joyful song of love and praise to Jesus—*Oh,* what strength He gives us!

Thank You Lord for this opportunity to make a joyful noise to praise You, and give You our worship.

Come on dancers with your tambourines, plug in those electric guitars, you musicians—blow the shofars so everyone knows it's a day for celebrating. It's a day for celebrating and feasting right across the land decreed and set by our King Jesus who loves to celebrate. He appointed it for a reminder for the people to remember their being set free from Egypt from a people who spoke a very different language, a language of slavery, and bondage.

Our Jesus is the same yesterday, today and forever. He takes our burdens and sets our hands and hearts free to worship Him. When we call, He comes and delivers us. When the world is crashing around our ears, He answers us in the middle of it. And when things look bitter, maybe He's just looking to see what we do with it—will we look to Him and trust Him to make it sweet? Yeaaaah!

Oh, but listen carefully, all of you; take notice.

Don't let anything become a God above Your King Jesus, especially not one of these demons that so many look to, like porn, gambling or alcohol, fear or worry. For He was the one who brought You out of that bondage, out of *your* Egypt, and

He is saying just open your mouth wide and give Him Your praise and adoration, and He will fill it—with all the best and choicest things you could ever imagine.

Unfortunately His chosen ones didn't learn to hear and listen to His voice, so Papa God left them to their own stubbornness, to walk in their own sweet ways.

Oh that they had learned to listen to Papa and walk in His ways, then He could quickly have put a stop to their enemies and have fought for them against any and all. But as for those who hate Him, who never learn any better—their fate never changes, either.

So what about you? Do you want the best and the sweetest to satisfy you? Do you want the bread of life[1], food that satisfies the spirit and truth like sweet honey[2] that causes the heart to laugh and rejoice? The choice is yours as to whose voice you choose to listen to and whose ways you walk in.

---

[1] Luke 4:4, John 6:35
[2] Psalm 19:10

Psalm 82

Oh, thank You Lord that You are the Lord of all Lords, and Judge of all judges—that You are the God of Justice and Righteousness, and You have ways of putting this world's judges firmly in their place.

Thank You that You don't judge by what Your eyes see or what Your ears hear, but You judge the needy with righteousness[1] and without partiality. Yeaaaah!

You judge the poor and the fatherless and see the destitute; those who have no voice, get justice. You deliver the poor from the wicked. *Oh,* thank You that this is Your kind of justice, Lord.

Many's the judge who knows and understands nothing of this kind of justice. That is darkness, and finally the very foundation of their society will crumble as a result.

Judges and rulers all—remember, you are appointed by the Most High, whether you recognise that or not. One day you will die like every other mortal, and your judgments will be your legacy.

Oh Lord, bring in Your Kingdom type of justice across the earth, Your Kingdom come, Lord. Thank You that the increase of Your government will never end, for You won all the nations and tribes for Your inheritance on the cross.

---

[1] Isaiah 11:3,4

Psalm 83

Help, Lord! I need You to speak to me, now is not the time for You to back off. *Oh,* I need You real close, I need to hear Your voice afresh, right now. Thanks. Thank You for Your promise to never leave us or forsake us[1]—to never leave me or forsake me.

Your enemies are starting mayhem, joining with those who hate You who are sounding off. I hear their plots and plans against those who love You:

"Cut 'em off! Destroy them altogether so no-one ever remembers them ever again."

They are all totally united on this; but it's against You that they are really agreed over.

What a list of peoples and nations they make, all so dead set against You. Ouch!

Whether it's the enemies of Israel who want to utterly destroy her, and are still saying "We will take possession of their land and drive them into the sea," or whether it is all the hosts of demons and their allies who have set themselves against those who love You, King Jesus, and Your Kingdom rule, they're still the same. We look to You our King to see they go the way of Israel's enemies in the past, like those wonderful tales in the book of Judges—the likes of Deborah and Barak[2], or of Gideon[3]. Lord, make them like tumbleweed that blows rolling out into the desert, make 'em dizzy with the spinning, or like chaff that just blows away in the wind. *Oh,* thank You for that mighty wind of Yours, Holy Spirit. Lord, we look to You to pursue them and terrify them, and turn

---

[1] Hebrews 13:5
[2] Judges 4
[3] Judges 6-8

everything they do to our good[4].

And in their jealousy, fill them with confusion so that they seek You, our Wonderful Jesus. Show them that they can never hope to win against You, so they are totally disheartened, and give up, disgraced.

We would love them all to come to know and love You, but recognise that this is always their choice. Help us to demonstrate You and Your ways of love while You supernaturally confirm our testimony. Will You reveal to them, King Jesus, that You and You alone are King of all the earth? You are so worthy of that honour, Lord!

---

[4] Romans 8:28

Psalm 84

Your place Lord, is just so, so beautiful—I long to come back to Your courts. It's not the beautiful architecture, but the beauty of Your Precious Presence—*Oh,* my body, my soul, and my spirit cry for more of You, Lord! More! More! More of You!

What a privilege for the swallow building her nest in the eaves of Your temple—bringing up her young in Your Presence—right near You Lord—*Oh,* my King, and my God.

Oh, that I could bring my family up in such sweet proximity to You—it's such a blessing to spend time with You—and inevitably praising and worshipping You, King Jesus.

Thank You Lord, for that precious privilege of being able to live-in-You all day, every day, while You equally live in me. That fills my heart with praise to You, King Jesus… Yeaaah!

It's such a blessing to have You living inside me, with Your Love, Your Grace, Your Courage, Your Freedom, Your Servant-heart, Holy Spirit—You're a freeway straight to Papa's heart. You just turn the valley of weeping into a fountain of Your Blessing and Grace that refreshes every aspect of my life. So I go from strength to strength in my love and knowledge of You, Papa God, as I worship You.

Oh, Wonderful Papa, thank You that You hear my praise and my worship; that my love for You King Jesus, Anointed One, brings Joy to Your heart. Yeaaah! What a shield You are, Lord; thank You for the incredible favour You lavish on me, Your little anointed one[1]. A day with You in Your Presence is

---

[1] Acts 11:26

so special, it's better than a thousand days any place else. I'd rather be a doorkeeper right on the threshold of the place than live richly, but surrounded by wickedness.

Oh, my King Jesus, You are my sun and my shield[2], You are the life of my life and the defence of my heart: the Grace and Glory You lavish on me is humbling—it's so totally out of proportion to what I deserve, and then You go on to promise that there's nothing that You would not want to give me—that all Your promises are Yes, Yes, and Yes in Your Son Jesus[3], as we walk every day with You, yes, every single one we can find! *Oh,* You're so Goooood!

Oh—How blessed, how rich is everyone who trusts in You, who You have made into a temple for Holy Spirit... Come, Lord, Come Holy Spirit and FILL this temple...

---

[2] Jude 1:24
[3] 2 Corinthians 1:20

Psalm 85

Wow! What favour You demonstrate daily to me! What Grace so totally underserved! When I completely blew it, You restored everything. You forgave my sin and didn't just cover it over, but obliterated all record of it[1]. And if that wasn't enough, You then promise to remember it no more[2]. I guess I'd better learn to take a leaf out of Your book, and do the same. Yeaaaaah!

All of Your judgment and the righteous anger that I so richly deserved You poured out on Your Son in my place.

Renew my first love for You—my King, my Saviour—Jesus, and please don't take Your Holy Spirit from me, but renew my knowledge, my love, and my understanding of You and Your wonderful ways. And Lord, the buck stops with me... I don't want my children and my children's children to have to face the consequences of things that I did, and that I have to take responsibility for. *Oh*, thank You.

Please renew my Joy in You once more. Lord I set myself to rejoice and to praise Your Mighty, Wonderful, and JOY-FILLED name—Jesus! *Oh,* thank You Lord for Your unfailing love—thank You that Your love never fails[3]. *Oh,* may all of my family and my extended family know You and the wonder of Your saving Grace.

Lord, I'm listening. Lord, I'm listening carefully to You—thank You for Your words of peace—Your peace that surpasses All understanding[4]—Your peace that You specific-

---

[1] Colossians 2:14

[2] Jeremiah 31:34, Hebrews 8:12, Hebrews 10:17

[3] 1 Corinthians 13

[4] Philippians 4:7

ally promised You would give, and leave with us[5] and would be a Mighty wall of defence all the way around for us, if we do our bit[6]. Do help us not to be so stupid as to ignore You and Your ways.

Oh, thank You that You save all who come to You—no exceptions—and changed hearts and lives bring great Glory to You and usher in Your Kingdom of Glory here too. Thank You that Your mighty angels of Mercy and Truth, Righteousness and Peace rejoice with hugging and kissing and a merry dance together with the saints in Glory, when they see men, women and children receiving You, King Jesus, as their Lord and Saviour, and being made into New Creations[7]. Oh, the whole of creation groans like a woman giving birth[8] to see such wonders.

Oh Jesus, You're so good! Righteousness and Justice went before You preparing Your every step, and they still do, 'cause You're the same yesterday, today and forever!

---

[5] John 14:27
[6] Philippians 4:6
[7] 2 Corinthians 5:17
[8] Romans 8:22

Psalm 86

Help, Lord! I'm so poor and I need You so bad[1]!

Lord, will You guard me? For it's in the blood of Jesus and You alone who I'm trusting in—for You are my Saviour, and my God. *Oh,* thank You Jesus for cutting such a powerful Covenant with Your Father on my behalf for me to draw on, for the assistance I need, day in day out. *Oh,* thank You that You're a God of Joy—that You're not a misery-guts, but You just laugh with Your children and laugh at Your enemies.

Oh, thank You Jesus, You're so Good and so Kind—so Full of Love to all who come to You. Thank You that You hear even my faintest whisper of a cry for help when I call, and You come and help me.

Who in heaven or on earth can in any way be compared to You, Lord? One day, all of the nations will come and worship You, King Jesus, and give You honour and glory. For You won that right on Calvary—You, wonderful King Jesus—You and You alone. Nothing is more wonderful, or more amazing than that You should lay down Your life for me. Rightfully has all power been given back to You, on earth and in heaven—now crowning You Lord of all.

Oh, teach me Your ways, Lord, that I may walk in them. Join my heart with Yours, Lord, that I may forever walk in holy fear and wonder, lovingly in step with You.

Oh, Wonderful King Jesus, I worship You with *all* my heart, my God, my Lord, my Saviour—*Oh,* I lift high Your Wonderful name 'JESUS'—forever! Your magnificent Lovingkindness is always pointing towards me. You and You

---

[1] Matthew 5:3, Luke 6:20

alone are my Saviour, You and You alone have Redeemed me from the slavery and depths of my sin and from its consequences of being eternally separated from You and Your love.

And now I come face to face with pride and ruthless-self that are dead set against the knowledge of You my King. *Oh,* thank You that You are so slow to get angry, and *Oh* so FULL of Mercy and Lovingkindness, when that's not what I deserve. More Grace, Lord, more Grace, and strength to be Your servant; Your handmaid, *Oh,* my Saviour.

Oh, show me, remind me of a facet of my life, a facet of my heart where You have changed me into Your likeness, that pride and ruthless-self will be put to shame, because of what You have done, and how You have changed me, and helped me.

Psalm 87

Thank You Lord that You have established Your people, those who know You and Your ways, as a mighty mountain of influence over all the earth. Thank You that as we come through the gates into Your Presence with Praise on our lips, we sense Your wondrous love and care for each and every one of us. And we sense Your Joy over us as we worship and enjoy You, and You come to inhabit the praise and worship of Your people[1].

What Wonder, what Glory, what Anointing, what Wisdom, what Servant-hearts are represented in our gathering before You, our King Jesus! Yeaaaah!

I personally know brothers and sisters from all over the planet, from Australia to California, from the UK to Florida, Fiji to Texas, all being able to boast that they have been born again into this precious family of worshippers. Indeed, one of the most common questions we ask is, "Where are you from?" as we celebrate our different cultures, and backgrounds, with You, our common Saviour and Lord.

And when the great Book of Life[2] is finally opened, then our Jesus looks up our natural birthplace, and our supernatural birthplace—both special reasons for celebration! Yeaaah!

Oh, the singers, the dancers, the musicians, the worship leaders all declare their Joy and Life flows from You our Wonderful Jesus—from You and You alone! *Oh*, how true my King—my Joy and Life flows from You and You alone.

---

[1] Psalm 22:3
[2] Revelation 20:12

Psalm 88

Mighty King Jesus, You are my Saviour, You and You alone. (Period!)

Day and night I cry out to You, and You seem so far away. Please listen and hear me.

It feels like I am absolutely overwhelmed in every area, especially physically, as my strength ebbs away, my muscles ache and that spirit of death starts to haunt my thinking. I've noticed that those who I thought were my friends are already working out life with me dead and gone. It looks like I've been already counted with the dead rather than the living, like those who no-one remembers any more, and are even cut-off from You.

Oh, this is a deep, dank and dark place—this really is the pits. Even Your hand feels so heavy on me, as wave after wave of despair and unbelief steamrollers over me—Ooooooh!

My friends are continents away and even they don't want anything to do with me anymore. Lord, I'm hemmed in, shut up, and the door slammed and bolted well and truly behind me. Even my spiritual eyes are struggling to see faith and life anymore—*Oh,* my Jesus—Heeeeelp! Yet I will praise You; I will yet lift my hands in worship to You my King and my Lord, 'cause I live by faith not by sight, 'cause I am a child of faith.

But Lord... I know that the dead are alive with You, praising and worshipping You in the Glory of Your throne room, experiencing Joy and Wonder beyond belief, Yeaaaaah!

But if I die now—then my death won't cry out Your Glory for all eternity, in the way that the act of Your healing me and raising me up again will forever declare Your faithfulness and Your lovingkindness. It will be evident for all to see—a sign and a wonder—a testimony of Your wonderworking love and power right here in the land of the living.

Help, Lord! Morning, noon and night I cry out to You. Please don't ignore me and hide Your face. I can't remember how long I've suffered like this—it seems like forever… with death just around the corner; terror and despair forever rolling in on me, wave after wave munching me. Lord, aren't You the one who is forever FULL of Mercy, and slow to anger, and quick to forgive…

As another tide of terror smashes in, Help! Lord. Those I love, my friends, my family have all left me—it's just You, Lord—it's just me and You… It's just in You who I trust…

And so Lord I thank You that You defeated terror and fear. That You spoiled *all* principalities and all of those demonic powers and made an open show of them on the cross—triumphing over them there[1]—that You demonstrated Your triumph by Your rising from that tomb. Now because You defeated them I turn to those waves of fear and doubt and despair, like You in the boat on the Sea of Galilee, and I say, "Shut up!—Peace, be still[2]!" And I say to myself, "You *WILL NOT* fear one moment longer. I trust in the risen Jesus of Nazareth!" And I say to you spirit of foreboding and spirit of death, "NO! Get you back where you came from! I will arise and give Glory and Honour to my King Jesus and will yet praise Him in the land of the living. Thank You Holy Spirit that You are the same Holy Spirit who raised Jesus from the dead, and You live in me and quicken this body of mine with the same resurrection life[3]. My life will yet be a testimony of Your saving Grace and Mercy."

Thank You Jesus, for all Your promises are Yes, Yes and

---

[1] Colossians 2:15
[2] Mark 4:39
[3] Romans 8:11

Yes, in Your mighty and precious anointing[4], and You command us to give no place to fear, but to allow Holy Spirit to come and rule in our hearts with His power, His Love and His Soundness-of-mind[5]. So Lord, I give my 'Amen' to You and to Your word[6].

Wow—thank You Lord... That was too close for comfort, thank You for reminding me of the part I have to play by resisting those things[7], so that they run away. *Oh,* thank You for the power of my words when I put Your words in my mouth.

---

[4] 2 Corinthians 1:20
[5] 2 Timothy 1:7
[6] 2 Corinthians 1:20 (second half of verse!)
[7] James 4:7

Psalm 89

All praise to You and Your Glorious name, King Jesus—FOREVER!

Throughout my time here on planet Earth and throughout eternity I will tell everyone of Your Faithfulness. Down through the generations my song will tell of Your Faithfulness to Your Covenant promises.

I declare that Your Love and Your Faithfulness stand forever—because this is who You are, and You don't change, and You have set Faithfulness as one of the very cornerstones of heaven itself. I'm reminding You Papa God that You made a Covenant with Your servant king David to establish the royalty of his family line forever and always, through all generations.

And it's true! King Jesus—You are forever known as the Son of David! And the increase of Your Kingdom will never end... Yeaaah!

As we look up at the night sky, the stars forever declare Your Glory and Your Faithfulness, King Jesus our Creator and Lord. What magnificence!

Who can be compared to You? There really is no comparison!

Oh, my wonderful King Jesus, Mighty God and Lord of All, Your heart is so rich in love; You are clothed with faithfulness; You wear it like a garment—this is who You are, and You don't change.

When pride stalks the earth and men arrogantly defy men, nation against nation, when the storms of war arise, You are the one who stills them. You took on the devil and all his demons and defeated them, breaking them and taking back the keys of this earth. You broke them and scattered them with the strength of Your character of love, so that it is all Yours—all of the heavens and all of the earth, and all the wonder of it. You designed it, You set this world up as such a special place with a North Pole and a South Pole and full of wonder in between.

Oh, the very mountains and seas, the skies and the deep rejoices in You King Jesus and the wonder of Your name. What a mighty creator! And yet through it all You aren't high and mighty, but Righteousness and Justice are the foundation of Your Kingdom, while Your smiling face speaks of Your Lovingkindness and Truth.

What Joy fills my heart when I hear the roar of the shofar calling me to come to You in worship! What a happy crowd we are who have learned how to walk with You, day by day; who know You aren't the "big-bad-I-said-NO!" or the God of fierce judgment on any and all infringement of some religious legal diktat. But You look on the heart and woo to Yourself a people who You transform into lovers like You! And You give them so much to shout and dance about, so much freedom and Joy! For You are our Saviour and King—King Jesus—the Holy one of Israel.

You raised up a man as an example to us all, of what You could do with Your anointing on one person. You found David and anointed him with oil and with You, Holy Spirit, and helped him and strengthened him, so that no enemy beat him; however wicked they were, they were never going to win. You took out his enemies and just demolished those who hated him. For You had shown him unequivocally what You were really like—so full of Lovingkindness and Faithfulness, that he learned to trust that You would come through for him. And because of that, You exalted him, promising through Your name Your amazing blessing on him and all his descendants:

I will appoint him to rule from the Mediterranean Sea to the Euphrates, over all the land I had promised to Abraham, that somehow they had never managed to conquer. And out of his relationship with Me he will learn to cry out to Me as a Father, as God and the Rock of his salvation—the foundation for his life. He will be to me like my firstborn, high over all the kings of the earth. Forever he will be covered by My Lovingkindness and our Covenant together.

Once and for all time, I have declared by all that I AM, that his family line will continue forever with a descendant after him, always on throne, like the sun and the moon—perpetual faithful witnesses in the sky, to this, My promise.

Always, Always, Always and Forever!

So Hey, Lord, How come? How come that now we appear to be utterly cast off, thrown out and that it looks like You are now totally mad with Your Covenant people. It looks like You now hate that covenant promise of Yours, treading this promise of perpetual royalty into the dirt. Just take a look at how the highways and byways are torn down, the countryside and strongholds now in ruins, and anyone passing by helps themselves. We're a byword to those round about us. It looks like You've raised up those set against us with the specific purpose of taking us down—we're the laughingstock of our neighbours.

Look what's happened to that wonderful anointed royal lineage... their swordplay—pathetic! Overrun in battle, now all that once shone in royal splendour is trampled into the dust. Their days are cut short as they hide themselves, covered with shame. Aaaah!

But how long, Lord? How long is it going to be like this, with You in hiding, Lord? Just how long is your anger going to burn? *Oh,* remember please, Lord, that my life is but for a moment; in Your timescales, just a moment. You can make everything about a man's life look so very futile. We all die one day, and what then? Who can live and not die one day? Who can deliver a man from the power of death? Aaaaah!

But Lord... But Lord, what has become of the Lovingkindness You boasted of, that You Covenantally promised so faithfully to David? Lord, remember—look around and listen to what's being said about us, about those who love You—all the mockery and pointing fingers by everyone, that burns deep inside. Listen to how they abuse even Your precious name, and mock the path You trod.

Oh, King Jesus how familiar this sounds as we look at Your people today. May we once more learn how to draw on Your Covenant promises for ourselves and for our nations, for this orphan planet. *Oh,* how much better, and Oh, how much more secure and proven is our New Covenant than ever the covenant David had with You—sealed with Your broken body and shed blood! We look to You our Anointed King Jesus, firstborn of many brothers[1]. You led captivity captive[2]. You demonstrated to us the Lovingkindness of Your Father[3], and that You are totally trustworthy. You have been exalted to the place of highest honour—high over all, and You have promised wonderful and amazing blessings on Your adopted brothers and sisters, throughout all generations. You have appointed us to reign in Your Mighty name from sea to shin-

---

[1] Hebrews 1:6
[2] Ephesians 4:8
[3] John 14:9

ing sea, from pole to pole. And You and You alone have redeemed and delivered us from the power of death[4].

All praise to You our Mighty King Jesus, Anointed One, forever and for always, Son of David, and we ask You Holy Spirit to once more turn back the tide and sweep across our nations with the knowledge and love of You and Your ways.

---

[4] John 11:26, 1 Corinthians 15:26

Psalm 90

Thank You Lord that before You even began this creation You had already prepared Your wonderful throne room for us all to come and join You, where one day we would come to give You the worship of our hearts—give You the Honour and Glory due to You, my wonderful King Jesus!—and for all eternity, yet to come... Yeaaah!

Oh, thank You Lord—wonderful creator[1]—You formed this whole gigantic universe with its billions of suns and galaxies, and somewhere in this little corner You set our solar system and formed this beautiful planet home of ours. You set up the mountains and measured the precise amount of water required for the oceans[2] to make this such a beautiful and special place for us.

And then, almost like we're the last on the list, You create man in Your own image to bring Your Kingdom here... Man, whose life is just a breath and we're gone in a moment, back to the dust from which we're made. When to You, a thousand of our years is just the blink of an eye.

To us, man springs up and turns round and our lives are over and done—just like grass in a meadow—springing up one day, but the next it's cut and dried for hay for animal fodder. So many simply see You as the 'big-bad-I-said-NO!', hugely angry at their every move, and live their lives terrified of putting a foot wrong as You count up all of their secret sins. And You really aren't like that at all! That's a picture of the one You took out on Calvary, and disarmed for us, and made an open show of, triumphing over him[3].

---

[1] John 1:1-5
[2] Isaiah 40:12
[3] Colossians 2:15

Their days are passed fearing Your anger—what a shame and a waste of seventy or perhaps eighty years, full of trouble and sorrow, and gone so quickly. What a curse that was on the people in the wilderness, who chose to believe that You couldn't take them into the Promised Land.

Oh, if only… if only all mankind would know Your anger—Your jealous anger that is not judgment, but Mercy! Such a jealous anger to love and shepherd and care for Your children, for those who bother to take the time to get to know You. It's as well to know, and to be somewhat fearful not to get on the wrong side of that anger[4]! Now that really is not clever[5].

Help us Lord to use our limited time we have here wisely—not to be fearful of how short it is, nor to put off to tomorrow things that are important, when tomorrow may not come. *Oh,* for more of You, Holy Spirit—Your Wisdom.

Remind us Lord of Your special, intimate, loving care and compassion for those who love You and honour You. Thank You for how You fill us up with Your unfailing love as we come to You and drink in Your Lovingkindness that is fresh and new every morning[6]. May we always be found singing and laughing all our days—overjoyed at Your totally outrageous Goodness extended to us. May You so totally transform us from the inside that we totally forget those wasted years of heartache and pain before we gave You our lives.

Oh, may we see Your miracles, Lord. *Oh,* thank You that we live in a generation when You are healing bodies and restoring lives—working wonders. Thank You that we are seeing things in this generation that earlier generations only dreamed of and never saw[7]. May our children see and touch

---

[4] Psalm 136:17-21
[5] Hebrews 10:31
[6] Lamentations 3:23

Your Glory—King of Kings and Lord of Lords.

Lord, may Your favour rest on us. May people comment of us, as they did of Peter, that we ain't that good, so we must have been with Jesus[8]. And all that You have set us to do, Lord, may it stand the test of time and bring You Glory and Honour; may it bring Glory to You, our wonderful King Jesus—You are so, so worth it.

And Lord, I want no part of that curse of a life limited to perhaps eighty years. Moses was eighty when You met him and appointed him to set the people free from Egypt[9]. And when he died at 120 "his eye was not dim, or his natural force abated[10]." And Caleb also, that faithful spy, when he finally made it back to the promised land declared, "I am eighty-five years old yet I am as strong as I was forty-five years ago, when, sent by Moses, we scouted out this land. I am as strong now for war as I was then, so give me my portion of the land—the mountain where the giants live in their strong walled cities, of whom the rest were so fearful. The Lord will help us drive those giants out, and enable us to possess it, 'cause that's what He promised". And Joshua blessed him and gave him Hebron as his inheritance[11]. Lord, You promise to satisfy me with a long life[12], and I take You at Your word. May it be said of me that "Your old men dream dreams[13]," so that I am still found dreaming of new things to bring You glory and honour, when others have long since stopped and gone on to Glory.

---

[7] Hebrews 11:39
[8] Acts 4:13
[9] Exodus 7:7
[10] Deuteronomy 34:7
[11] Joshua 14:11-14
[12] Psalm 91:16
[13] Joel 2:28, Acts 2:17

Psalm 91

Do you want to live absolutely safe and secure against all and anything... Do you want a place that's absolutely safe? Then here's how you build it... You have to pile-drive two deep foundation piles through as your foundation... Your relationship with the Lord, with Papa, Son and Holy Spirit, and the second is to align your words with that relationship. It takes time, energy and effort to drive these foundation piles deep, so daily you need to drive them down, further.

It is so easy to enter that relationship, to enter that secret place—simply ask Jesus to be Your Lord and Saviour, to forgive you for all your sin and to make everything new. But it takes a lifetime to explore His heart, and learn how to live His way. And what comes out of our mouths is a big key to that.

Here's your daily confession, to get your tongue in gear:
1/ You Lord are my refuge,
2/ You Lord are my fortress,
3/ You Lord are the one person who I trust, absolutely.

Lord, I want to live my life out of my relationship with You, with You at the centre. Thank You for that secret place with You, Papa God, under Your mighty shadow—Your amazing protection and loving care. *Oh,* thank You for the security You give to me, to my heart and spirit.

Today and every day I declare that You are my God, my refuge and fortress. I trust in You, Lord, and You alone. I still my heart before You in trust[1].

---

[1] Psalm 131:2

Oh, thank You my Lord, my King Jesus, that You will deliver me from every snare of the enemy, every trip wire, and all of the traps the adversary lays to catch me out... and from every sickness and disease that's running round, however contagious or nasty. And You don't stop there but cover me with Your mighty wings—now that's *real* protection to trust in.

Oh, thank You Lord that You are the Way, the Truth and the Life, and You are always, always True. Thank You that Your Truth is a big shield to cover every part of me, so fear has absolutely no part of my life, or my thought-life. Because of Your shield I have no fear of darkness or what may happen during the hours of darkness, or the arrows with my name on them fired in broad daylight. Equally I refuse to fear the disease that stalks the neighbourhood at night, and the plague that sweeps through at noon—whether it's cancer or Alzheimer's, diabetes or kidney failure, because You, King Jesus, my Healer, paid for my healing and wholeness with the lacerations of the lashes laid on You, lashing every part of Your sinless body[2]. You were reduced to being scarcely recognisable as a human[3], that I may know health and wholeness, and I don't want Your sacrifice to have been in vain.

When a thousand all around me go down with the latest flu, and ten thousand with this winter's cold, I declare it will not come to me, because You Jesus are my Lord and my God. *Oh,* thank You for this mighty promise, and the clear instructions as to how take the medicine—with Your promise on my lips. I will only be an onlooker to the problems and fruit of not knowing and loving You, my King. And it's all because of You, my High King—my King Jesus, my refuge! *Oh,* I

---

[2] Isaiah 53:5
[3] Isaiah 52:14

make You my refuge my hiding place, my home.

Oh, Thank You King Jesus for Your mighty guardian angels who You've assigned to take care of me. Thank You that with their care, absolutely none of these evil things are coming round my place, and no sickness or disease is putting up its bed for the night. Thank you—angels—*Oh,* thank you for all those times you've saved me from serious harm, and I never even thought it was you who steered things that little bit so it never touched me. Help me to pay attention when you are trying to help me and I'm too blind and stupid to realise. Thank you that you take care of everything I get up to.

My Warrior King Jesus, thank You that You have appointed me to exercise authority over every power of the enemy in Your Mighty name. You have appointed me to tread on lions and snakes, and trample the smaller ones underfoot. *Oh,* thank You for the power and glory of Your Wonderful name—JESUS! Thank You that no matter how evil their plans and purposes, we have Your word and promise that there's no way they can hurt us.

Oh, Jesus, I love You. You are my Lord, You are my God—You are the one at the centre of my heart. Thank You for Your outrageous promises to those who love You—

1/ You will deliver me,

2/ You will set me on high—all because I know and honour Your Wonderful name. "Jesus" [Your name is so sweet on my lips. I trust in Your word to me.]

3/ You will answer me when I call on You.

4/ You will be with me when I get into trouble and difficulties.

5/ You will deliver me from those situations

6/ You will then see that I get honoured!

7/ You will give me a long satisfying life.

8/ You will show me Your Salvation and Saving Grace.

Oh, Jesus, what a raft of amazing promises, of Your loving care—where would I be without them? Thank You for all those times when You have indeed delivered me from crazy evil and bizarre situations and circumstances. Thank You for how You have indeed brought me through with a testimony to share of Your Goodness and Mercy—with a crown to throw at Your feet—my King. *Oh* that You would have all of the Glory when I share what You have done in and through even me.

And Lord, I love LIFE. I want a long one! I have so many dreams of things I want to see and do for You. And Lord that list is growing faster than I'm knocking them off. I don't know just how long You have in Your book on my life, but You had better add a few pages, if You are going to satisfy me—LOL!

And *Oh*, there's so much more to Your Salvation that You won for me than I have even glimpsed at. Lord, I want to know You and understand more of all that You have done for me and for each of us. Lord, I want to know You so much more deeply than I do already. I want to understand what You accomplished for us so I can share it with others, that they too, can share in the Goodness You long for each of us to enjoy.

Jesus, I want to search Your amazing heart of love and reveal more of You to this world. The more I see, the more amazed I become—there really is no fathoming the depth of Your love for each and every one of us—so intimate—so free—so uncondemning—so enriching—so encouraging—so full of Your Glory, so kind. *Oh*, that I was better at demonstrating more of this—more of You Lord—*Oh*, how much more I need of You, Holy Spirit, in me.[4]

---

[4] 1 Corinthians 2:7-16

Psalm 92

Oh, You give us so much to thank You for, Papa, each and every day. It's so good to praise and lift high the wonderful name of Your Son—King Jesus—any which way we can; to tell everyone of Your Lovingkindness in the morning and Your Faithfulness every night.

Oh, bring on the instruments guys—give our King Jesus a song worthy of all He's done for us.

Oh Papa—You've put such Joy in my heart, doubly so when I remember the things I've seen You do—the people whose lives I've seen You transform—the people whose bodies I've witnessed You heal and restore. What You do is so, so special, Papa—Thank YOU! *Oh,* and what does that tell me about You and what You long to do... Restore, restore and restore, to make all things new—bodies, lives, marriages, communities... Wow!

How few ever seem to realise or understand You. Surrounded by people who don't know You, then it's hardly surprising they do all sorts of crazy things that are so counter to Your Kingdom, and when they do come in to stuff, they haven't a clue how to steward it so it really doesn't help them. They die and it all disappears with no legacy for anyone.

Oh, how different are You, Papa God, and Your ways! How really stupid to set yourself against such a loving God, but so many do! Surprise, surprise they come to nothing.

But what a different story for those who have set themselves to know You and Your ways... You have blessed me with such prosperity of soul, of my emotions, of my spirit, and such physical well-being—and then You anoint me with Your oh-so-precious anointing to bless others—to be the vehicle for You to reach and touch other people with the blessing You rain down on me—wow! Bring it on, Lord!

I've seen and heard what happened to those who set themselves against me... not a pretty sight. I didn't do anything, but You took 'em out like a flying rugby tackle. Thanks for that reminder to pray for them; I wouldn't want that to happen to anyone.

But those who love You, our King Jesus—who have received You as their Lord and Saviour—*Oh,* what a different story! You plant us like palm trees so we bend in the wind. We grow strong and majestic like a cedar of Lebanon. And You place us in Your house, in the very courts of Heaven itself; *Oh,* that's such a wonderful place to be! And not content with that, You then come and live in us[1]—*Oh,* thank You Holy Spirit. And You don't age, so we keep on growing and maturing, bearing fruit for You, always full of Your Life and Love...

Papa—You're so Gooood! We can never exaggerate Your goodness! What a privilege to be a walking demonstration of Your Goodness and Your Lovingkindness. You are my rock— You are the one I have built my life upon—You have been such a true, firm and sure foundation.

---

[1] Colossians 1:27

Psalm 93

Thank You Papa, for giving Your Son, King Jesus, *all* power and authority over this earth[1]. Worthy are You, Jesus, our Great Redeemer. You are so clothed with Majesty; You are so clothed with the strength of Your love—love that never fails. Nothing can slip past You and catch You unawares—You rule—OK! Before the beginning of space-time Your throne was established, so it's not about to change any time soon...

Hey—but You gave the rule You won at Calvary to us[2]...

The tumult among the nations of the earth has risen to a storm, with their strutting and posturing, the waves are getting bigger and bigger. *Oh*, thank You King Jesus that You still rule, and You rule over this tumult.

Thank You Jesus that we can look back on what You have repeatedly done in times past to bring peace to the nations and peace to Your special city Jerusalem[3].

Thank You Jesus that You are the same yesterday, today and forever[4] and You demonstrated that Your rule is of Righteousness, Peace and Joy[5], in the Holy Spirit.

So, as You have given Your rule to us, we address this tumult and say,

---

[1] Matthew 28:18

[2] Matthew 28:19

[3] December 1917 General Allenby, a Bible-believing Christian, entered Jerusalem on foot, leading the British Army as the Turks left without a fight, following the British dropping leaflets from planes. This was specifically done to avoid a fight in the streets of 'the Holy City'.
June 1967 The six-day war, the Israeli forces took control of the whole of Jerusalem including the Temple Mount, with very little resistance, and little loss of life or to property.

[4] Hebrews 13:8

[5] Romans 14:17

"Peace, be STILL! In Jesus' name!"

"Your nuclear bombs and aspirations—we dismantle you across the globe—in Jesus' name!"

"You fear—of terror, of nuclear war, of wars and rumours of wars—we recognise you for what you are and we bind you, and say—enough is enough—you cease—in Jesus' name!"

"Come Holy Spirit and sweep the earth with the knowledge and outrageous love of our Papa God as so well illustrated and demonstrated by You, our King Jesus, Anointed One. Your will be done here on planet Earth!"

Psalm 94

Oh, Mighty King Jesus, only You have the right to bring vengeance to the earth. Shine out! Why don't You do something? Lord, it's so tempting to say that this patient waiting for people to come to You isn't working, and won't You finally give the proud what they so deserve? I so readily forget just how patient You were and still are with me. But Lord... how long do we have to wait while the proud arrogantly boast of their prowess as they slaughter those who love You and blow up our places of worship to You? They boast of the widows and foreigners they've killed, and orphans they've murdered. They boast that You don't see or care, and that their demon god 'must be obeyed'. Ugh!

Wake up! you stupid people! Will you never learn? Does the very one who designed and created the ear not hear? Or the one who designed and created the eye not see? Get real! Will He who orders the nations not bring in His over-riding order and correction? Do you really want to be in His firing line when that happens? The very one who reveals to mankind what works and what doesn't—can't you see He knows all your thoughts and how limited, unimaginative and selfish they are?

Blessed is the one who You love and discipline, Papa God—the one who You reveal Your heart to, and teach Your ways to. You give them peace, rest and Your precious Shalom of body, mind, and spirit, till all the chaos is finished, and the perpetrators dead and buried. *Oh,* thank You Papa that You don't neglect the care of those who love You, that You don't bring sweeping judgment that would hurt the littlest one of Your family, who happened then to be at the wrong place, at the wrong time.

Thank You that those who showed Your Mercy will reap what they sowed. Those who demonstrated Your forgiveness will themselves be forgiven and be the peacemakers. So who in that light, who will rise up with me and say "Enough is enough" to these evil men? Lord, You know my stand against them is not for vengeance, pride, or my own ego. Left to me, I'd happily keep quiet. You remind me too often of how You are patient with me when I keep missing it. Rather, it's the sense of justice for the weak that You have built into me, as You have shown me Your heart, in those times of intimacy together—You and me.

Clearly You aren't going to allow this to carry on with its diabolical decrees—the very fact that they are ruling at all is an affront to You and Your Kingdom. They can't forever band together so specifically against those who love You, taking such delight in slaughtering them in such a barbarous fashion.

Oh, thank You Lord that You are my stronghold, the foundation and refuge for my heart; I need not fear their evil.

Thank You that their own ways will catch up with them. Thank You that You see to it that they will one day reap exactly what they themselves have sown.

But Lord... But Lord... are their hearts even beyond Your reach to speak to? Surely not! Can You not show them how much better Your ways of love are? Are You, even You, unable to remove the blinders from their eyes and hearts? Surely Your ways are so much higher than ours that You have ways of reaching these men—like You knocked Paul to the ground and unravelled the murderous plots he had planned for Your chosen ones[1] so that he became a passionate lover and warrior for You and Your name. Can You not do the same for these, too? Is that not the way of Your Mercy?

---

[1] Acts 9:4

Psalm 95

Come everyone—get out your musical instruments; let's make a mighty joyful noise to the Lord, the very rock and foundation of our hearts and lives—Jesus our Saviour!

Lord, we come to You with thanksgiving—*Oh,* You give us so much to be thankful for! Lord, it's a Joyful thankful song we sing to You.

For You Jesus are such a great God—indeed You are high over everything that pretends to be god, You so far surpass them all.

For You hold the depths of the oceans in the palm of Your hands and the mighty Himalayas too. You made the oceans, measuring just the amount of water to get the land and water at just the right ratio so this planet would work so beautifully for us—Your design is so intricate and beautifully interwoven.

Oh, wonderful King Jesus we worship You—we bow—we kneel to You—our Lord, and the love of our hearts and lives. You are the one who formed each one us in that secret hidden place in our mothers' wombs, making each of us so unique. And You are such a wonderfully Good Shepherd to each one of us, every day, as You call us each by name—You know us so well. *Oh,* help us to hear Your call! Help me to hear Your voice and not miss the blessings You have planned for me, through my hardness of heart, and lack of trust in Your unfailing love and provision—like the people of Israel in the desert grumbled and complained against You that there was no water, and Moses had to strike the rock for the water to come. In spite of all the incredible miracles they had seen and benefited from, they never learned Your ways, Your heart and how to trust You—they never learned that You loved them so much and wanted only the very best for each and every one of them.

Not too surprising then that You were a tad ticked off with that whole generation for forty long years, saying that they would never enter into Your rest. If they never learned to love You and allow You to love them, then they never could have known that wonderful and precious rest of heart and spirit that comes from knowing You. *Oh*, King Jesus—what rest and love there is in You… in knowing You. You so long and yearn for us to respond in faith and trust in Your unfailing love.

Thank You for that precious privilege of having You, Holy Spirit, coming and living in our hearts, with Your mighty Shalom—Your peace, strength and rest of body, mind and spirit. Come, Holy Spirit—I'm thirsty for so much more of You.

Psalm 96

Lord, today I sing to You a new song—a fresh song of my heart that loves You so. You are so good—so good to me, in all Your Wonderful Lovingkindness. *Oh* that everyone would sing Your praise—You so deserve it!

Oh, sing to Him a new song, everyone, that lifts high the wonderful name of Jesus! Shout out His Glory for all to hear, and the amazing and glorious things He has done!

Jesus—You laid down everything for me, Your life with Papa and Holy Spirit, even life itself to save me—what Love, what Grace, You extend to us every day. Greater love than Yours is quite impossible—You loved us so much, even when we hated and despised You—You still kept on loving—loving even me… Is anything more wonderful than all that You have done, and continue to do? You bore my sin so that I am forgiven. You bore my sickness and disease so I walk healed and whole. You bore my brokenness also, so my heart is restored to rejoice in Your amazing love. You disarmed fear so that I have absolutely nothing to be afraid of. You even became a curse that I may go free.

Who or what could be greater than that? Such Love—such Grace—*Oh,* You are so worthy of Praise—my King Jesus! And to think I could so easily miss out on such blessing, such wholeness and joy—ouch. What absurd things most people put centre stage in their affections! What idols! And what absurd things the nations and their politicians so avidly pursue… Doubly absurd when we have that amazing privilege of knowing You and Your Wondrous Love—Lord and creator of everything—and working with You, building things

Your way, and seeing Your incredible blessing as a result.

You have such Majesty—King Jesus. You are worthy of such Honour! Your Love is so beautiful, so strong... when we come to You, when we meet with You.

Come everyone and ascribe to Jesus the Honour, the Glory and the Strength due to Him. Ascribe to Jesus the Glory due to His wonderful, mighty and precious name. Come and bring Your sacrifice of Praise, come into His Presence with a song of thanks, with a sacrifice of thanksgiving.

Oh, worship our King Jesus, everyone. Come and worship Him with humble and grateful hearts.

Tell everyone that Jesus reigns—tell the nations, and show them with signs and wonders that Jesus is rightfully King of all the earth, and all power and authority has been given to Him. Tell everyone what He is like—that He is just and fair— that He is so full of love for all.

Is that Good News, or is that Good News? The heavens rejoice and the earth too.

Everyone and everything rejoices when You rule, King Jesus! The sea roars its praise to You and the fields—white for the harvest—rejoice. The trees of the woods sing for sheer JOY, both the wind through the branches and the wind of the Spirit through the elders of the nations standing tall in their worship to You as they honour You King Jesus.

Oh, Thank You Jesus that You are coming... that Your Kingdom rule is forever increasing. Thank You that You always judge righteously, and judge everyone with Your Truth.

Oh, Thank You that You are indeed the Way, the Truth and the Life.

Psalm 97

Wonderful King Jesus—*Oh,* thank You that it's You who reigns over this earth—and we can get happy and rejoice knowing that You are for us and not against us. That no matter what we've just heard on the news, or how we feel or what else in our own personal world may have fallen apart—that You are seated on the throne—and You are Good, Good, and always Good! *Oh,* thank You that You are a God of Hope, and You hope and trust in us, as we hope and trust in Your Unfailing Love!

So no matter where we are, how big or small our community, we rejoice in You, and our hearts can rest and be glad, King Jesus, that You are King—not just far away in heaven, but You rule here, and we give You place to rule in our hearts—to rule in my heart... Holy Spirit come with Your heavenly Shalom—*Oh,* thank You!

And thank You that we don't come to a mountain, burning with fire and smoke[1], or to a sight that made even Moses tremble with fear[2], where fire burns up anything its path... But we come to Mount Zion—Your Holy City—the heavenly Jerusalem where we join with countless thousands of angels and those who have gone before, rejoicing in Your love and in full-on Praise and Worship to You—our King.

But Lord... we thank You that You are the same and—just occasionally—You remind us as we glimpse that fire and smoke—we glimpse Your thick Glory cloud, and feel everything shaking at Your mighty Presence—and our hearts melt in awe at You as we are frozen prostrate to the floor.

Ahhh we so easily forget that it is indeed a fearful thing to

[1] Exodus 19:16-19, Hebrews 12:18
[2] Hebrews 12:21

fall into the hands of the living God[3]—that one day we all face You as Judge and King.

But whether we have ever experienced Your Fire and Glory, we have no excuse—we only have to look up and see Your Glory in the heavens, the myriads of twinkling stars in the night sky shouting of Your awesome creation, and of a wonderful creator.

How absurd to worship idols, whether they are manmade icons, movie stars or iPhones, and yet we so easily put other things before You, Papa God, our wonderful God and Father.

Oh, how Your people rejoice when You show up—when You do indeed change things in ways that demonstrate Your Lordship—Your judgments. *Oh,* how we love to see You restore broken lives, broken bodies, broken hearts, broken communities—thank You that You are still in the same restoration business today as You were on the shores of Galilee—for You King Jesus are our King so far above all the other things that compete for our affections. *Oh,* thank You for how You guard and care for those who love You and deliver us from all the things that would so easily take us out— especially our own foolishness! *Oh,* thank You for sowing Your Light and Life into our hearts—You give us such Joy… *Oh,* thank You Lord… thank You Papa, Thank You Holy Spirit that You are the Spirit of JOY!

We rejoice in You, Lord; we praise Your special and precious name, "Jesus"! *Oh,* thank You that ALL power and authority has been given to Your name[4], and everything is subject to Your Righteous name, and always will be… that You are the same yesterday, today and forever[5]…

---

[3] Hebrews 10:31
[4] Matthew 28:18
[5] Hebrews 13:8

Psalm 98

Oh, come everyone, and sing a new song to the Lord; He's done such amazing and marvellous things. Just stop for a moment and think of the incredible things He's done just for you and for me!

Oh, thank You Jesus that You stretched out Your hands and embraced that cross to become my Redeemer—that my name is engraved on the palms of Your hands. Jesus, Anointed One—what a Saviour You are!

And thank You Holy Spirit for revealing this wondrous love even to my cold heart, and for saving me. *Oh,* please sweep through the nations of the earth with this same knowledge that only You Holy Spirit[1], can make known and understood. And please remember Your love and promises to Israel Your chosen people, that even the very ends of the earth would see You blessing them so outrageously in every way, but especially in their coming to see You King Yeshua as their Saviour, as their long promised, anointed Messiah.

Give the Lord a big shout of Joy, everyone—*Oh,* that there could be a giant Mexican Wave of Joy to You King Jesus, right around the earth—You are so worth it! Make a jubilant song of praise—bring on the full symphony orchestra—King Jesus—You deserve the full works! Bring on the multi-chorus choirs—fortissimo! Trumpets and shofars—now it's your turn—give Him a joyful blast to wake the dead! Jesus the King of *all* Kings!

Oh, that all of this world would praise You Jesus—the sea, from pole to pole, and everything in it, dance for Joy... the rivers clap their hands and the mountains sing to You. For You

---

[1] 1 Corinthians 2:14

come to judge the earth... *Oh,* thank You that You judge everyone, and all people with such fairness and righteousness.

JESUS!

Psalm 99

Oh, thank You Lord that You reign! Sometimes it really doesn't look like it, sometimes it really doesn't feel like it, but I know that You, King Jesus, that You reign high over all... That to You has been given All power and Authority[1]... and You've given that to us[2]... *Oh*, teach us how to pick up that mantle! *Oh*, teach *me* how to. *Oh*, that people would realise one day they will be held accountable for their lives to You, that in ignoring You they miss out on so much here, and so much more for all eternity... What responsibility You entrust to us! *Oh,* thank You that it's You seated on the Mercy seat between the cherubim—and we know You are so *full* of Mercy. That when we should be shaking with fear in our boots, You always extend Mercy, Mercy and Grace and yet more Mercy!

Oh, King Jesus You are so amazing! You are forever the Lamb upon the throne[3]. You are so worthy of our praise and the praise of all the saints in Glory around Your throne. For You willingly gave Your life as a ransom for many... You laid Your life down for me. Worthy are You to be judge of all, ruler of all. Holy and high over all rule and authority—You are!

And thank You that You love Justice with a passion! Thank You that doing things right is one of Your hallmarks and as You establish Your Kingdom, You demonstrate a Kingdom of Justice and Righteousness.

Worthy... so worthy are You our King Jesus! *Oh,* what a

---

[1] Matthew 28:18
[2] Matthew 28:19
[3] Revelation 5:8, 7:10

privilege to worship You with our enemies placed under our feet as we sit at Yours—as part of that great company of heaven giving You Honour and Glory. Joined with the saints who we loved, respected and looked to, who have gone before us, together with the biblical saints—Old and New Testament ones such as Moses and Aaron and Samuel and John and Peter and Mary Magdalene rejoicing to see the fulfilment in You, Jesus, of what they glimpsed at during their time here.

As we remember them, we remember how You spoke to Moses in the pillar of cloud, that he so boldly walked right into—that he was known as one who spoke to You face to face. Thank You for the testimonies they left us of Your dealings with them—and reminding us that You are no respecter of persons, and we live under a far superior Covenant.

Oh King Jesus, we exalt Your wonderful and mighty name. We love, we worship, we lift You High with all the saints. Your love for each and every one of us is just so outrageous—so deep and so pure and true. You are so special—there's absolutely nothing You wouldn't have given to redeem each and every one of us.

What can we say, but thank YOU! We love YOU—Jesus!

Psalm 100

Come everyone and join me in a Joyful, Happy noise to the Lord—everyone, everywhere! *Oh,* come and worship our King Jesus with Joy-filled, happy hearts—full of joie-de-vivre—give Him a happy song—a *very* happy song! Doesn't our King Jesus make you happy?

Oh, thank You Jesus!

Thank You that You Jesus are God, and King of all the earth. You are the great Creator and Redeemer—You made us, and then re-made us with a second birth! Redeeming us to be Your people. So we are Your people. You are the Good Shepherd and we delight to be counted as Your sheep.

And thank You that the way into the very courts of heaven itself isn't difficult or shrouded in mystery, we just come through the gates with hearts full of thanks to You our wonderful King Jesus, Anointed One. And You invite us to come right into Your courts—the very courts of heaven as we give You our Praise! *Oh,* thank You Jesus—Thank You for the wonder of Your unstoppable love! I bless Your Mighty and Matchless name.

Thank You Jesus, You are so, so Good; Your Lovingkindness never fails; it never ends but goes on forever, and You are always, always, always, Faithful—that's just who You are!

Oh, thank You, King Jesus!

Psalm 101

Oh Jesus, I sing of Your Lovingkindness and Justice—these are so key to who You are. You are so special, King Jesus, Anointed One—what Joy to sing Your Praise! The praise of the one who laid His life down, that I may live.

Lord, I want to walk in a way that pleases You, and that brings Joy to Your heart. I so want You to come and live in me. I want my heart and my thoughts to be pure, even in those secret places, and secret moments, when no-one else is looking… especially in those moments, Papa. I could so easily look at things or spend my time or my thoughts on porn or other things just as vile that debase and de-value human beings and the splendour of what it is to be alive. They so easily attract and ensnare my thoughts, my affections and my appetite—Lord, I want nothing to do with these evil things.

You show me that even to slander someone in those secret places of my own heart is unacceptable to You. *Oh,* how easy it is to slip into haughty pride, arrogance, and judging others, which are so offensive to You—You who never condemned anyone, but believes in all the good in everyone.

Lord, I'll keep on the look out for those who walk in faith, trusting You. I'll take special care of them, bless them, and minister to them, and hear the word and the revelation You give them and receive it for myself, also. But those who deceive, gossip, manipulate and exaggerate—who big themselves up—these I'll keep clear of, or all too easily I'll become like them, picking up their horrible ways.

Every morning I come to You, Lord. I worship You, and fill my heart and my thoughts with You and the wonder of Your loving care. I silence all of those wicked, boastful, selfish thoughts and cut them off. King Jesus, it's You I want ruling in the citadel of my heart—You, Your Love and selfless Mercy and care for those hurting, broken and helpless.

Psalm 102

Oh, thank You Jesus that You hear my prayer when I come to You. Thank You that I don't have to keep spinning the same old prayer wheels—that You aren't deaf and You heard me the first time[1]. *Oh,* thank You that You know my need before I even think to bring it to You, but You still like me to come to You to request even our basic necessities[2]. But Lord…

It's not my needs that are eating at my spirit, but the state of Your people, Mount Zion[3], the gathering of the saints to worship You. We're in such a pitiful state, and You taught that we should pray, pray and not faint to see Your justice brought home[4]… that You are not an unjust judge. Come Lord, Come! Come, Holy Spirit, Come!

Lord, my days are slipping by with nothing to show for them—just wafting away like smoke. I seem to be sliding backwards everywhere I turn, and even my bones feel like they're catching the heat. And my heart that once was so passionate for You is now struggling to even sense Your Presence—I'm losing it, Lord. I even forget to eat—let alone stop for You and some bread-of-life to my spirit. This thing is just eating me up inside draining all life and energy for anything—even my skin feels like it's being stretched over my bones… I'm becoming like that lonely bird staring out into the desert wilderness, or an owl of the night scouring the scorched earth for a morsel. Ahhh—I'm like that sparrow left all alone on the roof, looking eerily around at what everyone else has seen and run from.

---

[1] Matthew 6:7,8
[2] Matthew 6:11
[3] Psalm 48
[4] Luke 18:1-8

I've now become a byword to my taunting enemies, while humiliation and grief, ashes and tears, are all that has fed my spirit. Lord, it feels like You've picked me up and tossed me aside, as I watch the evening shadow draw across my life, my spirit and my soul... I'm shrivelling up...

But You, Lord... But You... You live forever, and You will be remembered forever... And now is the time. Now is the appointed time to revive Zion—Your people. Lord, it's Your promised time to once again show favour and blessing on Your people. Lord, these living stones, these who love You, they are precious to me, so how much more precious are they to You, yet they are beaten down in the dust. Lord, will You put a new heart and spirit upon Your people? And build up Zion once more, that the nations of the earth may know that You are King of all Kings and worship You? That the nations of the earth would see that You respond to the poorest of Your children when they call on You.

Lord, I write this down for future generations so they will know You and know Your loving care. Lord—that a people not yet even a twinkling in their mothers' eyes will once more come and join in Mighty Joy-filled worship of You, King Jesus. Lord, I write that You looked down on us and didn't leave us as orphans and condemned, but paid the price to Redeem us and set us free[5]—You did it, Wonderful King Jesus—thank YOU! Thank You that one day Your people will once again gather and lift Your name high in honour, in worship and praise. *Oh* that Your people would once again gather in Jerusalem to praise Your name, King Jesus—Lion of the tribe of Judah—the tribe of Praise[6].

Lord, the brokenness of Your people has weighed on me and on my spirit, and shortened my days, but I look to You to

---

[5] Luke 1:68, Galatians 4:5, Titus 2:14, 1 Peter 1:18
[6] Revelation 5:5

give me back those years as I see You move once again. Lord, You and Your work goes on and on down all the generations, from laying the foundations of the earth and the heavens[7] till You wrap it all up at the end, but please remember that my life doesn't go on and on, but is very short. One day, this world, this universe, will grow old like a much loved and cherished threadbare tee-shirt, and You will make all things new[8] once more—for You don't change, and You have no end[9].

Thank You King Jesus that Your wonderful promises run down through a thousand generations[10]. Thank You that not only will we worship You through all eternity, but our children and theirs too will all be a part of that great gathering—lifting Your name high in Honour and Glory.

---

[7] John 1:3

[8] Revelation 21:5

[9] Hebrews 1:12

[10] Exodus 20:6, Deuteronomy 5:10, Deuteronomy 7:9,
1 Chronicles 16:15, Psalm 105:8

Psalm 103

I bless You—*Oh* Lord, my King Jesus! With all my heart and all my soul, with all that I am, I bless and praise Your wonderful and Mighty name! Jesus!

Worthy are You King Jesus! Worthy are You of all my heart, of all my praise, as I remember all the amazing things You've done for me, and promised to keep doing Forever. You forgave me! But You did so much more than just forgive me, You nailed that list of all the wrong things I'd done to Your cross, thereby cancelling, and blotting out the record of all the decrees against me[1], then You promised never to remember any of them ever again[2].

And through Your beating and lashing in the Praetorium[3] You paid the price for me to be healed of every thing that comes against this body of mine[4]. You heal all my diseases, from a stubbed toe, cancer, Alzheimer's… every sickness, every disease… every pain, every injury… You name it and Jesus heals it—wow!

You redeemed every aspect of my life. Even the crazy stuff I got into before I knew You, You've turned into a testimony for me to share with others about Your Goodness and Kindness. Lord—You're amazing! You truly crown me with Your love and care.

You don't just satisfy me, You lavish me with Your good things. I get to eat like a king—I'll have to watch my weight, but for now this is just renewing my youth so my dreams can take flight like the eagle. Yeaaah—I get younger and younger

---

[1] Colossians 2:14
[2] Hebrews 8:12
[3] Matthew 27:27, Mark 15:16
[4] Isaiah 53:5, 1 Peter 2:24

every day!

All that You do, Lord, is so good and right, especially the Love and Grace You give to those suffering for Your name.

Curious how Moses learned Your ways, but though the people equally saw what You did, they never understood You. They never understood just how merciful and full of grace You are—just how slowly You get angry, but how much more You love to be kind. The people were frightened because they saw Your flashes of anger, but never realised what they had been doing for so long that lead up to it. Thank You that You so quickly get over it and revert to Your kind, caring self once more. I need that so much!

Thank You that You haven't treated me like I deserved, reaping all the dreadful consequences of the stuff I was doing, but rather You lifted me out of the chaos and mess I was creating for myself. You sent the rescue helicopter in and winched me from the hole I was digging so furiously—thank You so much! I never deserved that.

When I look up at the stars spreading out across the night sky, I think of all Your blessing for me. Thank You that You're like this for *everyone* who comes to You. Thank You that having blotted out all the sins on that list You then removed them from my life—just as far as the East is from the West. I'm not sure just how big Your creation is, but my sins and their hold on me are well and truly gone.

Thank You that You're such a good Dad to *all* Your children—to *all* who come to You. You make sure no-one who comes to You feels left out, but everyone gets to call You Papa God. Thank You that You never lose sight of just how frail we are and how much we need Your loving care. We're here for a moment and in the blink of an eye are gone like a flower in the desert whose whole lifecycle is so incredibly short, before the scorching sun dries it up and it returns to dust blowing in the wind. Thank You that You remember that, and remember to bless with Your love and care, generation after generation of those who love You. And You see that their children and their children's children come to know You for themselves, following Your ways and remembering Your Covenant and covenant promises.

Thank You Lord that it's You who reigns for all eternity—King Jesus. I say, "Worthy are You to rule and reign. There's no-one like You—our Servant King—who bore my sin upon Yourself for me."

Oh, You angels—bless our King Jesus! You mighty messengers, as you go about your business for the King, delivering His messages, His help, His direction; praise Him!

And all you who have gone before us, now cheering us on from the heavenly grandstands[5], we know you're enjoying His Presence—give a renewed shout of Praise and Worship to our King! He's so worth it!

And all the wonderful miracles—changed lives, healed spirits, souls and bodies—you too, declare forever His Lovingkindness and Redeeming love—His rule over everything.

Oh, my soul… Wake up! Bless! Shout! Dance your crazy wild Glory jig!

Jesus Rules—OK!

---

[5] Hebrews 12:1

Psalm 104

Jesus—my King—I bless and I praise Your Mighty and Matchless name. You are clothed in Honour and Majesty, so I bow low as I come to You with wonder and bated breath.

I'm almost blinded by the light streaming from Your very Presence that carries on, streaming through space to join the light from the billions of galaxies that You arrayed around us like a curtain. When I see the beams of bright light shining through the clouds I am reminded of Your Glory—it's like this is Your home with the clouds being Your heavenly transport— Your time and space machine. I love the idea that You walk on the wings of the wind, or should that be that the wings of Your mighty angels carry You wherever…?

Curious that Your people used the same word for wind as for spirits—Your messengers. *Oh,* but Your mighty ones are so much more than that—they are like flames of fire!

Was it really You who laid the foundations of the earth, and placed it at just such a sweet spot that everywhere life could blossom? Lord—You are awesome! Then you brought water to it—just the right amount needed to keep everything in balance, organising the high mountain ranges and the trenches in the ocean deep. I imagine You telling them exactly where to go, because Your words are power and life, and they obediently followed Your instructions—You thundered and the valleys sank and the mountains rose up till it was just how You had intended all along. And You had got that balance of water just exactly right so there's just as much sea and just as much land as You originally planned. ["Who has measured the water in the hollow of His hand, or meted out the heavens with His hands?[1]" Who indeed!] Thank You Lord that You've set it

---
[1] Isaiah 40:12

perfectly for all time.

And the result of all this? Lord, as I look at the detail, it's truly incredible. As the mountains went up, so the valleys and rivers formed, twisting and turning and, *Oh*, so beautiful! And life everywhere! This just shouts of Your nature! The wild animals have places to drink, and the carpet of trees becomes the perfect place for the birds to build their nests and sing their praise to You among the branches. You set the whole ecology in motion from the clouds delivering their rain to the mountains through to food for the animals and plants and animals for us to eat too. And You even thought of the fruit of the vine—yes I do like a tipple—perhaps a bit too much (hic!)... and oil and makeup for the ladies to make themselves beautiful, and a steaming gorgeous loaf of fresh bread for my sandwiches. Lord, You thought of everything!

The interplay of all the different species on the planet speak of You, Lord, from the mighty cedars of Lebanon dripping from last night's rain, to the birds busily making their nests. Each has their own special niche in Your grand scheme of things—so the stork specifically chooses fir trees for her nest, while the wild mountain goats choose the high mountains and the hyrax the lower rocks.

You set the moon on its course to mark the seasons and the sun its course day by day. And the night You designed for so many of those forest creatures to go about their business in the darkness. Yeah—that sometimes leaves the young lions rather hungry, but their roaring tells all of their prey just where they are, so they keep well away. They have to learn the lion's ways, and wait for morning, and learn too that midday gets very hot, so to find some good shade and enjoy a break—just like we do. That is, except for those mad dogs and us Englishmen who insist on going out even in the midday sun. But even they enjoy the fruit of their labour come evening.

Lord, it is all so interwoven; it's truly wonderful how You thought it all through and made it all work so intricately. The profuseness of life everywhere shouts of Your nature!

I look to the sea, and I see the same there too—awesome! If I sail over the horizon I still find life everywhere—yes, even the sea is full of life—from tiny plankton to huge whales that leap out of the water slapping their tales as they crash back in again just for the fun of it. And they all know just where to go, season by season, for food and to have their young. And they are just as dependent on You as we are. If You stop the ocean currents and there's no food, they starve and die just like we do.

But You, wonderful Life-giving Holy Spirit, created them all. And You changed this whole planet from a desolate rock whirling through space to this amazing wonderful planet that is just so full of life everywhere in demonstration of Your glorious life-giving nature. *Oh,* may it carry on, forever bringing You glory and praise and making You smile. Look gently at this wonderful creation of Yours; it's all so delicately balanced.

As for me—well, I will sing Your praise, King Jesus, just as long as I live. Just as long as You still give me life, then I will rejoice in wonder at Your Mighty name.

And as for you—you would do well to follow my example, but even if you don't, you won't stop me from my praise and worship of that precious name—Jesus!

Oh, that everyone loved You King Jesus, Anointed One— that everyone turned to You as their Lord and their Saviour. You're so worth it! I bless Your Mighty name! All praise to You my King Jesus!

Psalm 105

Lord, it's so good to praise and magnify Your wonderful and precious name—Jesus!

Lord, we delight to tell everyone of the things You've done, as this gives us faith to believe You to do them again for us too, and to call You to come to our rescue when we need You.

It's fun to set them to song and sing of Your works, Your wonders. And to drink in again the Glory they give to Your marvellous name—King Jesus! We can't help but rejoice then, and wonder, and ask You what You want to do now in this present situation. Thank You for Your sweet and oh-so-Precious Presence here. *Oh,* thank You that You are alive and active and still ministering to the needs of those who call on Your name. And thank You that all You do is so Good!

Oh, and thank You that we have that so-special privilege of being adopted into Your family, with all the rights and privileges of adoption—all the promises You made to Abraham and the patriarchs are now ours too—wow—we too are Your chosen ones! And thank You that *all* Your promises are all Yes, Yes, Yes as we add our Amen[1]. *Oh,* You King Jesus are my Lord and my God—You are Lord of all the earth.

Thank You that You remember Your Covenant forever. As we break bread and drink the cup, we celebrate and remember Your body and blood, Your life poured out for us—for me. And all of those covenant promises pass down for a thousand generations, generation upon generation. Lord, we remember the ones You made with Abraham, that his descendants would be more numerous than the stars in the sky,

---

[1] 2 Corinthians 1:20

or the sand on the shore… And to Isaac that You would bless him outrageously and he reaped a hundredfold when everyone else was having famine[2]… And you confirmed both to Isaac and to Jacob that You would give their descendants the land of Canaan as an everlasting decree. And what does our Promised Land look like? Yes, the land You've promised to us? So much richer, so much more fulfilling than we would dare hope for, for ourselves—*Oh,* thank You Jesus!

And when those Patriarchs were just a few, and strangers in it, they wandered from nation to nation. Abraham even wandered right through into Egypt in his search for a land which had You for its foundation and builder[3]. And through it all You blessed them so lavishly, Abraham even had to tell the King of Sodom he wouldn't take any gift from him[4].

And no-one could lay a finger on them, and three times You rebuked kings for believing Abraham's story about his wife Sarah being his sister. Oh, they had egg all over their faces over that one!

Thank You Jesus that we walk in the same heavenly protection and provision, today, as Your little anointed ones[5]. And You command us to trust You in this and not avenge ourselves, but leave that to You[6]…

And thank You Jesus for the example of Joseph, sold into slavery by his brothers, jealous of the dreams You had given to him. Slavery and prison, false accusation, chains and fetters— through it all he remained faithful to trust You till You came through for him. And then Pharaoh set him free and appointed him over the whole kingdom—over everything! Joseph taught

---

[2] Genesis 26:12

[3] Hebrews 11:10

[4] Genesis 14:23

[5] Acts 11:26

[6] Matthew 5:38-40, Romans 12:19

them a thing or two! And through it You revealed Your purpose, to save a nation from famine, sending Joseph ahead to advise them on the necessary preparation. So he brought Jacob and all the family down to Egypt where they were treated like royalty, and You blessed them there; their flocks and herds and their families. Lord—when You are preparing and shaping us for the fulfilling of Your promises to us, remind us of Joseph and his faithfulness, that he didn't whinge or complain, and when the time came he so readily forgave his brothers, recognising Your hand of blessing was over everything, whether it looked like it or not.

But then it all went pear-shaped and there came a generation that forgot the blessing that these Hebrews had once been. The Egyptians turned to hate them and enslaved them for four hundred years, and You had to move once more to set them free by sending them Moses and Aaron. And one by one You dismantled the gods they trusted in, demonstrating Your lordship over each and every one of them with Your signs and wonders:

The water of the Nile turned into blood that killed the fish

Swarms of frogs—even in the palace!

Swarms of gnats and flies

Boils on the Egyptians

Hail instead of rain and flaming fire too

You smote the vines, and the fig trees

Swarms of locusts and grasshoppers that stripped every last green thing

The sun disappeared for three whole days

Finally their first-born died—right across the land

Except of course where Your people were, and those who put the blood of the sacrifice on their doorposts

And You led them out of the land loaded with the Egyptians' silver and gold and jewellery as they were desperate to be rid of them, because the fear of You was on them

Then You spread a cloud of covering by day and Your fire by night for light and warmth…

Quail for meat when they asked and manna for bread, day in day out…

Rocks opened up and water flowed out for them across the desert—twice!

For You remembered Your promises to Abraham, to make him a great nation and to give him the land of Canaan.

The people came out rejoicing, praising You and shouting for Joy; for You gave them other people's land. So they took up as their own inheritance what others had worked so hard to build, to build a new nation that knew You and Your ways and kept Your laws—"a people for Your own possession".

What a list! And these are just some of the highlights! Thank You Lord that this typifies how You so long to bless Your people, those who know You and will pass on their love of You and Your ways to their children and children's children. You so love to take them from slavery through total dependence on You, to a rich inheritance of more-than-enough.

And thank YOU Jesus for my own personal list:

You adopted me into Your family and grafted me into Your vine. You, Holy Spirit came and filled me and gave me my heavenly language.

You gave me a beautiful loving wife for 40 years, and four amazing children to pass on Your blessings to.

You've taken us through those same three stages, You the God of more-than-enough—*Oh,* how dependent we are on You! And what an inheritance You've given us to pass on to our children and our children's children!

You told us about Bethel, in Redding and enabled me to

go there so frequently and gave me many special friends there equally passionately pursuing You. *Oh,* what encouragement You give!

All Praise and Honour to You our Wonderful Mighty and Glorious King Jesus. We bless and lift High Your precious name!

JESUS

Psalm 106

Hallelujah! *Oh,* Thank You Lord that You are just so, so Good to all Your children—that Your wonderful Love and Grace is always outrageous—yesterday, today and forever... Who can possibly exaggerate the amazing and special things You do for us, or adequately praise You for Your Lovingkindness and care? You're too much, Lord! Much too much! Blessed—*Oh,* so richly blessed are those who have chosen You King Jesus as their Lord and Saviour and got to know You and Your ways of Justice and Righteousness.

Oh, thank You that You always remember to include me when You're doing something special, and come and help me out when I ask You. And thank You that Your plans are always to prosper us and have us enjoy happy, healthy, rewarding lives. *Oh,* thank You Jesus for paying such a price for us—that it is all paid-in-full by You when we deserved absolutely nothing. *Oh,* worthy, worthy are You, wonderful Jesus!

I sinned, just like everyone else, falling way short of the glory You had planned—*Oh,* it's just so easy to point the finger, and forget about the things I did before You saved even me, and the things I still do that cause such hurt and pain to You, and to those I love:

When the Israelites were in Egypt they gave You no thought about Your promises to deliver them, and gave up any thought of trusting you when they were trapped between the Red Sea and Pharaoh's chariots[1]. It was like they completely forgot all the plagues You sent on the Egyptians to set them free! And yet You still saved them, and showed them the

---

[1] Exodus 14:11, 12

wonder and power of Your mighty name by making a way through the sea for them... I so love it that You didn't just open up the way with the sea banked up on either side[2] but You sent a strong wind to dry the sea floor, and told them to wait until it was dry, so they could walk across on dry land[3]! *Oh,* You really are too much—just so thoughtful! And then, as though just to prove Your point, You collapse the water back onto the chasing army of chariots so that all of their enemies, all of their slave masters, drowned in front of their very eyes[4]— every single one!

It really took all of that for them to start putting their trust in You, that You would save them and deliver them[5]!

And they, just like us, have such short memories of what You do! They missed their smelly food[6] and meat, even though You gave them manna. And with all their lusting after their food, You sent a wasting and leanness in their souls and spirits in their grumbling against You. Ouch—Lord sometimes it's all too easy to grumble with the path, and plans You have for us.

Then there was the time that some got envious of Moses and Aaron—and Moses' role as leading the people, and Aaron's as offering the incense to You Lord on behalf of everyone. The earth opened up and swallowed Dathan and Abiram, their families, their little ones—tents and all... And then Your holy fire burned up 250 who thought they too could offer incense to You. Wow! Lord help me never to get envious of the ministry, mantle, gifting and responsibility You give to people who You have specifically set apart and chosen for what they carry for You. Help me, rather, if I see something I

---

[2] Exodus 14:29
[3] Exodus 14:21,22
[4] Exodus 14:28
[5] Exodus 14:31
[6] Numbers 11:6

especially appreciate in Your Giftings, Callings and Grace on someone, to seek You for it, with a clear and humble heart, recognizing that You are no respecter of persons. But above all, help me to see the part You have specifically, and uniquely, set for me to play—and to do that with all the passion, wisdom, faithfulness and anointing from You to do it how You want it done.

Then again at Horeb they got Aaron to make a golden calf—so they could worship that in place of You[7]! *Oh,* it's so easy to say "how stupid and silly!" but we, too, so easily put other things in first place in our hearts and lives and the things we feast our imagination over, and waste our time on. They exchanged You and Your delivering Glory for an image of a bull that eats grass! What a load of old bull is that? And they forgot once more that it was You who got them out of Egypt with that long list of miracles. It was You who destroyed their enemies behind them in the Red Sea. Not too surprising then, that You said You would kill them—were it not for Moses and Aaron instantly prostrating themselves before You, interceding with You on their behalf. *Oh*—what a reminder to seek Your blessing, Your compassion on those around us who don't yet know You, who just naturally do all sorts of things that we know are so far from You and Your ways—and to stand in the gap for them.

Then they had the gall to despise the green and pleasant land You had so specifically chosen for them, flowing with milk and honey, not believing that You would overcome the next set of enemies, giants and all, and enable them to walk in and possess it. More murmuring, grumbling and unbelief...[8] Till the Lord declared that indeed they would all die in the desert except for Caleb and Joshua[9], but that their children,

---

[7] Exodus 32
[8] Numbers 14:1-4
[9] Numbers 14:30

who they were so concerned to protect[10], would be the ones to go in and possess the land[11].

Then the men had sexual relations with the Moabite women and went to the sacrifices of their gods, thereby yoking themselves to these demons so that plague broke out in the camp. This time, Phinehas, one of Aaron's grandsons, out of his zeal for the honour of the Lord, drove a spear through an Israelite man into the Moabite woman, killing them both—but not before 24,000 had died of the plague. It took this act to stop the plague, and this act was credited to Phinehas as righteousness for all succeeding generations[12]. Curiously familiar wording as applied to Abraham, who believed God and 'it was credited to him as righteousness[13]'.

Oh, thank You Lord that for we who believe and trust in Your Son, King Jesus, that You raised Him from the dead, that we too are credited as righteous[14]. And thank You that You no longer require us to execute judgment and justice, but to declare Your mighty saving Grace and Mercy, that You so freely extend to all.

Then at Rephidim[15], a place of rest in the desert, wilderness of Zin[16] in Arabia, the people complained at the lack of water, and this was counted as rebellion to the Lord, so both of these occasions were referred to as 'Meribah'; places of quarrel and testing the Lord. And Moses had to seriously

---

[10] Numbers 14:3
[11] Numbers 14:31
[12] Numbers 25:7-9
[13] Genesis 15:6, Romans 4:3, 5
[14] Romans 4:24
[15] Exodus 17
[16] Numbers 20

intercede for them all, and in the end, his losing it the second time around, cost him his entry into the Promised Land. The first time, the Lord had instructed Moses to strike the rock, but the second time, the Lord instructed Moses to speak to it[17], and Moses in his anger at the people, struck the rock twice with his staff[18], saying, "Must *we* bring you water from this rock?[19]"

Oh, that was costly! Help, Lord! How often do I fall much more seriously than this! And You said to Moses, "Because you didn't trust Me enough to honour Me as holy in the sight of all the people...[20]" Thank You Jesus for Your forgiveness... May I trust You and honour You in all my dealings. Lord, I want to dwell in Your precious Promised Land. I don't want to miss out on the best of the promises You have for me.

Then when they entered the Promised Land they didn't destroy all of the inhabitants and drive them out as You had commanded, but allowed them to stay and infect the Israelites with their ways and their demonic idols. So, just as You had warned them, they started to serve these idols, even shedding the innocent blood of their sons and daughters in child sacrifices to these idols, defiling the land and themselves playing what was effectively spiritual prostitution. *Oh,* I know You are so long-suffering, but even You have to allow the inevitable eventually, and allow them to be overrun by the surrounding nations, and those who hated them. Many times You delivered them when they finally came to their senses and called on You, but it seemed they were hell-bent on rebelling

---

[17] Numbers 20:8

[18] The Lord loves variety, moving on and going deeper. Hitting the rock had been done already at Rephidim.

[19] Numbers 20:10

[20] Numbers 20:12

against You and Your ways. But Lord… *Oh,* but Lord—You were always so patient and remembered Your side of the Covenant You had made with their forefathers. You heard their pitiful cry to You and met them with Your incredible, forgiving, lovingkindness, and caused those who had them captive to show them Mercy…

Oh, thank You Lord that when I stubbornly go my own way You still guard me and care for me, and deliver me the moment I come to my senses and cry out to You. *Oh,* thank You for that precious Covenant that You King Jesus, cut with Father on my behalf at the cross. Thank You for the current revival sweeping the earth, across all the nations, sweeping men and women of every tribe and tongue, into a personal knowledge of You King Jesus, Anointed One, as their Lord and Saviour. And thank You Mighty King Jesus for that precious privilege to be alive to see it and be a part of it. *Oh,* how many generations prayed and longed for this time in history, but never saw or experienced anything like it. *Oh* King Jesus, we give You Glory and Honour—and delight to praise and lift high Your precious and mighty name—the name above every name—the name before whom every knee will bow—worthy, worthy is Your name 'Jesus'! *Oh,* how sweet to our lips and to our ears is Your precious name!

All praise and honour to You, King Jesus—the anointed one, the long-awaited Messiah of Israel. From everlasting through all the days of eternity to everlasting, we look forward to singing Your Praise and adding our "Amen!"

Hallelujah!

Psalm 107

Oh, thank You King Jesus—You're not just 'Good' You're 'the Best'. *Oh,* You are so, so good to me! You fill my life, my heart, my time and my relationships with such Life, Joy and Love. And thank You that Your covenant promises—Your amazing Lovingkindness—is guaranteed forever. I don't have to wait for some magic moment for it to start—You've demonstrated it time and time again, already! And it's promised forever and always—Wow!

And what does eternity look like? The redeemed, each telling their incredible story of Your wooing them to Yourself in such intricate and intimate ways... some while they are babes in arms and others on their deathbeds, and everything in between. You redeemed us from the evil one—from every tribe and nation, North, South, East, and West and gathered us into a family. But we don't have to wait for eternity to hear some of these stories—tell out yours...[1] Your story is so unique and special.

Oh, how many of us wandered in a wilderness of despair and chaos, hurt and in pain before we cried out to You, and You met us and led us to safety in You—to people who knew You who could help us, befriend us and teach us about You and Your wonderful ways. *Oh,* thank You King Jesus for Your unfailing, never-ending love that never fails[2]. And thank You for the amazing things You do for each one of us—for how You satisfy the deep hunger within us—hunger for more of You and of Your special love.

---

[1] For my story you will have to go to 'Your Invitation'
[2] 1 Corinthians 13

Some faced utter darkness as a result of their own misdeeds—rebelling against You and Your ways, despising Your plans and purposes... never a good idea! So You had Your ways of seeing they never ate the fruit of their labour as You dismantled their rebellious attitude with fruitless hard work until they finally fell down, crying out to You, with no-one to help them. And of course, then You saved them and brought them out of their darkness and death into Your marvellous light, breaking open their prison doors and setting them free, both spiritually and physically.

Some in their rebellion just show how stupid they really are, and often get sick because of their sin and stupid things they get up to. Some end up so loathing all food and that all but kills them, and causes them to cry out to the Lord for Him to save them. And of course You save them, Lord—Your word is all they need to heal them and deliver them[3]. *Oh,* that men everywhere would see how wonderfully kind our King Jesus really is and praise and worship Him as He so richly deserves. I bless You King Jesus! Worthy, worthy are You of all the honour, all the praise and all the worship I can give to You, my Saviour and my Lord.

Then there are those who sail the oceans of the world, whose job is sailing, and these see other facets of Papa's wonderful works. The deep sea is such a different place from terra firma, with its own wonders. And when You stir it up, You stir it! No matter how big the ship, it will go up and down and can be frightening, causing us to walk on the swinging deck like a drunkard! So just how fearful do we have to be to call on the Lord to save us? Which of course He can and does, as the waves grow still and we get happy as our ship finally arrives safely in port once more.

Oh, that everyone would Praise You, our King Jesus, for

---

[3] Psalm 103:1-5

Your incredible Lovingkindness—for Your Covenanted Assistance to those who know You and know of the Covenant You cut and sealed on our behalf at Calvary. *Oh,* join me, everyone! Let's gather and lift our King Jesus high with our praise, and with our worship. *Oh* King Jesus, You are so worthy—only You would give Your life as a ransom for us[4]— when we still wanted nothing to do with You[5]. Thank You Lord for the mighty gathering before Your throne—and our praises are joining with theirs, the myriads of angels and saints who have gone before us, all our praise in honour of You[6].

Only You can turn rivers into dry ground, turning lush pasture into a salt desert because of the wickedness of those living there. Equally You do the opposite to create pools of water in the desert and provide a place for the hungry to plant vineyards and crops to yield a harvest to feed a city—where they could grow in numbers, in prosperity and blessing.

Only You demonstrate Your righteousness by bringing down those in high places who don't know and love You, cutting down their numbers and humbling them with the absence of all those things that You so richly provide to those who love You and put You first. Just how humbled do you have to be to see it? They are oppressed with troubles and sorrow upon sorrow, wandering aimlessly, with no direction or purpose.

Oh what a different story for those who love You— wonderful Saviour! You set them high above wants and needs, sickness and disease[7]. You bless their families, not with addition, but with multiplication. The upright see it and give You praise and Glory, while such blessing well and truly shuts

---

[4] Matthew 20:28, Mark 10:45, 1 Timothy 2:6
[5] Romans 5:8
[6] Revelation 4:6
[7] Psalm 103:1-5

the mouths of those whose hearts are set against You.

So what was your path into His wonderful family? Stop for a moment and remember just how amazingly Good He has been to you, not just in saving you and delivering you, but in caring for you as one of His own... *Oh,* thank You! Thank You Jesus! Your loving care truly is amazing!

Psalm 108

Lord, my Joy is in You—in giving You Praise and Honour and Worship. In this my heart is fixed—*Oh*, my Gracious King Jesus! When I wake up I have songs and new songs running round my head and my spirit—I hear all the different parts of the various instruments… It makes me arise with the dawn.

Oh, thank YOU King Jesus—*Oh*, You give me so, so much to thank You for! Whether it's just me and You, or whether You give me the chance to lead the band and all the congregation in thanking You, streamed around the world, it's You I want to thank. My heart is so full of thanks to You for Your Lovingkindness and Covenant Assistance in every area of my life is just so outrageous… You're amazing. You've blessed us so we've never gone short as a family. You blessed my wife and I with four amazing children, all busy pursuing life and loving You. And we all love to make music and above all, to worship You our Wonderful King Jesus. In spite of my efforts, You tailor-made jobs just for me, where I could bless others and be a blessing, especially this last one. You've seen us through tough times—lots of tough times, but You've always proved Faithful. I've seen and experienced myself Your healing of body, mind and spirit—I'm wrecked for anything less than seeing You King Jesus being given Honour and Glory for all You won for us. And You blessed us with a knowledge of You, of Your Love, and of Your ways that spills over into projects like 'Living and Breathing the Psalms'—to bless others with the Wonder of knowing You. May the truth of Your love be known though all the earth and flood even the International Space Station! *Oh* King Jesus, I want to lift You high, high above the heavens, and Your Glory high above the earth—just as those astronauts see Your beautiful sunrises and sunsets from such a glorious vantage point.

Oh, that You would deliver and save the peoples of the earth who You love so much. You have declared that Your triumph on the cross was for all men everywhere—was for every tribe and nation, from the East to the West, from the North to the South—just like you assigned the land of Canaan for Your people with always enough to go round for everyone… Your triumph is enough for everyone! *Oh,* thank You King Jesus—thank You!

And thank You that You celebrate our differences, just as You celebrated the differences between the different tribes of Israel; Ephraim being their men-of-war while from Judah came their king, and ultimately You our King—wonderful Jesus. And You celebrate our trust in You, and treat with contempt those who set themselves against You; Moab—a dirty washbucket, and Edom a place for throwing off dirty sandals. And over you, Philistia; one day the Lord's triumphant shout of victory will be heard as you bow the knee in adoration and love for our High King Jesus.

As these places look closed and fortified against Your Good News right now, we thank You that this is but for a moment… That You will show the way to bring Your light and love even into Edom. *Oh,* thank You that Your love is just so much greater to the tearing down of satanic strongholds[1]. But this is not in man's strength or wisdom, but through Your mighty weapons that cast down every high thing that exalts itself against the knowledge of You, King Jesus and the wonder of Your Mighty Love[2].

Thank You for the co-labouring role You give to us. Thank You that You have entrusted to us the responsibility to bring the wonderful Good News of Your Resurrection Life

---

[1] 2 Corinthians 10:4
[2] 2 Corinthians 10:5

and Love to every tribe and nation, everywhere[3]... and You equip us to tread on everything that rises up to oppose that[4].

Oh, how beautiful are the feet of him who brings Good News; who proclaims peace, who brings the wonderful truth of Jesus' victory to all, declaring and demonstrating that King Jesus reigns![5]

---

[3] Matthew 28:19
[4] Luke 10:19
[5] Isaiah 52:7

Psalm 109

Oh, Papa God, why have You gone strangely silent, just when my heart needed to hear Your voice once more? Haven't You heard all the lies and deceit railed at me by those evil and wicked men? Haven't You seen how they are attacking me with absolutely no reason, surrounding me with their words of hatred. In return for my friendship they have become my accusers.

But Lord... But Lord I throw myself on You, and You alone. I'm shutting my mouth to listen to You; don't You see how they repay me evil, cursing and lies for the good I try and do for them, and they repay my friendship with hatred?

What do I hear You trying to say to me? "Bad company corrupts[1]..." "Will you pour out a list of curses on your enemies? That makes you no better than them. Actually it makes you worse 'cause you know better; they don't. But continue for a moment, if nothing more than to get it off your chest—OK—tell me what they are saying about you."

Give this jerk a wicked boss and an evil adversary forever at his right hand. Whenever he is judged, see he is declared 'Guilty!' May the moments he thinks to pray be only cursing and condemnation. Shorten his days; with his wife a widow, see he is unceremoniously removed from his position and replaced by another. May his children have none of their own, but end up wandering beggars driven from the ruins of their homes, while their creditors seize all that's left, and strangers run off with the little that's left of the fruit of his labour. See that no-one takes care, or has pity on his fatherless children, as

---

[1] 1 Corinthians 15:33

You cut off his descendants completely, blotting them out entirely from the next generation. *Oh,* remember the evil of his fathers and don't think of blotting out the sin of his mother! Always remember their sin while You blot out their names from the earth. Remember how this guy never thought to show kindness to anyone, but rather persecutes the poor and needy and how to finish off those broken-hearted already.

Oh, and remember this guy's filthy language! Bring his cursing back on himself. And, just as it never entered his head to bless anyone, see he gets none, himself. He is clothed in his cursing like an overcoat... he drinks this stuff for breakfast. It's like oil that lubricates his tongue. This is what this guy is clothed with, belt, braces and all.

Lord this is what my accusers are railing me with... and You know how I hate that kind of rhetoric; I wouldn't want that on my worst enemy. But Lord, it drives me back to You. You and You alone know what, if any of this, is indeed true and deserved, but I thank You for Your Forgiveness and outrageous Lovingkindness that You continually show to me. Lord I daren't plead my righteousness before You[2]. But You— please deliver me. For regardless of what it may seem on the outside, my heart is deeply wounded, while my spirit is poor and needy—*Oh,* how I need the fresh breath of You, Holy Spirit, to bind up, heal and restore. My life is passing like a sundial's shadow, lengthening as the day draws in, while I'm tossed around like a locust in the frying pan. Lord, You know how I'm weak at the knees and look quite anorexic from all my fasting. I'm becoming a byword to them as they shake their heads when they see me.

---

[2] Isaiah 64:6, Romans 3:23

Help, Lord! Help! *Oh* Lord, save me from such a fate—I plead afresh Your Mercy, Your Lovingkindness, Your Covenanted Assistance. And Lord, can You do it in such a way that everyone has to acknowledge it is Your doing?

While their cursing and railing at me is their (super)natural reward that they are heaping on themselves, I'm struggling, Lord. I'm struggling to pray that You bless them instead. Will You see they are at least put to shame while I rejoice in You and Your love? Will You see that these accusers of mine are clothed in shame and disgraced?

Oh, my King Jesus, I praise and lift high Your Wonderful and Mighty name, "Jesus!", Lion of the tribe of Judah, Lamb forever on the throne, King of Kings—*Oh,* how I love Your names. Thank YOU Jesus—for saving me, for redeeming me, and for ALL You do for me—I know I don't even know the half of it!

Jesus, I take You as my advocate. Thank You that You are the advocate for all who seek You, the advocate before any accuser.

Psalm 110

Oh, what a shout of praise must have greeted You, King Jesus, when You stepped over Heaven's threshold—Victor of Calvary, Golgotha and the cross—what a roar of praise from all the hosts of heaven gathered to greet their servant king— the Lamb. No wonder Papa God said, "Come and sit at my right hand till I make all Your enemies Your footstool." *Oh,* worthy are You King Jesus to be forever the Lamb upon the throne. And Papa God has stretched out His holy Sceptre—the sign of His rule and authority over Zion—His redeemed and holy people—to fulfil that directive.

You are saying to each of us, "Go and implement My rule in the midst of Jesus' enemies." *Oh,* Papa God, we say, "Worthy is our King Jesus to be given all rule, power and authority, over everything!" *Oh,* give us wisdom, grace and anointing to bring in Your Kingdom rule here, today, Lord. We gladly, we willingly, take up the mandate You give to Your people—to those who have washed their robes white in the blood of Jesus[1], our sacrificial lamb. We present ourselves as arrayed in Your holy robes of righteousness at the dawn of this new era, but please recognise and remember that we are but babies—we have only just been born-again.

But what role is this that I hear Papa God announcing over You, King Jesus? Ah—You are a priest forever! *Oh,* thank You that we forever have You interceding for us at Papa's right hand. Thank You Papa God that You have declared it, and You will never change Your mind over this. A priest forever like Melchizedek—the Priest and King of Salem, the city of Shalom, who had no genealogy yet Abraham honoured

---

[1] Revelation 7:14

His priestly position in giving him a tenth of the spoil of his victory over the kings—the King of Righteousness[2].

As we think of what the nations and kings of this world deserve on the day of Your judgment, may that spur us on to demonstrate and usher in Your Kingdom Rule to all who will hear and receive. The crushing of the nations and their rulers at the great Armageddon, the valley running with the blood of the dead, brings You no joy—nor me.

Oh, thank You Jesus that we can bring You Joy and lift Your head and Your Spirit as we crush the adversary under our feet[3] and assert Your Kingdom rule in Your mighty name—the one name above every name[4], to whom has been given *all* rule, *all* power and *all* authority[5]. "Jesus"!

---

[2] Mechizedek can also be translated as King of Righteousness
[3] Luke 10:19
[4] Ephesians 1:21, Philippians 2:9
[5] 1 Corinthians 15:24

Psalm 111

Hallelujah!

Oh Lord, worthy are You of all my praise, all the worship and all the honour that I can bring before all the saints as we gather to worship You. All that You do is so special and good—You make it such fun to seek out the things You do, and what they tell us about You. 'cause *all* that You do tells of Your Glory and Majesty. *Oh,* Thank You that Your Righteousness, the loving 'rightness' of *all* You do, goes on through all eternity.

And Thank You Lord that all You do is Gracious and full of Mercy, and You do things in such a way as to make them particularly memorable. *Oh,* I need that, with my memory! And thank You too Lord that You give food to those who know You and love You, not just food for our bodies, but food for our minds and our spirits to feast on and chew over—that You remember Your Covenant with us forever and always— Jesus our King and our Redeemer.

Oh, Thank You Lord for showing us the power of what You do—giving Your people the Promised Land flowing with milk and honey was a prize illustration; driving out those who had worked it and prepared it and cared for it, and giving it to Your people as an inheritance. All that You do speaks of Your Faithfulness and Justice as examples for us to follow for all time; done simply truthfully and right—just as the testimony of what You've done, is a prophetic picture of what You long to do again.

Oh, thank You King Jesus, for being our Redeemer, for redeeming us from the slavery of sin, and cutting such an incredible Covenant with Papa God on our behalf—*Oh,* so much more than we could dare to deserve! *Oh,* Holy, Holy and awesome is Your wonderful name—"Jesus!"

The fear of You, King Jesus, the fear of missing out on Your best for us, is the beginning of wisdom. Those who follow Your directions soon start to understand You and Your ways, You make them so straightforward for us to follow. All Praise to Your wonderful name, Jesus, forever. Thank You so much for all You've done for us, all you continue to do for us, day in, day out—and forever.

Psalm 112

Hallelujah!

Blessed and happy is the man who's learned to know You and Your ways, and to enjoy that intimacy that You call us to, communing with You and drinking in Your Presence. *Oh,* Thank You Holy Spirit for searching out our Papa's heart and revealing Papa to us[1]. Anointed is the one who has learned how to co-labour with You to bring Your Kingdom, Your wonderful rule, here to planet Earth. Thank You that our children grow strong and influential with a rich inheritance to pass on, just as they have themselves benefited from the riches and blessing You brought us. Thank You that Your ways are always right, and You don't change.

And when the world darkens, and descends into war, anarchy, evil and lawlessness, it's Your people who arise, demonstrating Your ways, Your blessing, Your Grace and Mercy. Thank You Lord that Your blessing is always on those who are generous and lend to others. And thank You that regardless of our circumstances we can trust in You, and You not only take care of us, but see we are respected and remembered forever.

Thank You that time and again You said "Do not fear![2]" and we don't need to fear evil rumours or news when we have You to trust in. Rather, our hearts can remain fixed on You, knowing that in the end we will see You triumph.

Thank You Lord, that You bless us so we in turn can bless the poor, which is not only the right thing to do, but returns honour back on us. The wicked just look on, clutching their

---

[1] 1 Corinthians 2:10
[2] Hebrews 13:6

wallets, bewildered, frightened and angry. They see the things they longed for and worked so hard for, manipulated and twisted others for, simply run through their fingers and come to absolutely nothing.

Psalm 113

Hallelujah!

Oh, join me in giving Praise and Thanks to our King Jesus—all of You who love Him and have given Yourselves to Him—lift high the Wonderful name of "Jesus"!

Oh Lord, You are so, so worthy of our love, our praise and our adoration now, tomorrow and through all eternity.

From those wonderfully glorious sunrises when You paint the sky with such an amazing palette of colours, all through the day, till You repeat it again at sunset—*Oh* Jesus, Your name is so worth praising!

For You are indeed King of this world, King of Kings and Lord of Lords. You won Your crown, not with swords or bullets but by laying Your life down as a ransom for each and every one of us[1]! *Oh,* how much more Glorious—Lord of Love!

Who can compare in any way with You? You are just so much higher. Worthy are You, King Jesus, seated on Your throne at Father's side[2]! Yet You don't just look down from Your heavenly throne, but Your heart still beats with Your love and compassion for this orphan planet. You are so intricately involved...

You have such a heart for the poor to raise them up from their rubbish tips and grinding poverty. You seat them with royalty—the royal children of Yours who know and love You their King—who You send to help them.

And especially Your heart is for the barren; these You delight to bless with Joy, surrounding them with laughing,

---

[1] Matthew 20:28, Mark 10:45

[2] Colossians 3:1

happy children for them to love, care and provide for[3].

Oh, Hallelujah!

Oh, ALL Praise to You King Jesus!

---

[3] Isaiah 54

Psalm 114

When Your chosen ones Israel left Egypt, those people with such a barbaric language of slavery and bondage, You dwelt with them in the cloud by day and the fire by night, so they became the place where You dwelt in Your holiness. And now once more Wonderful Lord You dwell with Your people— You indwell Your people so we become Your living sanctuaries. *Oh,* thank You for that precious privilege of having You, Mighty Holy Spirit, come and dwell in me!

The Red Sea saw the pillar of cloud and fled, and the Jordan was driven back, stopped in its tracks. *Oh,* that the nations, that sea of people, would see Your Glory dwelling in such earthen vessels and run in response—to You, rather than away! And the river of life, of trade and commerce of the business of our world, and the news and news media—stop and be driven back, that You the King of Glory may come in... may enter this Promised Land, with Your blessing and truth.

The mountains leaped like rams, and the hills skipped like lambs, *Oh,* that the mountains of influence and the hills of culture would leap and skip in Your Presence. As the earth trembles with Your Glory and Majesty, King Jesus—the God of Abraham, Isaac and Jacob[1]—may the nations tremble in anticipation of Your Wonderful Kingdom rule.

Just as You brought flowing water out of the rocks in the desert, turning hard rock into springs of life and refreshment, turn this world into a spring of Your Living Water—a River of Your Life and Love to all nations. Thank You that the increase of Your government will never end[2].

---

[1] Matthew 22:32
[2] Isaiah 9:7

Psalm 115

Oh Wonderful King Jesus, we don't deserve any glory, but You do! You deserve it *all*! You are always so full of love for each and every one of us, and always full of faith in Your love, believing the best of us and for us, and always so faithful. *Oh, worthy, worthy are You King Jesus, Anointed One.

What a ridiculous question the nations of the world ask in their unbelief, "Where is your God?" *Oh,* thank You that You are seated high above all, in heavenly places, and You take such great joy in blessing and loving us all, especially on those who love You.

How absurd to worship silver and gold, and things made by human artistry. All those buddhas—they have big mouths but they can't speak! They have big ears but hear absolutely nothing; likewise their noses don't smell a thing. Their hands feel nothing and their feet can't take them anywhere—totally incapable! What a big noise they make with their throats—not even a pip-squeak! Those who make them and those who worship them have as much sense between the ears as their images!

And as for those who have more refined tastes and idolise the latest football player or media hero—go on and idolise them, but they won't come and bless you! You can pile up your silver and gold, your antiques, or CD collection but they won't love you back! Do you really think they satisfy the longings of your heart?

All you who have been born again and come to know Jesus as your Lord and Saviour—put your trust in Him, and you will readily find Him to be a wonderful friend, helper and shield from all of life's fiery darts.

All of you who have invited Holy Spirit to come and live in you—put your trust in Him, and you will find He is such a wise help and strength for the inner man.

And all who have come to love Heavenly Papa God—*Oh,* put your trust in Him. *Oh,* thank You Papa that You are so Trustworthy and True, such a Mighty Help and Protector from everything that assails us.

Oh, thank You Papa God that You are always thinking about us and how You can bless us best[1]. Thank You King Jesus for You too are always thinking of us and transforming us from one degree of glory to another[2]. And thank You Holy Spirit for how You are always searching out more of Papa's heart and love and revealing more of Yourself to us[3], anointing us to share Your love with others. *Oh,* thank You that You are absolutely no respecter of persons[4]—You so love to pour out Your blessing on all who will open their hearts and their arms to receive more.

Oh, thank You Lord that You take such delight in seeing we increase in every good thing, and not just us, but our whole family—our children and our children's children too… Bless You Papa God, bless You Wonderful King Jesus, bless You Glorious Holy Spirit for making this earth such a special place for us. The highest heaven belongs to You—where Your throne is—*Oh,* we look forward to joining the crowd worshipping You there, one day[5]. But here, this earth You have given to us to rule in Your name—You won it back and then gave it back to us[6]—wow!

---

[1] Psalm 139:17
[2] 2 Corinthians 3:18
[3] 1 Corinthians 2:10
[4] Acts 10:34
[5] Revelation 4
[6] Matthew 28:18, 19

And there's something You especially love about the praises of those who love You here. You know their worship is one of faith and trust in You and Your word, out of choice to believe You, in the face of many contradictions. Those who praise You around Your throne see Your Glory face to face and can't help but Wonder and Praise You. For them it is very different.

Oh, join me in praising our Wonderful King Jesus!

Thank You that You are such a fountain of Blessing and Life to those who love You, Mighty Jesus!

Hallelujah!

Psalm 116

Oh, I love You my King Jesus! I love You so much because You first loved me, and You know my need before I even open my mouth—*Oh,* thank You that You love me to come and talk and commune with You, and You listen every time I come to You and You help me. *Oh* Jesus, I will call on You every day of my life.

Death was staring me in the face, its tentacles clawing at my throat, while trouble and sorrow stalked my spirit. There was a time when it took that to make me turn and call on You, my Jesus—how stupid of me! But then I called on Your mighty name—*Oh,* thank You that You stripped the adversary of the keys of death for You are the Lord of LIFE! And when I finally called on You to deliver me, You did just that, restoring my life. You are so Gracious and Right in all You do—so full of Mercy—Your Covenant Assistance. You show such special care for the helpless—that was me, and You saved me.

Now I can rest—*Oh,* thank You Jesus—You've been so good to me. You delivered me from death, from so many tears and given me my life back again—now I can walk with You once more in the land of the living. Thank You for helping me trust You when even I was saying "I'm so ill, I'm going to die." It looked like everyone and everything was lying to me.

Oh Papa, how can I repay You for restoring me? You give me back so much. Thank You Jesus for cutting Covenant with Father on my behalf. I will celebrate Your Covenant with those who know and love You—I will lift high the Passover Cup that You declared was "the cup of the New Covenant in

My blood which is poured out for you[1]." You said, "Do this in remembrance of me[2]." *Oh,* I gladly do this to remember You, and to remember all You poured out for me, that I may have life—*Oh,* thank You Jesus!

Oh Papa, how special and precious each of us is to You; You make our life here Wonderful and then, when You translate us into eternity, that has to be *the* best moment of our lives. *Oh* Jesus, I'm Your love-slave, the true son of another of Your love-slaves. How can I be elsewise when You have set me free, and given me my life back?

Oh, thank You, thank You my King Jesus. May my life be a sacrificial thank offering to You, my Saviour, my Healer, my Redeemer, my Lord.

I will remember our Covenant, Holy God. As Your Son King Jesus asked us to, I will remember Him, and remember that You are a Covenant-making and Covenant-keeping God. So with all the saints I will break bread and drink the cup, and remember You Jesus, our Covenant maker. I will remember the price You paid, that I may have life, and have it more abundantly[3]. Papa, I will come into Your Presence; I will enter Your gates with a thankful heart and with songs of thanksgiving, and I will come into Your courts with praise and join that heavenly host in worship of You. Thank You Lord, for the LIFE You've so richly lavished on me.

Hallelujah!

---

[1] Luke 22:20
[2] Luke 22:19
[3] John 10:10

Psalm 117

Oh, come and join me everyone, to give our Wonderful King Jesus the praise and honour due to His Mighty name! *Oh,* that all men everywhere, from every tribe and tongue, would come and give You Praise—my Precious Saviour King. For You gave Your life as the Covenant offering for each and every one of us.

So great is Your love that You gave Your life for us—You left Your throne of Honour and Glory and came here and even while I was so set against You, You laid down Your life for me[1]—Wow!

And not just laid down Your life, but endured such humiliation, such beating and battering and finally such an agonising death on the cross, all so that I may be forgiven and know Your kind of Life and Love; Wholeness and Health in every aspect.

Such is Your love for me, and for everyone—*Oh,* thank You Jesus! And thank You that Your love for me endures forever—throughout eternity; for ever and always.

Oh, bless You King Jesus! Thank You so much!

Hallelujah!

---

[1] Romans 5:8

Psalm 118

Oh, thank YOU Lord that You are always, always, always Good and planning the very best for me and my family, and all Your people. If I dare let my thoughts stretch out to eternity I know You will still be just the same, planning wonderful things for us to enjoy and wonder at—of Your Goodness towards us. Well—You gave us Your Son, so how will You not also freely give us all things[1]?

All you who have been born again and come to know Jesus as your Lord and Saviour—join me in declaring how Jesus' love is always the same, wonderful same, yesterday, today and forever and always.[2]

All of you who have invited Holy Spirit to come and live in you—put a new song on your lips and song in your heart that His lovingkindness will always be a growing river of life and love pouring His life out, through you, to those around you.

And all who have come to love their Heavenly Papa God—*Oh,* come join me in saying "Thank You" for the love He so freely pours into our hearts fresh and new every morning—such is His Faithfulness to each and every one of us! *Oh* Papa, You are amazing! Thank You so much!

I was hemmed in and surrounded by a multitude of enemies, and when I called out to You Lord from my distress and fear, You came and made a way wide open for me. *Oh,* thank You Lord that with You on my side I will not fear 'cause there really is nothing that man or the adversary can do

---

[1] Romans 8:32
[2] Hebrews 13:8

to me. With You my King Jesus on my side, that gives me a rather unfair majority against my foes regardless of the size of their army! Thank You Lord that together we will see Your victory, Your rule and reign established.

How much better it is to hide in You Lord under the wonderful shield of Your mighty pinions than to trust in people—they can be so fickle. *Oh,* thank You for the wonder of Your name King Jesus that every power, rule and authority has to bow to Your name[3]. In Your name every one of those enemies that swarmed around me like bees had to stop. Everyone is subject to Your name—Wow! Your name on my lips was like a flame-thrower, they went up in smoke at the whisper of Your name, "Jesus"!

For a moment they were pushing me so hard I looked dead set to fall; when I felt You at my back and I put Your name on my lips—*Oh* Jesus, why did it take me so long? "*Oh* Jesus, You are my strength and my song—You are my Wonderful Saviour!"

Glory! Bless YOU King Jesus! What a shout I give You my King! What a song of joy and victory. Come on, join me all of You who know the wonderful power of the name of Jesus. *Oh,* thank You Jesus for what You do—the mighty things You do. Your right hand is High over all and will hold me fast[4]... *Oh,* thank You for the wonderful and mighty things Your right hand has done in framing the universe[5] down to taking this wonderful loving care of even me!

I really thought this time I was a goner—I deserved to be. But You saved me, King Jesus, so that I live now for You and You alone, and You give me this incredible time to tell

---

[3] Matthew 28:18
[4] Psalm 139:10, Isaiah 41:13
[5] Isaiah 48:13

everyone of the amazing things You have done for me. *Oh,* thank You! I thought You were being really hard on me, but You weren't; it was just me. Thank You for restoring me; thank You so much!

Open up you Gates that I may give my thanks and praise to my King Jesus, before His throne. *Oh,* thank You Jesus for the gateway of thanksgiving, that this is always open when we come with thankful hearts in honour and praise to You. *Oh,* thank You that when I turned and called out to You for help, You saved me. I was fit for nothing, but somehow You so worked on my heart and spirit as to make me a cornerstone for what You are doing. *Oh* King Jesus, You are amazing!

Oh, come and rejoice with me at what the Lord has done—today! *Oh* Jesus, You know just how to make me so glad! Thank You!

Oh, thank You Jesus, for making today such a special one—join me everyone, in rejoicing and praising our King Jesus—*Oh,* You make me so glad and happy to be alive. Save, and help me again in all You have given me to do today.

Oh, blessed is any and every one who comes in King Jesus' precious name—we bless you from His holy place. He has shown us His nature and His ways of life. So Lord, my heart is forever bound to Yours with ropes of thankfulness—I am forever Your living sacrifice[6], to exalt and lift high Your Holy and Wonderful name, King Jesus, with a heart of great thankfulness.

Oh, join me everyone in giving our Wonderful King Jesus the thanks He so richly deserves. *Oh,* You are so, so good, Lord—all the time, in every way. Somehow You redeem every situation, for Your lovingkindness goes on and on—it never fails.

---

[6] Romans 12:1

Psalm 119

Each section of this rather long Psalm starts in turn with each letter of the Hebrew alphabet.

Aleph

The one who knows Your anointing and walks perfectly in step with You, Jesus, is blessed indeed! So too are those who remember the wonderful testimonies of the things they've seen and heard You do, and are pressing in to see You do them again.

These humbly live life Your way, before You, out of that hunger for more of You and longing to see You love on people and heal and restore hearts and lives.

Oh, thank You for making it so simple for us in giving us just two instructions—to Love You, and to love my neighbour as myself. Now that may be hard, but at least it's simple! *Oh,* help me Jesus to do them better, then I will never be put to shame. *Oh,* thank You King Jesus for coming and transforming my heart from the inside so I can at least start to love myself in the amazing way You love me, 'cause it's only then I can really start Your step two of this simple process.

Oh Jesus, I so love Your way of doing things, I just wish I was better at following them. Please help me, I need Your help so much.

Beth

How on earth can a young person navigate the path to adulthood in a way that is right and pure? It is actually simpler than we think; it is by taking notice of what God's Word says—both the written and the Living Word—and putting it into practice. *Oh* King Jesus, I seek You with *all* my heart—to know You better and to follow You more closely. I search Your Word, memorise it and meditate on it, that I can align my heart and life with You.

You are so blessed, King Jesus; please teach me Your ways so I too can share in those blessings. All praise to You, Jesus, that Your ways are so good, and so easy to share— loving You and loving my neighbour as myself really isn't difficult to put into words—or to share the wonderful resurrection power of Your name King Jesus. *Oh,* thank You that there's healing and deliverance in Your wonderful name—JESUS! *Oh,* thank you King Jesus for the wonderful stories of those who have gone before us from David the shepherd boy who You made King, right down to friends and family and how You took care of them and revealed Yourself to them; these are infinitely more precious than money. I love You My King; I will meditate on You and Your wonderful plans for my life. I will take great delight in seeing what You do and how You do it, so that You can do that through me too… And above all I will remember Your word, to feed on it, to read it, and to listen and take to heart Your living Word to my spirit, and act accordingly. *Oh,* thank You King Jesus that You are the Word made flesh[1]—I always have You as such a simple and direct example, and Your voice to learn to hear.

Gimel

Lord I need Your hand of blessing on every area of my life. Without Your blessing, it's all so worthless. If I've learned anything, it's that Your way is a pathway of blessing and I need that, especially if I'm going to be fuelled to stick to doing what You say to do, I need to see Your outrageous blessing result. *Oh,* show me things from Your Word that fuel my spirit to keep me pursuing You. I know there has to be so much

---

[1] John 1:14

more there that no-one has yet seen or connected the dots—and Lord "I want it!2" Thank You Holy Spirit for what You've been showing me in the Psalms, I hope this helps others see and understand just how good, how generous, how loving and forgiving You really are. Lord, I realise my time here is short so please make things obvious for me; most times I'm so slow and hard of understanding. I know You only hide things for us, and not from us, but I do so easily miss the glaringly obvious. I don't know what I don't know, so most times I don't even know what questions to ask3. My soul is tearing apart with longing to know You so much better—to know You and Your ways, that I may be better at bringing Your Kingdom here to planet Earth.

The arrogant who think and live like they are above the law—even above Your law—carry a weighty curse... *Oh Jesus*, help me never to set a foot on that path and help me to guard my attitude so as not to slip into scorn or contempt, but rather simply stick to a heart full of thanks to You for all You've done for me.

And even when those over me gossip and slander me, I will keep my mouth shut from self-justification, but remind myself of Your unfailing love and care, and I will remember to pray for them and bless them4.

Your ways are always so special and precious to me. I so love to hear testimonies of what You've done in changing other people's hearts, lives and bodies—these are food for my heart and spirit... these direct my thoughts to see You do it again.

---

2 Jeremiah 33:3
3 Romans 8:27
4 Matthew 5:44

Daleth

Oh Jesus, I'm eating dirt right now—I'm that low. It feels like everything is about to crack up, fold up and give up—please help me!

I poured out my heart to You—thank You so much for listening and showing me the things I'd missed along the way. *Oh,* You have so many blessings planned for me every day and I bungle along so poorly, I miss so many!

Help me to understand... The Israelites saw the same miracles as Moses, but somehow they never understood You and learned Your ways like Moses did. Lord, I want to meditate on the wonderful things You do, and have You teach me, and show me, Your nature, Your heart, that in them and through them, I may know YOU. *Oh* Jesus, Anointed One, You healed people, You set the demonised free, You healed the broken-hearted, You gave sight to the blind, hearing to the deaf—Lord I want to learn how to walk in that same anointing that You demonstrated. After all, You said we were to do the same things as You did, and more[5].

Lord, it is written that You healed all who came to You... How much more I need You, Holy Spirit.

But right now, Lord, my spirit is weighed down—heavy with sorrow because of the discrepancy between what I understand of Your ways and the ways of those around me. Now in the face of such opposites I really do need You to show me Your best, Your way of life, and then help me put it into practice. Lord I need You to show me in Your word and then back it up with Your Rhema, Your word of life, to my heart and spirit. I have seen that You are a God of Faithfulness, and that You highly regard faith, so I choose faithfulness. I choose faith—I choose above all to believe You and Your word[6], even when that looks absolutely crazy to me.

---

[5] John 14:12

King Jesus—as I cling to You and to the testimonies of what You did, and the wonderful things I see You doing today, I trust You—Period! Thank You that You will never shame me. I rest my heart on that, and that even through me You will heal, restore and deliver. Lord, You know how I'm running after Your heart—enlarge mine with Your Love, Your Compassion, Your Faith, Your Vision, Your Hope that accepts no impossibility with You[7].

He
Oh, teach me Your ways, King Jesus, that I may follow You *all* the days of my life. Show me Your heart and Your nature so that my heart follows Yours. Lord, put a spotlight on the path in front of me 'cause Your ways are always such fun when I catch the drift of what You want me to do, or more correctly, what You want to do through me.

Lord, I so love the stories of the things You do. Lord, I want stories of my own to share, rather than be always envious of other people's. And help me to seek out the best in everything, and to bring out the gold in others, like You do.

And Lord I really do need You to confirm Your Word to me; Your promises are so outrageous that I scarcely dare to believe them, but I really do want to, and to be truly in awe of all that You long to do in and through even me.

Oh, thank You Jesus that disgrace is never part of Your plans for those who love You, for All Your plans for us are so Good[8], and so much higher and better than we would dare to dream of[9]... *Oh,* how I long to understand them more clearly, so I can co-operate with You so much better.

---

[6] Proverbs 3:5
[7] Matthew 19:26, Mark 10:27
[8] Jeremiah 29:11
[9] Ephesians 3:20

Vav

Oh Lord, I need You so much! Holy Spirit, fill me and fill me some more, as the seal to my salvation[10], just as You promised[11], then I can answer anyone. Lord, it's Your word I trust in. And may I never contradict Your Word that is always the Truth, for all my hope is You King Jesus, my Living Hope, and in Your Word. And may I live life as Your Word directs—always—for that way, and searching out Your ways, is truly a path to life and liberty.

I so love the things You ask us to do—they are such fun, when I pluck up the courage to do what You've asked, 'cause then You do such wonderful things. And Lord I won't be ashamed to tell everyone, whoever they are, however high and mighty, of the special, amazing, loving things I get to see You do. Lord, I lift my hands in worship to You, for You to anoint with Your Power and Love to bless those around me as You direct. *Oh,* what Joy to my heart and spirit to remember the things I see You do—*Oh,* thank You King Jesus!

Zayin

Oh, King Jesus, I remind You of the promise You gave me. You gave me Hope when mine had all run out. And the one thing I cling to as everything around me fails is Your promise—the Hope it brings me, and truly preserves my life. The arrogant are merciless in their mockery of me, but I have nowhere else to go or turn to, but Your Word, and Your ways. Lord, I remember and remind myself of Your old-fashioned Gospel, that I was a sinner with a heavy price on my head and no way to pay the penalty. I was headed straight to hell and busily creating it around me as I went. But Lord... You died for me, and Your blood paid for everything. *Oh,* thank You

---

[10] 2 Corinthians 1:22
[11] Acts 2:38-39

Jesus! *Oh,* thank You for Your forgiveness, for Your Love, for Your healing, for restoring even me.

Lord, when I see people so loudly pushing their right to do wrong, it makes me boil inside. *Oh,* remind me I was just as bad, and they need the same heart transformation You so freely gave me. Help me to find ways of reaching them with Your Truth to show them in their language what they will inevitably reap if they carry on that way, together with the love and the anointing to open them up to receive You, my Wonderful Saviour King—Jesus.

Thank You Lord that You always put a song of Joy in my heart, whatever I'm doing—a song of Your love, Your truth, Your ways, and of what You so love to do... And as I lay down to sleep, I remember Your Wonderful name—Jesus! *Oh,* just remembering Your name and all You've done for me— that keeps me on the straight and narrow—no problem!—my thoughts too!

Heth

Lord, You've given me so much, You've shown me so much of Your heart and Your ways, how could I possibly do anything else but follow You? Lord, it's Your Face, Your Favour I seek with all that I am—I long for more of You. Lord it's Your Mercy—Your Covenant Assistance—I need, just like Your Word promises. Lord, I thought for a moment about what I was pursuing and then You reminded me of some Testimonies that absolutely stopped me in my tracks—oops! Lord, You know how I stopped straight away and changed my behaviour and the words out of my mouth. *Oh,* may I always do that when You show me stuff and be quick to change and make amends.

And Lord when I'm bound by whatever—*Oh,* remind me of what Your Word says on the matter so regardless of the inconvenience or the time, I can thank You for Your simple way and have You set me free once more.

Lord, I love all those who know and love You, and are living Your way. The earth is so full of Your love, Lord *Oh,* help me to learn and follow Your ways—they are so much more in tune with Your creation, and they work so much better.

Teth

Oh Lord, You've been so outrageously good to me, so much more than I could ever have deserved. Will You show me more of Your heart and how You weigh things, what's important and what isn't, what's of value and what isn't? Lord I trust You.

I scarcely want to remember what I used to be like, and sick with it too, but I said "Yes" to You and it all changed— what I couldn't do, You did—You made it so easy and so obvious to live life Your way when You first changed my heart on the inside. *Oh,* Thank You Lord, You are so good, and so, so Good to me. Show me and help me to walk Your way, *Oh,* how I need You to keep being good to me!

I think I'm learning, Lord, to understand and walk Your way of love, with Your love in my heart, even when slandered by proud and evil colleagues; their hearts must be so calloused and hard. But I'm learning to delight in Your love and Your Presence, Lord—thank You so much, and to trust You and Your anointing and favour on my life. As You always do, You even turned what was meant for evil, to my good[12], because I really learned how amazingly trustworthy You are. When I put everything into Your hands, trusting You with it, You took care of it all for me—*Oh*, thank You!

Your promises to me are so precious, as is Your Word of life to my spirit—Lord these are worth so much more than any

---

[12] Romans 8:28

amount of money—money really can't buy Your approval, Your Wisdom or Your anointing. *Oh*, knowing You is so much more valuable!

Yodh

Lord, I haven't a clue how You formed me in that secret place in my mother's womb, to be who and what I am. Which just reminds me how clueless I really am. So Holy Spirit please give me Your Wisdom and Understanding on things that really matter.

May those who know and love You rejoice when they see me as a living demonstration of how You take care and outrageously bless someone who loves and trusts Your Word and places all their Hope in You. *Oh* Papa God, what a privilege to know You and to know that everything You do is right, through and through. When I was seriously sick, You remained faithful and true (how could You be anything else!) and You healed and restored me. *Oh* Papa, Your unfailing love is always so comforting—there's nothing I can ever do to earn it, all I have to do is turn my heart to Yours, and remember Your promises to me, for You are always the same.

Lord, I trust in Your Covenant Assistance, Your Mercy, that I may live. *Oh,* how many times have I needed You to heal and restore me. Your promises bring me such Joy, *Oh* Lord, I delight in them, and watching You bring them to fruition in my life. Similarly, when brought really low by what those around me have said and done, You saw me through and raised me up. You justified me right in their faces. *Oh,* thank You Papa, You, Your Lovingkindness, Your such loving ways—*Oh*, You give me so much to think about and meditate on.

May those who are seeking more of You and seeking to understand You and Your ways so as to follow You, may they look to me as an example of what You do. And may I be found mature, even as You declare me perfect[13]. In stretching out for Your high calling on my life[14], I never want to be ashamed[15] or to be ashamed of You[16] and Your Wonderful Good News[17].

Kaph

How much longer, Lord? I'm cracking up inside with longing for You my King Jesus. All my hope is in You and Your Word... the promises You gave me. It's been so long, I'm having a job remembering and seeing in my mind's eye what those promises spoke of. When Lord? When?

I think I can just remember when You first filled my heart and my life, Holy Spirit, with Your wondrous love, Your Grace and Your Faith—*Oh,* I was stretched to bursting with Your new wine—but look at me now, *Oh* Lord, I feel like a smoky shrivelled-up wineskin. But Lord... But Lord I'm still clinging to You and following Your ways. Just how many days here do I have left, Lord? Just when are You going to vindicate me?

Lord, You know how every which way I turn, I'm surrounded by deep pits deliberately set for me to fall into by proud, arrogant opponents who don't care a fig for You or Your ways. *Oh,* thank You that *all* Your instructions, *all* Your ways, give me such clear signposts through this minefield. Help, Lord, Help! You know they have no cause to pursue me like this! They almost took me out, and would have if I hadn't been so careful to follow what You had laid so on my heart. *Oh,* thank You Lord!

Thank You Lord that Your Love never fails, and I can trust You to take Your usual, never-failing care of me, that I

---

[13] Colossians 1:28
[14] Philippians 3:14
[15] 2 Timothy 2:15
[16] Mark 8:38, Luke 9:26
[17] Romans 1:16

may do the things You've called me to do.

Lamedh

Oh, my King Jesus, the Word made flesh—You are eternal, and Your Word never changes. One day this wonderful creation of Yours will be rolled up and discarded, but Your Word will still remain the same—forever True and Faithful—because You are the True and Faithful one to all generations. You are the one who created everything[18], and You hold it all together[19], this whole creation.

Oh, what a privilege it is to know You, Lord—*Oh,* thank You and to learn Your heart and Your ways. I would surely have died if I hadn't learned of the price You paid that I may be healed[20], and have life; the scourging, beating and mockery[21] to the point that you were scarcely still recognisably human[22]— *Oh* Jesus—my Lord and my God! I can never forget what You laid down that I may have life, and have it so abundantly[23].

Lord, I'm Yours. It's in You and the blood You shed for me that I trust, and only in You. The arrogant, the trivial, the wicked, the inconsequential have all stalked me to take me out, but I will remember, and remind myself of the stories of what You have done, especially the things I've seen You do with my own eyes, and the changes You've made in my own life and heart, and the times You've healed my body too.

Oh, thank You Jesus, that You are the same yesterday, today and for every day in Your wonderful presence in eternity. Your love is so strong, so pure, so perfect; through all eternity I will continue to explore You and Your love.

---

[18] Colossians 1:16

[19] Colossians 1:17

[20] Isaiah 53:5

[21] Matthew 27:26-30, Mark 15;15-20

[22] Isaiah 52:14

[23] John 10:10

Mem

Oh Jesus, I love You. Who can compare to You and Your incredible Love, and Lovingkindness? You spell out so clearly and so simply for us just how You want us to live every day—loving You and loving those around us as we love ourselves. Your simple laws of love make me look so wise, and so much wiser than those who always seem to set themselves against me. And thank You Holy Spirit that I have You inside to help me interpret just what that's supposed to look like in every situation—every day. You give me so much more understanding than those around me, more even than those who are supposedly my teachers, as I remember and remind myself of the things You did in response to religious bigotry, self-centredness and evil. You always had an appropriate answer or response to everyone and every situation, which I do very well to follow.

It often looks like I even have more understanding than those well on in years all because I have got used to walking this way—Your way. Many times You've checked me and saved me from taking the wrong path all because I had stored those stories of You in my memory, and You reminded me just in time. *Oh,* thank You Lord for helping me this way, and teaching me day by day, so that I keep my love on all the time.

Oh, Holy Spirit, I so long for Your direction, Your words-of-life to my spirit. *Oh,* they're the best! They're sweeter than honey, all the way down deep to my inner man, speaking to me of Your incredible love for me and for everyone. And as You unfold to me the reality behind the crazy situations that I find myself in, You give me such wisdom, and insight, such wise responses, that any other response would be totally out of the question.

Nun

Oh, thank You Jesus for being such a flashlight for me on the way ahead. So many times I have had such difficulty seeing the way ahead, and when I turn to You, You illuminate everything so clearly for me; thank YOU so much! It's so easy to promise that I'll always do what You ask, but sometimes... But sometimes it looks really stupid, really crazy—*Oh,* help me to trust You in those situations; I so want to *always* be obedient to Your leading and prompting.

Just look at me right now: I feel so weak, so ill. *Oh* Lord, quicken Your life to me afresh, please... and I mean now, not tomorrow or next week. And what do I hear You saying to me—to praise and worship You with a thankful heart? Really? You evidently still have lots to teach me! But OK Lord, if that's what You say to do, then I'll start. Thank You my King Jesus—thank You that You bore my sin, You didn't just cover it over, but You, the sinless one, paid my penalty for me. You have forgiven me and removed all of the consequences of my sin from me—wow! You died the death that I should have, and in its place You gave me Life, and life with You, the Resurrected One. You took on Yourself my unrighteousness and ascribed to me Your Righteousness[24]. *Oh,* thank YOU my King, my Lord—"Thank You" seems far too little to say in response to all You've done for me. You bore my sickness and my disease, so I breathe in more of You Holy Spirit—You the very breath of God—I breathe You into every part, every organ of my body, every corner of my heart, every corner and crevice of my spirit. I breathe You—the same Spirit who raised Jesus from the dead—into my mortal body, with the same resurrection life[25]—*Oh,* thank YOU! Come, Holy Spirit—Come! I know I don't deserve this, I don't deserve You, or anything, but I do know Your love, and Your promises, and You want this for everyone. And I want You

---

[24] Romans 4:24
[25] Romans 8:11

Jesus to have the reward You so justly deserve, for all Your suffering, and that's to see us rejoicing in the LIFE You give us—body mind and spirit.

Oh, You're showing me how I hold my soul, my heart and my emotions in the palms of my own hands—You give me such power over my own life, it's awesome—it's really quite frightening just how much responsibility I have for *me*... OK Lord, I will remember, and remember too the importance of what comes out of my mouth, especially when my enemies lay snares and traps for me to fall headlong into.

But Lord, I will remember those stories of You, remembering that they aren't fiction, or fairy-tales, but Your demonstrations specifically recorded for us, forever. I love to read afresh, and remind myself, how You answered some of those traps so carefully laid for You... "Should we pay taxes to Caesar?"[26], and the woman caught in adultery[27]—hey—what about the man?

Lord, I hear You... I hear You. You gave Your disciples some very specific instructions, such as 'Heal the sick, cleanse the lepers, raise the dead and cast out demons; freely you have received, so freely give...'[28] And You gave them a very specific mandate after You had risen, in the light of You having been given *all* Power and *all* Authority in heaven and on earth—to go and teach every tribe and nation, baptizing them in the name of the Father, the Son and the Holy Spirit; teaching them to do and to teach exactly the same as You taught them...[29]

Thank You Lord that we have Your promise that You are always with us, backing up our witness and testimony to the

---

[26] Mark 12:14
[27] John 8:3-11
[28] Matthew 10:8
[29] Matthew 28:18-20

Name of Jesus[30].

Samekh

Thank You Lord, that Your law of love is so simple and direct and never double-minded[31]. Double mindedness sure is a recipe for disaster, and not one I like, either. Thank You Lord that Your promises are always "Yes, as we say our Amen."[32] And You always do answer us when we call on You, single-mindedly in faith, believing You[33]. Lord, it's in You and You alone I've learned to trust, and to hide myself in You. You are such a wonderful shield, not just from the fiery darts of the evil one[34], but so many things that would cause me serious harm. Lord, all my hope is in You.

I resist you evil—you evil thoughts, unbelief, unforgiveness, bitterness, and strife, and I address you and say "you leave in Jesus' Name[35]". Lord, I choose to believe and trust in Your Word and Your ways. I readily submit my thoughts to your thoughts, so I refuse to harbour unforgiveness of others or myself. Thank You so much for forgiving me. I refuse bitterness and strife, as I thank You for the Wonder of Your ever-faithful Love and care—just how You watch over me so tenderly. *Oh!* Help me, Lord! Help me to guard the soil of my heart, to give no place to things that have no business there, but to tend carefully the seeds You've planted, the promises You've made to me. And Lord, may I never be ashamed of the Hope to which You've called me, and all the saints[36], my brothers and sisters.

---

[30] Matthew 28:20
[31] James 1:8
[32] 2 Corinthians 1:20
[33] James 1:5-8
[34] Ephesians 6:16
[35] James 4:7
[36] Ephesians 1:18, Ephesians 4:4

Please help me, Lord. With You looking after me I'll be safe, no matter what comes. *Oh,* may I never forget Your so simple instructions. They may not be easy to follow, but they are simple, and simple to remember.

It makes me shiver to think of what happens to those who reject You and Your ways. All that they do is deceitful, like sleight of hand; You throw them away like slag. Thank You for showing me, Lord, the responsibility You give to me to guard my own heart—that makes me tremble. *Oh,* how much better are Your ways.

Ayin

Lord, You know—*Oh,* thank You that You *do* know the honesty and the dishonesty of my heart. Thank You that there's nothing I need, or can hide or cover up from You. But Lord, You know how I've learned to love Justice and Righteousness, so I ask that You don't leave me to face injustice and unrighteousness by myself. Rather, will You promise me that I won't have to face the proud and arrogant.

Lord, right now I'm struggling to see You Jesus, my King, and to remember Your word and promises to me. Please will You remember Your Lovingkindness to me, and remind me of Your ways. Lord, I am nothing but Your servant—I do my best to follow what You tell me to do, but I long for so much more. Lord, I long to understand Your heart and why You do what You do, so I can co-operate and co-labour with You. Now looks like the time You need to step in and do something, Lord, 'cause Your law is being rampantly flaunted, mocked and disregarded.

And Lord, I so love Your instructions, and Your ways; they are so much more valuable than money or prestige or material possessions, because they lead to Your Wonderful Shalom, to Your Peace, health and wholeness for every part of who and what I am, and for my family too, for all those who I love. Thank You Lord for showing me just how valuable and special You are, and Your ways. I despise all these other routes to happiness—they may look good, but they are all shortcuts that lead to pain and problems, anguish and angst.

Pe

Lord, I so love the stories of the wonderful things You've done. I love to tell them to people, and to meditate on what You were really doing and why—so as to understand You better. *Oh,* thank You Holy Spirit for the light You pour into my heart as You show me, and give me this understanding. You make even simple me look wise!

And what You show me so simply fuels my hunger to know You more… my mouth's wide open for more of You! *Oh* Lord, I'm panting, gasping for More! Please turn and show me Your Lovingkindness to me one more time, as I see that You always do for those who so love Your name—JESUS.

Oh, Holy Spirit, please turn that flashlight back on again so I can see clearly from Your Word the right way to go—and please give me the strength and the grace to do it and not get overtaken by the lusts of the eye and the lusts of the flesh, and the heart, that would derail my efforts so easily.

Oh Jesus, my Redeemer, please redeem me from the diktats of man, their expectation and manipulation—it's You I want to be obedient to. *Oh,* how I need to see Your face smiling on me—*Oh* Jesus, how I need Your approval; I know I can never earn it, but I would like to. Lord, my eyes are full of tears as I turn to You in love, and away from the oppression and the bullying stupidity of so much political correctness that goes under the guise of tolerance and being open-minded. *Oh,* thank You Jesus, I have You to turn to.

Tsadhe

Oh, thank You Lord that You are always so good and right,

always right and good in all Your ways and in all Your instructions to us. Loving You and loving others as we love ourselves—that's good. Good and simple for all of us, and always the right thing to do. *Oh,* thank You that the stories of what You do so underline and remind us that everything You do is always, always right, and we can fully trust You that they always will be.

Lord, the fire of love for You that You've ignited in my heart—it's burning me alive as I see those set against me take absolutely no notice of Your so precious words, that are pure Life to my spirit. Without them, Lord, I'm done for—I live for them. Little ol' me, hiding in a corner I may be, but Lord… But Lord I don't forget Your promises to me. I know that from everlasting to eternity Your word will be fulfilled, 'cause You are faithful and true to fulfil it.

In the middle of trouble, and everything falling apart, I will remember Your Word to me, and hold it close as the one thing that I can cling to that is secure.

Lord, I so love the stories of how You intervene to change hearts and lives, healing bodies and relationships, and restoring nations. *Oh,* show me—show me Lord the what, the how and the why, that I may co-labour with You more effectively to see Jesus get His full reward.

Qoph

"Help, Lord! Help!" Lord, I'm crying out to You with all of who and what I am—with *All* my heart, "Help!"

Lord, I so want to do things Your way, and bring You Joy, but Lord, I so need Your help to do that. Lord, I read the stories of times past and the wonderful things You did for those who loved You—the things You did through them—and Lord I want You to do the same through me—so I need You to help me, to change my heart and anoint even me.

Lord, I'm awake before dawn, remembering that Your

Mercies, Your Covenanted Assistance for me, is new afresh *every* morning, especially *this* morning. Lord, my hope is in You and Your Word. That's why evening finds me still meditating on Your promises. Lord, if You are going to work through me, then I need You to quicken my heart and my spirit—to pour Your Life and Love into me, even as You are Life and Love. Lord, I'm surrounded by evil voices and those who don't care a monkey about You and Your ways, so please help me to hear Your voice in the midst of the clamour, for I know You really aren't far away, my King Jesus. *Oh,* thank You that all Your ways, and all those stories, tell of Your amazing Goodness and Lovingkindness. They always have and they always will, because that's just who and what You are.

Resh

Lord, look at my situation and rescue me. King Jesus, my Redeemer, will You take up my case with Papa God, for I remember how You paid the price for me to be healed, delivered and set free, in body, in mind and in spirit, and Lord, I want You to get the reward for what You paid for. Please quicken me—pour Your Love and Life into every part of me, as You promised. Holy Spirit fill me, even as You are the same Spirit that raised Jesus from the grave, to the highest place of honour at Father's right hand.

Lord, I know this is not available for those who don't know and love You and Your ways. But Lord… But Lord, Your Mercy, and Lovingkindness is so Great, even to the likes of me, just trying to learn and such a novice at these things. Lord quicken me—light that blaze in my heart for You, flood me with Your Holy Spirit—just as Peter said You wanted to do, and promised on the day of Pentecost—to those listening and to their children, and to all who are far away, even as many as the Lord our God shall call[37].

Lord, I don't have to remind You of the enemies I face, both within, and without, especially doubt and unbelief, but You know how I have kept on meditating on those stories of what You did… and believing You to do the same again. Lord, I see how those voices so oppose You and Your Word, it grieves me—it cuts me up inside.

But Lord, You know how I love You and love Your ways: quicken me afresh, Jesus, with more, more, more of You and Your Lovingkindness, with more of You Holy Spirit.

For all Your words, from the very foundation of the creation of the cosmos with those wonderful words "Let there be light!" right through till You roll it all up at the end, they all speak of You and that Your words are creative Life, that they are True, and You are *always* true to Your Word.

Shin

The rulers of spiritual principalities and powers of darkness have pursued me—they clearly have their reasons, but I don't know why. Lord, my heart isn't moved by them, but it is by You—Lord, I stand in awe at the might and the power with which You back up Your word. Indeed all things are subject to us in the Name of JESUS! *Oh,* my King Jesus, that makes me HAPPY! Happy, happy, happy! Lord, the promises you've given to us, especially in Your commission, are priceless[38]! *Oh,* thank You that You promise to always be with us, even to the end of the age[39]… that You will never leave us or forsake us[40].

I so love Your Word, Lord, because it is full of Truth even as You are always True[41]. Lies and liars—Ugh!

---

[37] Acts 2:39
[38] Matthew 28:18-20
[39] Matthew 28:20
[40] Hebrews 13:5
[41] John 14:6

Lord, I lose count of the number of times every day I have to stop and praise Your Wonderful name, "Jesus"! I see the truth and the transforming power of Your simple instruction to love, to love, and to love—Lord, it's so simple—You are amazing! Those who get a hold of this can't help but know Your Precious Shalom in every area of their bodies, their minds and their spirits—Your wholeness, Your healing, Your restoration, Your Peace... There's just no way then, that we can get tripped up.

Jesus—You and You alone are my Hope and my Salvation. Lord, I simply follow You and Your wonderful example to us. I so love the stories of the healing and deliverance You brought to people, especially those who interrupted and stopped You along the way, like Jairus, and the woman who touched the hem of Your garment when You were on the way to Jairus' house to raise his daughter back to life[42]. And there are those lepers[43] and blind Bartimaeus[44] Lord, I look at these and I study them dearly, that I may know Your heart and Your ways, that You, Holy Spirit, may do the same through me. *Oh,* I so love blind Bartimaeus—he was not going to shut up until You stopped for him. Lord, I need You to stop for me; You know how hungry I am for more of You.

---

[42] Matthew 9:20, Mark 5:25, Luke 8:43 & 44, Matthew 15:27, Mark 7:28; Luke 19:1-10
[43] Luke 17:11-19
[44] Mark 10:46-52

Tav

Are You listening, Lord? Do You have any idea how hungry I am to understand You and Your Word[45] and Your Heart? This is the cry, the song of my heart, Lord.

Lord, I set this before You, that You would set my imagination and my understanding free to know and understand You—The Word made flesh that dwelt among men[46]. *Oh* that I could adequately express my high praise and worship to You, King Jesus, Anointed One, as You show me more and more of Yourself hidden in the pages of the written word. *Oh* that I could turn these into songs of worship to You.

And thank You that You always hold me by my right hand[47]—You are always on hand to help me—no wonder then, that I choose You and Your ways, Lord.

I will sing my Praise to You, King Jesus, while I still have breath to sing—You are so, so worth it. Your law of love is so simple, so true and such a help—especially when You pour Your love into me like You do. I had messed my life up just as badly as anyone, but You are always the 'Good Shepherd[48]' and You came after me—*Oh,* thank You Jesus!

I will never forget Your instruction to go and tell everyone everywhere of Your amazing Love and saving Grace and tender Mercy for all, regardless of colour, race, gender, age, or rank.

---

[45] John 1:1
[46] John 1:14
[47] Isaiah 41:13
[48] John 10:11-18

Psalm 120

Oh, thank You Jesus for being my help when I call on You. I was in such a spot and You saved me—thank You so much. *Oh,* save me from lies and deceit—and keep them from coming out of my own mouth too. Thank You that You hate these even more than I do, and You have Your special and wonderful ways of bringing these evils back on the heads of those who live by them, whether it's war, fire or whatever.

Woe is me, for I live in a land so far from the Kingdom, so far from Godliness, it's like I'm a refugee in a tent in the wilderness. Too long have I lived here among those who hate peace. I long for peace, but the moment those around me open their mouths they want war, war and more war.

Lord, in the middle of a people who are so far from You, and whose thoughts are so far from You, please help me keep my thoughts aligned with You and Your wondrous love.

Psalm 121

Help, Lord, Help! I need Your help again, Lord! Some look to the mountaintops where the idol worshippers have their altars—Ugh! I look to You Lord Jesus—the maker of the heaven and the earth.

Lord, I don't take these blessings as simply falling out of the sky, but I declare them. I thank you for them in faith, as an expression of my trust in You.

Oh, thank You that You take such good and special care over those who love You. You make sure we never go 'slip slidin' away', but rather You never sleep and are watching over Your children *all* the time.

Oh, thank You Lord that You watch over each and every one of us so minutely, being a sunshade for us as You hold our right hand in the midday sun, and You take equally close care of those moonlit night times.

Oh, thank You Lord that You keep us from everything and anything that would harm us—over every aspect of our lives; over all our toing and froing, our driving, our flying, our walking and running, right now and forever.

Oh, thank You Jesus! Thank You that I have You as my helper, my shield and my defence.

Psalm 122

I was so happy when my friends, my brothers and sisters who love You, suggested we have a praise party and come to You, King Jesus. And here we are standing right at Your gates, the gates of Your Holy throne room. It's like a huge really dense football crowd, everyone packed in close as we gather before You. This is where the people from every tribe and nation come to worship You, and to praise Your wonderful and mighty name, just as You ordained, a place for us to come and give You our thanks—JESUS!

Oh, thank You that You are here seated on Your glorious throne, and even assigned us to sit beside You[1]. Wow! And as You have set thrones for judgment there, we thank You that being justified by faith, we have peace with You[2] and are saved from Your anger[3]—totally undeserved, but all because of Your precious blood—Lord Jesus!

So Lord we pray "Your Kingdom come, Your will be done" for our brothers and sisters that they may know Your wonderful Shalom in ever deepening measure, on every aspect of their hearts and lives. *Oh,* thank You that the increase of Your government shall know no end[4]. Come and rule and reign in our hearts—Holy Spirit—and the hearts and lives of all who know and love You—those on the earth, those gathered in the heavenly throne room cheering us on, and those right here standing shoulder to shoulder with me. *Oh,* how much we need You, King Jesus!

---

[1] Ephesians 2:6
[2] Romans 5:1
[3] Romans 5:9
[4] Isaiah 9:7

Psalm 123

Lord, in quietness and confidence[1] I am looking to You. Ahhh it's so good just waiting in Your precious presence and enjoying You.

Lord, just as a servant is on the lookout for direction from his master, or a maid is looking how she can help her mistress, so I am looking to You; waiting on You, my wonderful King Jesus. Thank You for that amazing privilege of being able to co-labour with You; that You give us a part to play in bringing Your Kingdom to our world.

Thank You for Your Lovingkindness—always extended to us when we come to You with a servant's heart.

When my soul is raw at the scorn of those at ease, or at the contempt of the arrogant, I thank You that I can come back and be at ease with You; that I can come and re-calibrate my heart back in tune with Yours, spending time in Your sweet presence, once more.

---

[1] Isaiah 30:15, Isaiah 32:17

Psalm 124

Oh, thank You Lord that we have You on our side. Phew—if we hadn't had You on our side we would have been totally eaten alive by that bunch—their raging anger just flooded over us, sweeping away everything in its path.

Oh! Praise be Your wonderful name—King Jesus—thank YOU—You never let them even scratch us! Instead we escaped like a bird escaping from a snare—You broke it and we escaped—Yeaaah! We just flew away! Just how? I haven't a clue!

Oh, thank You Jesus—Your help is amazing—It's in times like these that You show You are indeed the awesome creator of heaven and earth[1], and know just how to look after those who love You.

---

[1] John 1:3

Psalm 125

Lord—it's in YOU who I trust. And I trust in You because You are the same yesterday today and forever—immoveable, and the place where the saints gather to worship You is equally the same trustworthy place as always. I'm not going to wake up tomorrow and find You've decamped to someplace else.

But rather, those beautiful mountains that I gaze at in wonder, that have taken aeons of time to rise up, and the snow covers them one day, and the sunshine the next—they remind me of the mountains around the New Jerusalem—that place where You dwell for all generations. And that's what You are like around Your people—generation after generation—Your promise of blessing was for a thousand generations.

Lord give us Godly government and leadership where Your values, such as Mercy and Truth, are held in high esteem, so people will be encouraged to follow You and Your ways rather than be led down the path of compromise and sin that masquerades as political correctness.

Lord, I look to You for health, life and prosperity for me and my family—those close to me whom I've come to love and care about—those who love Your name—King Jesus. May we find in You the Grace and Strength and Wisdom to walk full of Your anointing and Power in the middle of an evil generation.

But those who don't know and love You don't have Your truth, so it's natural that their lifestyle and values forever change in the wind—slip-slidin' away. That's a terrible way to live, that carries dreadful insecurity and a frightening set of consequences. Lord, I really don't want that—I don't ever want to be jealous of anything that others boast of, lest I run after it myself and suffer the same dreadful consequences, and end up missing out on Your so precious Presence.

Psalm 126

When You set us free, and returned us to our true homes as free people—*Oh*, we dreamed! This was so much better than the wildest dreams we had had as captives in that foreign land. Our true home was, and always is, Your place, Lord—Mount Zion[1], full of laughter and overflowing with all that our hearts had longed for—full of joyful singing and shouting our Praise and our Worship of You, our King Jesus. We couldn't help but tell of the wonderful things You had done, so that those people and nations around us couldn't help but say "Wow! The Lord certainly has done amazing things for them!"

Yes He has! He's done amazing things! He's taken our points of deepest sorrow and pain and given us His Fullness-of-JOY in exchange! Lord—will You restore these wild fancies in our hearts so they become the bedrock of our life with You? This sudden change is like a rushing river in the desert after a mighty clashing thunderstorm, that sweeps everything before it, and leaves behind seeds sprouting with life that turn into a carpet of beautiful colours, where once was nothing but desert sand and rock.

And now as it's You who have set us free, we will go out once more and sow the last of our seed into this rich soil, watering it with the tears of our hunger, 'cause we so dearly need to eat it now, ourselves. But we trust that in good time we will return and reap a mighty harvest of blessing because this is who and what You are. This is just what You do. We are giving life to the dreams that You've lavished on us that they will indeed come true so that in due time, we will come back to this place with shouts of praise and worship to You our

---

[1] See Psalm 48

King Jesus—that one day we will return, struggling with the abundance of the harvest that these dreams have brought—with all that You have given to us. Thank YOU Jesus.

Psalm 127

Oh Lord, unless You are in on what we do, that sure is a heap of wasted effort! Unless You're watching over it all, it will all be a complete waste of time. It's so pointless to get up early, work my butt off all day long and go to bed late, only to know I have to do it all over again tomorrow. *Oh,* thank You Jesus that You give sweet, precious sleep to those who love You.

Thank You Jesus for the children You give us. They may be exhausting, but they are a wonderful and precious heritage. Help us to give them the time, attention and love that they so richly deserve as the gifts direct from You that they really are.

Children, especially those born to us when we are young, so help accelerate our maturity as well as increase our stature and influence. He's a blessed man indeed who has lots of them. They are huge strength as they come alongside when fighting life's battles and difficulties.

Psalm 128

Oh, thank You Lord—You so bless those who love You and are listening out for Your every direction. You so bless the fruit of our hard work so that we prosper and are able to bless those around us. You make my wife to be so fruitful—so much sweeter than wine, and our children adding blessing on blessing—like oil and wine.

Oh, thank You Jesus that this is the blessing You so richly prepare for all those who love You.

May the Lord bless you too from His rich storehouse. May you help build up the Lord's family helping it to grow from Glory to Glory[1], all the days of your life. May you too live to see your children's children be a double bonus to your heritage.

Shalom shalom to all our Papa's wonderful family.

---

[1] 2 Corinthians 3:18

Psalm 129

Lord, how often my own life seems to mirror Israel's when I think back and remember my younger days. I was oppressed and beaten up by all sorts because I didn't know You and how to live life Your way with You living in me. When they remembered You and Your covenant promises then You delivered them, blessed them and took care of them, but they were dragged through it well and truly when they forgot about You. But even then You saw to it that they never quite got totally beaten. Just like me—I have to admit those hurts were half of the reason why I finally asked You into my life, Lord. Like Israel—boy oh boy they were deep furrows, and long.

Oh, thank You King Jesus, my Saviour, my Lord—You set me free from all the bondages that my sin tied me up in, just like You set Israel free when they turned back to You, each time. *Oh* Jesus, Your mandate is so good—it never changes. You are always the one who sets the captive free[1].

Lord, I know You don't shame anyone, but they bring it upon themselves. May those who hate those who love and worship You be so covered with shame that they daren't come near... May they be like mown grass that's cut down and withers in the hot sunshine before its time; and when the reaper tries to collect it up it's too short for proper armfuls—absolutely useless to everyone.

Thank You that it's a very different story for those who know and love You. They just attract a blessing from every passer-by, whether that's "Happy Christmas", or "Happy Easter" or something more specific and formal such as "May the Lord bless you and keep you—make His face to shine

---

[1] Isaiah 61:1, Luke 4:18

upon you, and give you His Shalom."[2] *Oh,* thank You King Jesus that Your blessing sticks, and Your face shining on us with Your favour is so, so precious. You bring so much more than just harmony and peace, Your favour brings prosperity and good friends to share it with—it brings more-than-enough so there's plenty left for the orphan and refugee…

Your favour brings health and long life so we can enjoy helping pass on our heritage to our children's children, teaching them the wonderful things You've done for us so they too know the Wonder, the Love, the Grace, the Power and Authority that's in Your name—"Jesus"! Thank You that they grow up knowing You!

---

[2] Numbers 6:24-26

Psalm 130

Help, Lord! Help! *Oh* Lord, You seem so far away. This hole I've dug for myself—it's so deep—*Oh* Lord, why am I so stupid that I've done it again? Please, please hear me, and pull me out one more time.

Lord, thank You so much that when I confess my sin to You, You blot it out from Your book, and promise me you'll never, never ever even think about it again[1]. How else could we ever come and have a relationship with You—we'd always be so aware of our guilt and shame—but You are always so full of forgiveness. Help me to grasp how You so long for us to realise we really are forgiven when we come to You, and all the guilt and shame and habit You totally wipe away, giving us new life in exchange.

Lord, I know I deserve absolutely nothing, but when I read about Your forgiveness, and You washing me clean in the blood of the Lamb[2]—Your Son—Lord, Your word gives me Hope. I wait on You Lord—I wait for You Lord.

Like a watchman on the city walls scouring the darkness and waiting for morning, I'm waiting for You Lord. Lord, inside I'm desperate for first light—far more than those watchmen, my heart and my soul are desperate for signs of Your light breaking through the darkness. *Oh* that those who profess to know You would once more fully put their hope and their trust in You King Jesus—and drink in Your Lovingkindness and all Your special promises to set them free and bless them outrageously more than they would even dare to ask You for.

---

[1] Jeremiah 31:34, Hebrews 8:12, Hebrews 10:17
[2] Revelation 1:5, Revelation 7:14

Oh, thank You Papa that You're not a skinflint, or miserly with Your blessings, but rather You are such a hugely generous and loving Daddy to all who come to You. And yet You are so much more than that—You, Jesus, are our Redeemer too—redeeming us from all the consequences of all our sins—every single one.

Oh Papa, as the first light of dawn breaks through into my heart, may this not just be for me, but for all who know and love You—may they know afresh Your Forgiveness, Your Rescue, Your Cleansing, and Your Empowerment and Grace to never go there again. May we realise the magnificence of the great exchange, that You, Jesus, bore our sin and our shame—that as You became sin, Your Righteousness is now imputed to us, so that we lose all of that sense of sin-consciousness, but our thinking becomes totally transformed into seeing ourselves as Righteous—just as You see us. And may we all join with our brothers and sisters in worship, to give You the thanks and the praise that You, King Jesus, so richly deserve. And may those who don't yet know You be so jealous of the JOY and Life they see You've poured into our hearts, that they too come running…

Psalm 131

Thank You Lord for reminding me I'm a rather simple guy. Lord, I'm happy with that. It's so easy to get proud and haughty when I really have absolutely nothing to be proud or haughty about! Lord, I happily leave to others their theological discussions and high and mighty ideas and notions way over my head.

Thank You Lord for the simple wonder of knowing You, and knowing Your peace—deep inside. When the whole world is in turmoil around me, what greater blessing could I possibly imagine or need than You and Your Peace, Lord—thanks a million! Lord, I'm stopping and quieting my spirit before You, right now. I'm reminded of our children when they had suckled their fill at my wife's breasts, resting, smiling—full—content—loved—secure—peace personified! Lord, that's a special, good place to be with You. Thank You.

Oh—if You know Holy Spirit—drink deep, drink your fill[1]. Rest in Him and tank up on His Life, His Love, His Joy, His Peace. He always has more than enough—ALWAYS! Put your hope in Him.

---

[1] 1 Peter 2:2

Psalm 132

Lord, I share David's passionate heart of love for You and for Your honour—how he vowed to You, King Jesus, that he would not rest, he would not go to bed to sleep until he'd found and made a place for the Ark of the Covenant to dwell—the place of Your Presence, Your Love, and Your Mighty Power, You the Mighty Covenant-keeping God of Abraham, of Isaac and of Jacob. And that place had to be at the very heart of his kingdom. Largely abandoned and ignored during the reign of Saul[1], David's heart was to make You a home in Jerusalem and create a place where You would be worshipped 24/7, centre-stage. Lord, we have no Ark, but all that we have and are is Yours—our King—come Holy Spirit and make a home in our hearts, and may our bodies be Your dwelling place[2]. May we worship You and have You centre-stage in our lives. May we be the living temples You long for[3].

David heard You were in a field in a forest—well, the Ark, anyway, and set out to find You and worship at Your footstool, the Mercy Seat between those mighty Cherubim. His cry was to bring You and Your Ark home, and I say my "Amen" to that—*Oh,* come and fill my home, King Jesus. Come Holy Spirit, may we too, as priests to You[4], be found clothed with Your Righteousness and Resurrection Victory, singing and shouting with the sheer Joy that You bring.

Lord, I love David's heart, even as You do. What a promise You gave him, that one of his descendants would be on his throne, and if they kept Covenant with You, each

---

[1] 1 Chronicles 13:3
[2] 1 Corinthians 3:16,17, 1 Corinthians 6:19, 2 Corinthians 6:16
[3] 1 Peter 2:5
[4] 1 Peter 2:5 & 9

teaching the next generation You and Your ways, then one of David's sons would always be on his throne—forever and always. And Lord I think You even exceeded that! King Jesus You are forever known as "the Son of David"—forever through all eternity.

And thank You King Jesus for choosing me and those around me who love You to be a Kingdom of priests to You—a temple of living stones—a place where You are truly enthroned on our praise, and on our worship. And thank You that You blessed abundantly those who lived nearby on Mount Zion, and You bless us so abundantly too. And thank You Lord that You remember practical things like blessing the poor with food, but You don't stop there, You bless us with the sweet knowledge of You, and Your saving Grace and Mercy... and as we respond with faith in You—You give us fresh songs full of Your JOY! Yeaaah!

Thank You that there on Mount Zion, David's kingdom and rule grew strong and was established, and in You King Jesus as His royal successor came a light of Kingdom revelation to us Gentiles[5] of You and Your Wonderful, Loving nature—truly You are the Glory of Israel.

And while Your enemies are clothed with shame, we look to You King Jesus, and Your crown of thorns—a crown of shame for a moment, but a crown now radiant with Glory! Worthy, worthy are You—forever the Lamb upon the throne.

---

[5] Luke 2:32

Psalm 133

Oh, my Wonderful King Jesus, it's so good, so sweet when my heart and Your heart beat together as one. May that same sweet fragrance of unity spill over to all those who also know and love You. You do something so, so special when we finally put aside our differences and crown You King Jesus as our Lord and our King, and join in the same unity You, Papa and Holy Spirit enjoy.

Oh, Your anointing flowing down, Holy Spirit, is like thick anointing oil running over our faces and beards, down our shirts and clothes right down to our feet—*Oh,* how much we need that—how precious, how special it is! *Oh,* what a fragrance! It's like the dew on Mount Hermon that gathers and flows down in joyful rivulets watering a parched and weary land. It's like the dew of Heaven watering parched and weary spirits!

Oh Jesus, bring it on—for it's here You command the blessing—it's here You bring Healing, Joy, Refreshing, and LIFE. And Lord because that's the way You are—thank You that it's always like that, because You are like that.

More, Lord! More!

Psalm 134

Oh, King Jesus—I delight to give You Praise—my Saviour and my Redeemer... my Rock—the foundation for all that I am. *Oh,* come join me everyone and let us lift the Wonderful name of Jesus High in our praise, in our thanks, and in our worship. Gathered in Your house Lord—who cares how dark the night is getting outside—we have the Wonder of Your Light and Love shining and illuminating our spirits!

Oh, with all that I am, I worship You, Lord. I raise my hands, I dance, I want *all* of this body of mine to somehow express my love and my worship to You, and to lift You high, just as I want my mind and my spirit to sing and to dance in worship to You.

Thank You Lord that You are enthroned in our Praise; that we can bring Joy to Your heart... That is reward enough of itself, but *Oh,* we thank You Lord that You put such JOY back in our hearts too. Your blessing, Your Life and Love is so much more than we deserve, or could ever earn. Thank You Lord, for the river of that creative blessing that flows in response to our Joyful Praise and Worship of You the Creator of Heaven and Earth, You the Healer of broken bodies, Restorer of broken lives, Healer of the Broken Hearted, *Oh* the freedom, You release to set the captives and the prisoners free... *Oh,* thank You our King Jesus—Lord of All!

Psalm 135

Hallelujah!

Oh, Praise the Lord's name all you worshippers, all you who love and serve Him—"JESUS"!

Worthy, worthy are You King Jesus! Anointed One! Worthy is the Lamb who was slain to receive ALL Honour, Glory and Power.

All you worship leaders—all of you gathered here with me to worship Jesus, Praise His Wonderful name!

Lord, we join with those who've gone before us, who are with You around Your throne, too numerous to count—and we declare that You are Good—You are always Good, outrageously Good, especially to those who love You, who have asked You to come and live in them...'cause that's exactly what You do—WOW! Lord, we sing, we shout, we dance, we rejoice and praise You, that You are Good to each and every one of us—and *Oh,* it's such fun, it gives us such Joy to praise and worship You, Jesus, in total abandonment.

Oh, thank You for choosing each one of us. We do acknowledge that we didn't choose You, but You chose us— even me—Thank You Lord, thank You so much! You chose us to be the bride for Your Son, to be His inheritance for eternity; You grafted us Gentiles into Your chosen family nation—Israel.

Lord, You really are amazing! You are so good, so great— just so much better, so much higher, so much more generous than anything we can ever dream of, or imagine! *Oh,* thank You Lord, that You do whatever You want to, where and however You want to, and You love us so much, not because you have to, but purely because You *love* to, simply out of the love You have for us…

Oh, thank You Jesus for the order and intricacy of this whole wonderful creation—the clouds and the rain, the thunder and the lightening—You designed it, You created it and it's still subject to Your Word—Yeaaah! You sent signs and wonders on Egypt in the face of Pharaoh culminating in the death of all the firstborn, including even the animals. The kings and nations that stood in the way of Your people entering the Promised Land, such as Sihon[1] and Og[2], were no match for You with Your backing Israel's army.

Similarly all the kings of Canaan had no chance—for You had covenanted all of Canaan to the patriarchs and their descendants as their inheritance forever.

Your name, "Jesus", endures forever. Your name, Lord, will be lifted high in honour and made known to every generation. Thank You King Jesus for how You vindicate, how You stand back of everyone who knows and loves You, for You have such love for each one of us. Thank You that we have got to know You and we humbly and readily worship You, while those around us worship their bank balance or credit rating, and other stupid man-made idols. They have mouths that can't talk, eyes that can't see, ears that can't hear and not a molecule of breath in them! And those who make them end up becoming just like them, as do all who spend their lives serving them.

---

[1] Numbers 21:21-24
[2] Numbers 21:35

Oh, but all You who love Jesus—give me a "J!"

You fathers in the house—give me an "E!"

You sons in the house—give me an "S!"

All of you who love Him—give me a "U!"

All of you who stand in awe at His Greatness and Majesty—give me an "S!

What does that spell?

"JESUS!"

What does that spell?

"JESUS!"

Hallelujah!

Psalm 136

Oh, thank You King Jesus, that You are so, so good to all of us, even those who don't know or acknowledge You—You died for them too, just as You died for me, while I never acknowledged You. You still went and cut an everlasting Covenant with Papa on our behalf—You still bore our sickness, our shame, that we may have Life and have it more abundantly.

Oh, thank You Jesus for going through with it—worthy, worthy are You to be given all power, all authority on earth and in heaven—*Oh,* thank You that You are High over all—that You rule OK, 'cause Your love never fails.

Thank You Jesus that You are Lord of Lords and are forever the "Lord of Love". *Oh,* thank You that all that You do is always motivated by such a deep, deep heart of love towards each one of us.

Thank You Jesus that other powers work wonders, but only You perform Great Wonders—wonders that heal our hurt and our brokenness, while at the same time setting us free to be all that You created us and intended us to be.

Thank You Jesus as we acknowledge You as the great creator, thank You that You planned and engineered this amazing and intricate creation we live in. You're the one who set the galaxies in their places, the sun in its place and this beautiful life-supporting planet Earth in its place—with the sun to give light for the day, and the moon and stars by night. *Oh,* You think of everything!

And it was You who finally released the demon of death to strike dead all the firstborn of Egypt—animals included—as the final plague that freed Your people from their slavery. It was Your mighty hand, Your outstretched arm that delivered them. And it was You who divided the Red Sea so the people could walk through, but saw it sweep back over Pharaoh and all his army, totally destroying their slave drivers. *Oh,* thank You that You delight to do the same today, taking captivity itself captive[1]. You set us free so there's absolutely no going back.

You led Your people through the wilderness—the Fire by night and the Cloud by day—*Oh,* thank You that Your word is still a flashlight to my path ahead[2]—You still direct and lead those who look to You.

Out of the love You had for Your people, You slew mighty kings and their peoples, removing them from the land for Your people to inherit; Sihon, king of the Amorites, Og, king of Bashan, to name but two.

You really don't want to stand right in the way of the Lord and His wondrous Love of those who honour and love Him, for He is and always will be King of all Kings. *Oh,* thank You that every knee has to bow to Your wonderful and mighty name, "Jesus", the Prince of Peace"!

Your Covenants are eternal, the land forever assigned to Israel; Your Lovingkindness and Covenanted Assistance[3] are beyond belief!

Oh, thank You Lord that You remember us when we are really brought low—You are our comforter—Wonderful Holy Spirit[4]! You still free us from every bondage or prison[5], whether we deserved it or were taken captive—it doesn't matter to You. And You are the one who feeds every creature,

---

[1] Ephesians 4:8
[2] Psalm 119:105
[3] See 'Mercy - God's Covenanted Assistance' by this author.
[4] John 14:15-16, John 14:26, John 15:26, John 16:7
[5] Luke 4:18-19

and provides us with Your wonderful bread-of-life for our spirits, too[6]—for Your love endures forever.

Oh, thank YOU! Thank You King Jesus that it is You who are the King of all Kings and Your love never fades or changes, but Your passionate heart for us—for me—is always seeking my good, and You never change for all eternity.

---

[6] Matthew 4:4, Luke 4:4

Psalm 137

When we feel we're a long way from You and Your wonderful Presence, when we're beaten up and can stand no longer, Lord, it's hard to remember and sing again those songs of joy. When our cheeks are running with the tears of distant memories of what it was like to be Praising and Worshipping You in the midst of a passionate company of wholehearted believers, Lord, it's tough to get out the musical instruments and sing those songs yet again.

We can sympathise with those Jews taken captive to Babylon and asked in mockery by their captors to sing again their joy-filled dancing songs of worship to You. *Oh,* how can one sing those songs in a foreign, alien land. No wonder their cry was may they never forget Jerusalem, even if they forgot the songs and how to play them, may they prize Jerusalem above everything else—where Your Magnificent temple stood housing the Ark of the Covenant, the place of Your Special Presence.

Lord, remind me that You never leave me or forsake me. Remind me that You are really never far away, regardless of how I may feel. Remind me that a sacrifice of praise is always precious and of inestimable value to You, and it's always and only to You that I want to sing those songs—*Oh,* how I hate 'performing' them. It's to You I give myself in worship—You my King Jesus, and You alone.

Lord—do You remember the voices of those who tore down the precious and wonderful thing that You were doing, with their words of bitterness, unbelief and compromise? They still ring in my ears, and grate on my spirit, like the Edomite onlookers cheered on the Babylonians as they ransacked and stripped Jerusalem and its beautiful temple to its foundations.

Lord—keep me from cursing—somehow—may Your love flow even through me. However deserved, that was a dire curse those captives sang over their captors—one I don't want to repeat, even here.

Thank You King Jesus that Mercy triumphs over justice[1]. That Love never fails[2]—Your love always wins through, and it's in You I put *all* my trust. Thank You Lord that You end up laughing[3] at how You twist the craziest, most evil situation to still work for my good[4]. I will yet sing those songs of love and worship to You. I will yet put Your Joy back on my lips, and laugh at hurt and pain, and grief. For You will yet turn my mourning into dancing, and make me glad once more[5].

---

[1] James 2:13
[2] 1 Corinthians 13:8
[3] Psalm 2:4
[4] Romans 8:28
[5] Psalm 30:11

Psalm 138

Oh, thank You Lord, for the wonder and strength of Your passionate love for me; a love that dreamed of me long before even the world was made, and You wrapped me around a dream of Yours! You died to redeem me from the evil one and rescued me, and filled me with Your so precious Holy Spirit… With *all* my heart, with *all* that I am, I give You my thanks, and before everyone, I will sing my songs of love and praise to You, my Glorious King Jesus. Before You I bow in worship and adoration.

You promised to dwell in the temple in Jerusalem forever[1], so even now I still gladly turn towards Jerusalem as I offer my song of thanks to You, and praise Your Wonderful name "Jesus" for Your amazing Lovingkindness that sought out even me, and wooed me to Yourself. And thank You that You are always Faithful and True, with Your promises to us always Yes, Yes, Yes and Yes, as we add our Amen[2].

Thank You Lord that You have chosen to honour Your Word over and above even Your very name. Thank You there's no going back on Your Word. And thank You that You delight in us when we take You at Your word and act on it, nothing doubting. *Oh,* thank You for how You delight to honour Your Word. *Oh,* help me to be careful with my words and to honour my promises to others, and myself, and above all to honour my promises to You, my King.

Thank You that on the same day that I called to You for help[3]—You came and encouraged me—*Oh,* thank You Holy Spirit for all Your encouragement and strength You pour into

---

[1] 2 Chronicles 7:16
[2] 2 Corinthians 1:20
[3] Daniel 10:13

my spirit, to my inner man.

One day… One day, all of the kings of the earth will similarly thank You, King Jesus. They will honour You because of the true and faithful words and promises You similarly give to them—*Oh,* make it soon Lord, that those kings of the nations, and those kings of the different aspects of our world, of commerce, of the arts, of science would acknowledge You and Your Words of Life. *Oh* King Jesus— thank You that You are "The Word of God, made flesh."[4] And may they sing of You and of Your Greatness; of the Wisdom, of the Truth, of the Life of You and Your wonderful ways.

Thank You Lord that even though You are high and lifted up, surrounded in Glory, You still have such love for the poor and humble of heart. And those who think themselves to be high and above others, You still see them, and see the motives of their hearts.

Thank You Lord that though I'm currently walking right through the middle of a load of trouble directed right at me— thank You that none of it can even touch me, because You take such wonderful good care of me. Thank You that You keep the anger of those so set against me at Your arm's length, and You have a long arm! *Oh,* thank You for Your promise that You hold me by my right hand[5] so I don't have to cling to You for all I'm worth, but I can relax, because, like a good Dad, You have a hold of me.

Oh my King Jesus, thank You that You sort it all out; all this horrible angst and mess—You make it all straight and sorted. I really don't know how You do it Lord, but in Your Lovingkindness, I even come out of it smelling of roses! You're amazing!

Oh Lord, please don't forget that we're like clay in the

---

[4] John 1:14
[5] Isaiah 41:13, Isaiah 42:6

potter's hands—thank You that You are such a skilful potter[6] with our lives, with our souls and with our spirits—with all that we are.

---

[6] Jeremiah 18:6

Psalm 139

Dare I look into Your eyes, King Jesus?

One look and I know You have seen right through me—right through all my pretences, and pretensions. You see everything I do—nothing can be hidden from You. And yet my eyes are drawn back to Your deep, deep wells of love, and to let You see into the very depths of who and what I am. Thank You that You don't violate my privacy, and the privacy of my internal world.

Thank You Lord that there's no guilt or shame in Your look of love for me, no disappointment or hurt as You see and understand my thoughts and my heart. Thank You that I sense only a love that draws me to You and yearns for You to come and search out my heart, my motives, my longings, my loves. *Oh,* come and bring Your love, and Your wholeness to the broken places, Your peace to the fractured, and Your Joy to my heart.

Lord—I give You all my ways, I want to open all of my heart to You—as if I really could hide anything anyway. For You know what I'm about to say before I've even formed the words. You formed and shaped me with such a loving touch from Your hand—Lord, the magnitude and detail of Your loving care is incredible—it's far too big for me to get my head around.

Where can I hide from You and Holy Spirit? I'm having a hard job thinking why I would want to right now, but there are times when I'm hurt and angry and lashing out… If I go and take a ride in the International Space Station, You'll still be there with me, and I seem to remember that You made quite an impact on those who went to the moon. If I drop down in some underwater capsule to the depths and darkness of the Pacific

Ocean, I won't have left You behind. Similarly if I jet off into the sunrise and set up home on some distant island, that gentle tender touch of Your loving hand will never be far away, and Your right hand will never let go.

If I think to myself that surely some blackout curtains can turn the day into night, and You'll never be able to see me, then even when I can't see my own finger in front of my face—it will still be as bright as day to You. LOL!

Oh my King Jesus—how did You create me in my mother's womb? You really are amazing—how You formed each part of my anatomy so uniquely, and my soul and spirit too. Even identical twins have such unique souls and spirits— they're still totally unique to You. Just how do You do that Lord? *Oh,* everything You do is so wonderful—that has to be pretty obvious to everyone with eyes to see! All Praise and Glory to You!

Thank You that I wasn't an accident and hidden from You as I was coming together, but rather You had Your creative hand of genius putting me together totally in secret. You saw those cells growing and multiplying and already You had all my days written in the Lamb's book of Life—Wow!

Oh Papa God, Your thoughts for me—they're so precious, so good, so big! And so many I could never count them if I tried—way more than the grains of sand on every seashore... When I stop my dreaming and wake up—*Oh*—*Oh,* thank You. my King—You're still with me and thinking of me.

Oh that my thoughts were like that, Lord. You know the bloodthirsty, selfish, angry, proud thoughts that assail my mind inside, like my enemies outside who despise Your name: "Jesus". *Oh,* You know how I hate them both, Lord. You know how I am so easily ensnared and seduced by their train of thought, and entertain them far longer than I should. *Oh,* how I hate them, and how they pollute my thought life.

Lord, search me. Lord, come in and walk with me through every aspect of my heart and life. Lord, I *want* You to know me, to know me better than I know myself. I want You to show me anything that displeases You—anything, Lord.

Lord, I can't change me—but *You* can change me. So Holy Spirit—show me and help me tend the garden of my heart with Your royal care. Help me to spot and weed out the weeds, the lies, the dishonesty, pride and fear. And help me to watch over and care for those shoots of Lovingkindness, of Wisdom, of Humility, of Hope, of Faith and Trust in You and of Your Love—Your special Agape, selfless kind of love. And help me to grow my heart to steward more of You, Holy Spirit—to grow in maturity and favour with those around me, and especially with You, Lord[1].

---

[1] Luke 2:52

Psalm 140

Help, Lord! Help! *Oh* deliver me Lord from evil men, and from evil. It sure does get tough when I'm confronted by the living embodiment of evil to hate the sin, but still love the sinner. Lord, please protect me from the violent and those who plot evil mischief, gathering others like-minded to war against the saints. Guard me too, Lord, from those who quietly plot evil mischief that they then get others to do. Like a snake, they speak with forked tongue—honed and sharp—with very poisonous venom. Ugh!

Guard me, my King Jesus, from the scheming of the wicked and especially from the violent—those who set out to devise multiple ways to trip me up. Thank You Lord that You see their arrogance in hiding snares, trip wires and pits along my way to trap me. Grrrr!

Oh, my King Jesus—You and You alone are my God, my Lord, and my strong Saviour. Hear me, Lord, it's You I trust in, not in my own wisdom, ability or strength. Thank You for Your helmet of Hope—You will see me through when things get really tough—all my hope is in You, Lord. You, please, direct my path so that none of their plans succeed, or they will boast something shocking.

Listen Lord to the proud boasting all around me, pressing in on me. Lord, may the burning coals they had destined for me fall on them, as they fall into the deep dank pits they had dug for me. Thank You Lord that for them there's no escape.

As for slander—Lord, please see this boomerangs on those who peddle this stuff. Thank You that You see to it that no slanderer will ever amount to anything, but they are taken out by those who are worse still.

Thank You Lord that You always plead the cause of

the poor and justice for the needy. *Oh,* thank You that justice is just so important to You—that You rejoice when those who love You take up the plight of those who have no voice for themselves. Thank You for how You back those who help the poor, and pursue justice on their behalf.

Those who love Your ways and who love justice, *Oh,* they praise and magnify Your wonderful name, King Jesus. If anyone knows injustice, it's You, Lord—at every step of all of those fateful trials You were denied justice. You know exactly what it feels like. And thank You Lord that You, the Righteous One, You became sin for us in Your sacrifice, so that You could impute Your Righteousness to us. Wow! *Oh,* thank You Lord—we bless and praise You for giving us this wonderful privilege—this everlasting invitation to live in Your sweet and precious Presence—now and for all eternity—*Oh,* thank You, Lord!

Psalm 141

Help, Lord! *Oh,* my King Jesus, how much I need Your help, and quickly. Thank You that You always hear my cry for help, and are never far away.

Lord, I want my time spent with You to be like the incense from the evening sacrifice—my hands rising up in worship to You, like the smoke of the incense as a sweet smell that You appreciate. Lord, I need this time with You, time to rest and reflect, time for You to re-calibrate my heart and my affections, for You are my Lord, You are my Wonderful, Mighty King, my King Jesus.

Lord, will You set a watch over my mouth—I so easily say all the wrong things, or with the wrong tone, and I really need Your help so that my words carry only Your Life, Your Love and Power—Your power to heal, bind up and restore. Lord, please check me before I say things rather than afterwards when it's too late—it's so hard to correct things afterwards.

And I need Your help with my heart, too, Lord—it's just so easy to be carried along on the spur of the moment with those around me who don't know You. Their envy and jealousy so quickly leads to taking what isn't mine, and dissing others out to get it. Lord, I really don't want that, and the fruit of that always leaves such a nasty taste.

Oh, help me to have an open and listening heart, Lord; one that 'hears' Your correction, or the correction of my brother or sister who knows and loves You. Help me to appreciate in the middle of the hurt of their correction, that really they're doing me a favour so I don't keep making the same mistake over and over.

May those around me stand or fall by You, the Rock-of-

My-Salvation[1]—the stone the builders rejected. *Oh* that they would 'hear' Your sweet words of love and forgiveness. *Oh* that Your plough would plough in those words of life so that they sprout and bear fruit, rather than break them into pieces on their way to hell. That's never what You want.

But Lord… But Lord I look to You, my Wonderful King Jesus. *Oh,* hide me in that same rock. Keep me from being caught by the trap they've laid so specifically for me, and also from all the others I would so easily fall for… May they fall into them, themselves, while You help me see them, and navigate a safe path, giving them a wide berth.

---

[1] 2 Samuel 22:47, Psalm 18:46, Psalm 62:6-7, Psalm 89:26, Psalm 95:1

Psalm 142

Help, Lord, Help!

Oh, my King Jesus—Help! Can't You see the trouble I'm in this time? Do I really have to spell it out for You?

Lord, my spirit is just fainting away... Please watch over me, and breathe Your life back into me once more. It feels like I'm about to fall headlong into a deep pit carefully planned and dug just for me. I look to the right and to the left and there's absolutely no-one around—that's surprising in itself and, Lord, it feels just like that in my spirit too—does anyone care for me?

Lord, I have no other place to hide, but in You. Lord, You are my refuge, You are my hiding place. *Oh,* that sounded good! Lord, I shout that to You, "You are my refuge, You are my hiding place, I hide myself in Yoooooou!"

Lord, I'm so low, I feel like I'm just a shadow, fading away. But Lord, I want what *You*'ve got for me, and *only* what You've got planned. Thank You that I know that You are my deliverer[1] and You will rescue me. Thank You that You set the captives free, and You will bring me out of this prison, and set my spirit free once more to soar with You—to rise up, as it were, on the wings of eagles.

Oh, thank You Lord, Thank You my King, my King Jesus! Thank You that You are always so strong to save to the uttermost[2] those who trust simply in You and Your unfailing love—Your love that *never* fails[3].

Thank You that the righteous, that those who know and

---

[1] 2 Samuel 22:2, Psalm 16:1, Psalm 18:2, Psalm 34:1, Psalm 40:17, Psalm 144:2, Romans 11:26

[2] Hebrews 7:25

[3] 1 Corinthians 13

love You are pressing in and cheering me on; at last I think I can almost hear their cheers[4]. *Oh,* please keep cheering—I so need your cheers to keep me running. *Oh,* thank You Lord, that You have such wonderful things planned, not just for me, but for all who love You.

---

[4] Hebrews 12:1

Psalm 143

Oh, thank You King Jesus that You always hear even the whisper of my cry to You, 'cause You are always, always Faithful and True. Thank You that You didn't come to judge each of us, but to save us[1]—please don't judge me, but save me. Every one of us only deserves Your judgment, for we've all fallen so far short of the glory You intended for us[2].

Oh, my enemy has lassoed me, pulled me to the ground and is dictating my life, inexorably pulling my very life away from me. Lord, my spirit—that spirit that You have redeemed and made new within me—is getting fainter and fainter, weaker and weaker.

Lord, I'm desperately trying to remember the miracles... the miracles recorded in Your Word, and the miracles I've seen and experienced myself. I want to remember and think about the wonderful things You do, the Wonderful things You've done—even in my own life...

Lord, I spread out my hands wearily before You. I lift them up to You in worship, heavy though they are, like my heart. I'm so thirsty for more of You—Holy Spirit, Come—please Come once more... Yeaaaah!

Please hurry, Lord, *Oh,* my King Jesus; I can almost feel my spirit wasting to nothing. Please show Your face to me one more time, Your wonderful loving smile, once more—I'll die without that. Can You give me a word as I wake in the morning? I so need that to see me through the day. Lord, it's in You I trust, no-one else—only You. Please help me to know Your path of life, the path You have ordained for me to walk

---

[1] John 12:47
[2] Romans 3:23

in. Lord, even as I lift my hands to You, I lift my soul and my spirit to You—my King Jesus—Lord of Love, Lord of Life, the Great Deliverer—as I worship You afresh.

Oh, my King Jesus, please deliver me and set me free once more, for You are my vindication. Lord, You know how I have run to You to hide myself in You.

Oh, please teach me to walk the path You have for me—to delight in it and not get led astray again. Lord, You are my God—thank You that You are so, so Good, and so, so Good to me—thank You, Holy Spirit. Please fill me afresh and retune my heart to Yours. Holy Spirit—You lead me straight and true, please.

Oh, my King Jesus, how much I need Your Life and Your Love afresh—please quicken this mortal body with more of You—for the sake of Your wonderful name—JESUS!

Lord, You know the love in my heart for You—even as You are always right—so please lift me up once more and deliver me from this. And Lord, because You are always so full of Lovingkindness, will You extend that to me once more and cut this lasso off of me? Will You so set me free that I can truly trample on this thing and then be able to set others free from it too?

Lord—I'm Your love slave—in serving You I find perfect freedom.

Psalm 144

All praise to You my King Jesus, my rock, the very foundation of all that I am. Thank You Prince of Peace for Your wonderful ways of peace, and yet You teach my hands to war and my fingers to fight. *Oh,* thank You that our warfare is not against flesh and blood, or against other people—though there are times it really does look like that. Thank You that our weapons are so infinitely more powerful to address the real roots of conflict, the spiritual forces of evil[1]. Thank You Lord that You put in our mouths the sword to cast down imaginations, thoughts and dreams and every proud thing that exalts itself against the pure humility of knowing You—that our words carry this power to bind and to loose, to shut up and to set free[2]—*Oh* the power in Your so precious name, "JESUS!" Lord, I need much teaching from You to learn how to be effective in that warfare. I see so much shadow boxing that saps the life and joy from my spirit, taking me away from my focus and love of You.

Oh, thank You Mighty King Jesus that You spoiled every principality and power that raised itself against You and made an open spectacle of them in Your resurrection march of triumph to the throne of grace[3]. Thank You that You are the one with the keys of the Kingdom, the keys of death and hell[4].

Oh, thank You that You Jesus are Lovingkindness—that You are such a fortress all around me, for You deliver me from everything that would put me down. *Oh,* You set me on such a high tower above those things. *Oh,* what a shield You

---

[1] 2 Corinthians 10:3,5
[2] Matthew 16:19, Matthew 18:18
[3] Colossians 2:15
[4] Revelation 1:18

are to me when I come and hide myself in You! Thank You that You have appointed me to crush and trample on serpents and scorpions and their likeness in the spirit, and there is no way they can hurt me. *Oh,* thank You that when Your disciples grasped this point, and put it into practice You got so happy![5] *Oh*, how You want us to tear these things down and trample on them… but I thank You that my name is written in Your book of life[6]—*Oh,* guard me from doing anything that could in any way blot that out, ouch!

But Jesus, what is it about mankind that You have any thought for us? Why on earth would You take on human form and become one of us? We're like a breath of wind—one puff and we're gone—a shadow that leaves absolutely no trace of its path behind it.

Oh, thank You Mighty King Jesus that You did indeed rend the heavens and come down[7], and all of heaven and the earth had to bow and bend to Your intent. That in due time, when You, Papa God, opened the heavens and declared that Jesus was indeed Your beloved Son in whom You were so delighted, that You, Holy Spirit, flew down and rested upon Him[8]. Yeaaah!

Oh, thank You that all those mountains of influence, of power and of evil have to bow the knee to You, Jesus. Send Your light to illuminate what was hidden in darkness, and scatter them as You rout them. And Lord, will You hold me and pull me out once more from the lies, deceit, selfishness and greed of the rulers of this earth and the world they've created. I sing my songs of praise to You my God, my Rock, my King Jesus—it is such a joy to sing and make music to

---

[5] Luke 10:17-21
[6] Luke 10:20
[7] Isaiah 64:1
[8] Matthew 3:16, Mark 1:10, Luke 3:22

You, that lifts You high.

Thank You for the wondrous privilege of having You teach me how to rule and reign in life, to give me victory through every situation, and give You Glory and Honour through it all. Thank You for how You deliver me and rescue me from those with very different ways of thinking and of living, full of deceit.

And as I learn how to rule and reign, then my children learn too, and are saved the crazy mistakes and problems I created for myself. *Oh,* thank You Lord that I live to see my sons rise up and take their place as wise adults over their families, and my daughters grow in beauty, both physical and spiritual, and be the pillar of their families and communities.

Thank You Lord, that as I have aligned myself to You and Your ways, You have provided for me so I have more than enough, in every area of my life, with plenty left over to bless others and further Your Kingdom.

Thank You that Your Kingdom is one of prosperity for all, where there is no forcible breaking in and destroying, or stealing another's property—where there are no protest marches over injustice, because there is none, but everyone is happy, happy, happy! Fulfilled and happy!

Happy are the people who know You, King Jesus, 'cause You somehow manage to bring this Joy, this peace, this prosperity of soul to us, even in the midst of a generation that is running away from You and Your ways.

Psalm 145

Oh, my King Jesus—my Lord and my God,

Oh, I bless and I praise Your wonderful, Your Matchless, Your Mighty name, "JESUS!" *Oh,* there's no other name that gets close—there's no other name like Yours! *Oh* Lord, I will bless and praise Your name every day and for all eternity.

For You are so good, always so, so good, and so loving to all of us, though none of us deserve it. *Oh,* my King Jesus I love how You are able to twist and turn everything to my advantage, even when I get things so horribly wrong—*Oh,* that's really brilliant—*Oh,* what a creator You are, to create such beauty out of pain, sorrow and hardship. No-one can search out the depths of just how Wonderful You are!

It's fun telling our children of the things You've done for us, how You rescued us and saved us from disaster time and again, how You transformed us with Your Lovingkindness, how You are always, always, always true to Your promises. I daren't imagine what my life would have been like without You. *Oh,* I want them to know You and be saved from all that pain, grief and loneliness. Thank You that You don't have any grandchildren.

Thank You Lord for the peace that floods my heart when I think about the amazing things You do—that You laid aside Your Glory to become a man, to be our Saviour. You laid aside Your Glory to take on human flesh, born of a virgin, and to demonstrate and show us Your Father's nature, to love, to love, and to go on loving regardless of the cost. That You bore my sin, and my shame, and paid the price for me to be adopted into Your family, and to be declared righteous the moment I received You as my Saviour—*Oh,* what a King You are— Jesus!

Everything You do speaks of Your Wonderful and Awesome nature. We just have to look around us at this wonderful creation that You designed for us; from the size and majesty of the universe to the details of the absurdly small particles that make up matter. Or the loving and tender care You show for each one of us, but yet the freedom You give to us to mess up, or walk away from You, they all shout, "Lord, You're Good." Everything You do simply shouts, "You're so Good!"

We only have to stop for a moment to wonder at just how amazingly Good You are, Papa—adopting us into Your family, and welcoming us in, even when we were so mired and dirty from the life we had been leading. But You took us and washed our sin away, You cleansed us in the blood of Your Son, and gave us new and clean hearts and spirits. I can't help, then, but sing Your praise! All that You do is so right and good.

Oh, King Jesus, You are so Gracious and so full of Mercy to each one of us… You are so slow to get angry with us— even when we seriously deserve it—Your Lovingkindness just goes on and on, You are so good to everyone. Your such-Tender Compassion caps all that You are.

All those who have come to know You can't help but thank You for all that You have done, and bless and praise Your Mighty and Wonderful name, "JESUS!" Your ways are so Glorious, Your Kingdom is so full of mercy and truth and Your creative and loving care. Your Glory illuminates everything through all eternity, shining on Your Faithfulness and Truth.

Oh, King Jesus, my King, Your Kingdom will last forever—stretching through all eternity. Your wonderful rule and reign of selfless love spans every generation. And All Your promises are Yes and Amen, for You are totally trustworthy, totally faithful—always.

Oh, my Wonderful Jesus, look how tenderly You restore those who fall, and bring a smile back to those bowed over with pain, anguish or grief. There's no condemnation from You, no pointing the finger or blame. No wonder everyone looks to You—Your words are Life—they are food that nourishes my spirit, and out of the sheer generosity of Your heart You satisfy that need in every living thing... in all our uniqueness and individuality.

Oh, thank You that everything You do is so, so right; all Your ways are so right—every aspect of Your Kingdom so, so right, and gracious—You are always so faithful. And You are always so close to each of us when we call on You—Most Faithful and True.

My Lord, I give You my dreams and longings, for You— Your selfless love and Your humble Glory—have captivated my heart and my imagination. One day—in Your good time— I know You will find, in Your so imaginative way, a way of fulfilling them far more beautifully than I would ever have dared to dream or imagine.

And when it's all getting too much—thank You that You always hear my cry for help, Lord. So many times You've come to my rescue—thank You so much. Lord, it's in You I trust as You watch over me and over all those who love You.

I daren't think what happens to the wicked who reject Your Love and free Salvation, I really don't want to go there.

Oh, my King Jesus, I will forever sing and shout Your praise. I will forever praise and lift high Your Wonderful name. *Oh* that every creature would praise Your Holy name— "Jesus" forever and through all eternity. *Oh,* there's no-one like You Lord, no-one close to deserving the praise of our hearts, like You, King Jesus. Thank You. Thank You for all You are, and all You are to me.

Psalm 146

Oh my soul, get a hold of yourself! Praise our King Jesus! Lord, I want every breath of my life to be a Praise offering to You. *Oh,* my King Jesus, You are so, so worthy of my praise—my Saviour, my Life, my All!

Don't trust other people to help you, however high and mighty, whatever their influence. Honour them and help them, but don't put yourself in a place where you depend on them and their help. The moment they complete their last breath, their thoughts and ability to help die with them. Far happier are those who have learned to trust in You, King Jesus, my Redeemer, and lean on You for help—just like Jacob did[1].

For You are the great Creator—You made the heavens, the stars and the galaxies, and You made this wonderful planet Earth with all its beauty, its complexity and its Life. And like creation goes on forever, so You are True forever and always, and Your ways stay the same. You execute Justice for all and give food to the hungry. You set the prisoner free, and give sight to the blind[2]. You lift up those bowed with grief, and love and especially watch over and care for those who love You. You care for the outcast, the lonely, the widow and the orphan by adopting us into Your wondrous family. But that contorted route of those who despise You and Your ways, You add extra twists and turns—LOL!

Oh, my King Jesus—Your Kingdom lasts forever—from that first Easter through all eternity! What a Wonderful reign!

Oh, people of God—you who have learned to know Him and love Him—join me in singing His praise—JESUS!

---

[1] Genesis 48:15
[2] Isaiah 61:1-3, Luke 4:18

Psalm 147

Hallelujah! Hallelujah!

Oh, my King Jesus, Anointed One, You are so, so good, so worthy of our praise and our worship, and as we lift You high on our praise, Your presence lifts and thrills our hearts too. You make it such fun to rejoice and dance in worship to You. Thank You that You so love to celebrate and party[1]!

Oh, thank You that You are a God of such Joy and Laughter and Freedom that, as we gather in worship, You build up and encourage Your people—we even join with the Heavenly Jerusalem[2]! And You move to gather to Yourself the lonely and broken, and broken-hearted, binding their wounds and healing them.

And yet You count the stars and know each one by name—*Oh* Lord, You really are amazing, so much more than we can comprehend, and yet You look after, and lift up the meek and humble while bringing down those set against You and Your ways. Thank You that You so freely share Your heart with us, giving us You, Holy Spirit, to come and live in us—You the very same Spirit who raised Jesus from the dead[3] to the highest possible place of Honour and Glory, who searches out Your heart for us too[4]. Thank You that while You are so far above our understanding, yet You passionately want us to know You, Your heart and Your Amazing and Wonderful Love[5].

---

[1] Luke 15:10,1 Peter 1:8

[2] Hebrews 12:1

[3] Romans 8:11

[4] 1 Corinthians 2:10

[5] Matthew 11:27, Matthew 16:17, Luke 10:22, 1 Corinthians 2:10, Ephesians 3:5

Oh, my King Jesus thank You for Your wonderful heart-restoring love, for giving us Your Spirit, Your Life, Your Love—*Oh,* how much we need You! Thank You that You set the sun to rise and the rain to come on those who love You and equally for those who hate You[6]. You see the whole of this beautiful blue planet is just so full of life in all its intricacy and interdependence—from the oceans to the clouds to the thunderstorms and rain to give life for vegetation that feeds the animals, each with their own niche in Your scheme of things. What a picture of this world that You created is for us, of how You so want to bless us, and bless us with abundant variety. You so celebrate diversity and uniqueness!

You don't place value on someone's strength and physical prowess—but rather, You look for strength of character and spiritual prowess—in their trust and hope in You and Your Lovingkindness—in their boldness to proclaim and usher in Your Kingdom rule.

Oh, I bless You my King Jesus—*Oh* everyone—please join me in praise, in worship, in thanking Him for all He did and all He keeps on doing... *Oh,* Thank YOU my King for giving Your life, that I may live, that I may have LIFE and have it so abundantly, so richly—that I may experience such freedom to be me. *Oh,* thank You for revealing Yourself to me so I could choose YOU! *Oh,* join me all of you who have chosen King Jesus! Join me in Your praise and worship—in Your own personal thanksgiving...

Oh, thank You Jesus that You are my defence—that You have strengthened our family, and our family ties. You have shown us Your ways and Your priorities, and they really do work! They bring peace and prosperity to us and our children, and their children after them. Thank You that Your ways are ways of prosperity where everyone has more than enough and

---

[6] Matthew 5:45

with plenty left over to help those not so fortunate. *Oh,* thank You that Your ways satisfy! *Oh,* how they satisfy every part of who and what I am, and in style 'cause You are the King—and not just *the* King, but King of *All* Kings.

Thank You that You are still revealing Yourself to us, and still showing us how to live life Your way. And when Your word, Your fresh revelation comes, it seems like everyone has it at once—it seems like everyone passes Your Word on real quick. That's just as well, as You set seasons for life[7], just as You set the four seasons of the year, and doing the right thing in the wrong season can be lethal! Who can survive for long without the right gear in the middle of winter's snow, ice and frost? That's not the time for summer clothes and outside parties! But when You ordain springtime has come, and the wind of Your Spirit is blowing in the trees and river of life is in full flow—that's the time to jump in wholeheartedly. *Oh,* thank You that You reveal these things to those who love You, so they can co-operate with You with what You want and with what You have in mind to bring about.

And those who don't know You have no idea! They have no idea of the time[8] or the season. How can they?

Oh, thank You Lord for bringing me into Your family, and showing me Yourself, and Your ways—*Oh,*

Hallelujah and Hallelujah!

---

[7] Ecclesiastes 3:1

[8] Romans 13:11, 2 Corinthians 6:2, 1 John 2:18

Psalm 148

Hallelujah!

All of Your creation, Lord, declares Your praise and Glory!

All you His angels, His messengers—give Him your praise—together with all the hosts of heaven! *Oh,* King Jesus You are so worth it—giving Your life as a ransom for me, and for all of us.

Sun and moon, stars and all you wonderful heavenly bodies; black holes, white dwarfs and red giants, galaxies upon galaxies—what praise and Glory You give to our King! What creator makes such a varied and wonderful creation— you all say so much about Him and His character and His ways!

And you, heaven itself—far higher than the universe we see—what Glory do you shout of our Creator King? You must have seen Jesus speak the word and seen our universe spring into being[1]! GLORY! All Glory to You, King Jesus— establishing this creation, decreeing it will last forever[2].

What Praise does this earth give to You, Lord? *Oh* that it all would give You the Glory and the Honour You so richly deserve. And like the variety in the heavens the variety here too speaks buckets of You! There's the sea creatures in the depths of the ocean, humble plankton and giant squid and everything in between! Then there's lightning, hail, snow clouds, twisters—*Oh,* what a variety of weather You created! Then there's mountains and molehills, fruit trees and giant cedars, wild animals and domestic ones, gnats and birds to eat 'em— *Oh,* the list goes on!

---

[1] John 1:3

[2] This is what the Hebrew says. I wonder when cosmology will agree?

Oh, but how much more precious is the worship and praise from the hearts of those who have come to know You, Jesus, and love You! *Oh,* join me you kings of the earth, you princes and princesses, you rulers, men and women, young and old, come and give King Jesus your praise and worship! *Oh* Jesus, Your name alone is High over ALL! Your Glory is so much brighter!

Thank You that the heart-given praise and worship of Your people, Jew or Gentile, male or female, is so special and so valued by You. Thank You that You've given such a faculty to us to bless and enrich Your life, King Jesus— through all eternity—surrounding Your throne.

Oh, Hallelujah and Hallelujah!

Psalm 149

All Praise to You, King Jesus!

Lord, I sing You a new song—a song fresh with the Love and Joy You pour into my heart—a song that celebrates You, that everyone who loves You can join me in the chorus.

Lord we rejoice and thank You that You are the Mighty Creator and Restorer. We're all so glad that You've gathered us together for this time of praise and worship of You our King.

In song and in dance it's You Lord Jesus we're celebrating—our hearts are so thankful for all You do for us, for how You delight in us! Thank You that You crown the humble with the victory You won—You're amazing!

Come on, everyone, rejoice at the Glory and Honour that He crowns you with! When you get it, you can't stop singing in the shower or when you're trying to go to sleep—the songs just keep running round your spirit and out of your mouth!

Oh, take our praise from praise to 'High Praise', Papa! Put Your powerful two-edged sword in our hands to cut through the injustice that's so rampant throughout the nations and bring those responsible to account. Lord, give us wisdom in how to cut off those ruling spirits that have ruled and blinded nation after nation, how to remove their power and hold and bind them once and for all. You've given all of us who love You the mandate to usher in the rule of Your Son Jesus our servant King. Help us to serve the nations well, in a way that brings Honour and Glory to Him.

All Praise and Honour to You, Lord! Our King Jesus!

Psalm 150

Oh, Mighty King Jesus, Anointed One, I bless and I praise Your Mighty, Your Matchless, Your Wonderful Name—JESUS!

Thank You that You sit enthroned on the praises of Your people so the moment any of us turn our hearts to praise to You, there You are. Lord You are truly Wonderful.

How You've demonstrated over and over, so powerfully, Your amazing love of me, and not just me, but everyone! You are indeed High over all.

Bring out the loud trumpets, bring out the guitars and all those stringed instruments and the flutes and the saxophones, now bring on the dancers with their tambourines. Let's celebrate our Wonderful King.

Hey, someone—give me the biggest cymbals you can find, I want to have everyone jumpin' out of their skins! Our King Jesus is so worthy!

Thank You Lord that You aren't frightened by loud noise!

Oh, come on, everyone—give it all you've got now, in praise of our JESUS!

King Jesus—You are so worthy of *All* our Praise and Worship.

Psalm 151

As I come to the end, I can't help but add my own heart's cry here. [JVE]

Oh, how long? How long, Lord, will Your so-precious name be trampled underfoot, and the nations and kings of the earth rage against You—my Wonderful Servant King JESUS?

Oh, how long? How long will those who love You so struggle to find a family where they can party in Praise and Worship of You, Jesus? Where can they dance and sing, shout and let their hair down in abandoned, extravagant, outrageous worship and praise of You, the Crucified and Resurrected One[1]?

Oh how long? How long will the refugee, the poor and the broken-hearted search for a home, and the incurable-sick search for healing and find church doors barred to them by a people who are themselves chained by unbelief and worse, rather than finding You, Mighty King Jesus—always strong to save and heal, and deliver? But Lord… it's so easy to point the finger. You direct them to my door, or lead me to theirs, and I trust You to give me Your Boldness, Your Wisdom, Your Insight and above all, Your Anointing that it's not me they meet, but YOU.

Oh thank You King Jesus that You Love the mess and chaos of the delivery room; giving birth is a messy business. And thank You that You equally don't mind the mess and chaos of setting the captive free and healing the broken. *Oh* thank You that this is Your kind of order—filled with Joy and Laughter! Hysterical Joy and Hysterical Laughter—Yeaaaah!

---

[1] Oh, Thank You, Georgian and Winnie Banov, for your example.

342

Lord, as the tsunami of Your next move sweeps across the earth, please don't leave my nation out, but may we be transformed into an irresistible invasion force of Your saving Grace and Mercy for the nations around us—bringing many into the knowledge of You and Your ways. Lord, may I be found kite-surfing this next wave of Yours with a joyful shout of Praise to You, Mighty King Jesus, as You, Holy Spirit, flood my kite with as much wind as I can handle. May I cut a straight wake with a cry to all, "This is the way to Father's Heart—follow me."

If you have been impacted by this book, and find it helpful, I ask that that you recommend it to others. For that, then there's a very vital part you can play. Please go back and leave a review on Amazon. This is a very key part of passing the message on, as well of course recommending it to your friends. Your reviews count very strongly to people evaluating whether a particular book is worth reading. Thank you so much.

I am currently working on a fresh paraphrase of the epistles, amplified to explain their meaning, and comes with study questions and notes. The intent is to make for easy reading or convenient study, in a new easy-reading format. *Living and Breathing Hebrews to Jude* is now in print and available from Amazon. Currently *Living and Breathing Romans to Galatians* is being edited, so is nearing completion, to be followed by *Living and Breathing Ephesians to Philemon*. [I am trying to complete the printed versions, before going back and re-editing them for Kindle, as the Kindle version's notes will require a major re-edit of the whole document.]

For updates on progress with this and my other books, please go to our website and subscribe to the blog:
www.landbreathingt.com

About the Author

Jim Edwards is a passionate lover of Jesus, He lives on the South Coast of the UK, with his wife Val. Married for over forty years, they have four amazing and wonderful children.

Recently retired from being Technical Sales Manager for a high voltage power supply company he had made regular visits to his USA customers and on to Bethel Church in Redding California. The role was to explain the details of the electronics to technical and non-technical people alike. Now remember, you cannot see electrons, so the role translated to that of explaining the operation and details of things that you cannot see to a wide variety of people.

His hope and prayer is that you have encountered Father, Jesus, and Holy Spirit through this book. They love you dearly. Jim would always love to hear that story. He can be contacted via Edwards Family Publishing on Facebook.

This was the third of a number of books, there are more to follow—watch this space.

Additional Books by the Author:
[All available from Amazon]

Living and Breathing Hebrews to Jude

Living and Breathing Hebrews to Jude is an easy reading paraphrase of the Epistles. Here are letters written to us from those who knew Jesus intimately, who were brought up with Him, or spent years with Him as His disciples.

Guarded, and carefully copied through the centuries for us, they are now unravelled in a fresh way, in the everyday language of today. They are here amplified to explain the truths those early followers of Jesus were so concerned to pass on to their fellow believers.

The reality of the promises, the prayers and the truths of the wonderful good news that Jesus paid such a high price to bring us, is vibrantly brought to life. While Holy Spirit's life-changing, heart-changing, healing power to comfort, to save, to deliver, to restore, and to bring hope is here laid out for us.

Alongside the text, are thought provoking study questions, notes and cross references, to unveil the enormity of all that Jesus won for us, and to reveal our Heavenly Father's wondrous heart of love; His longing to know and be known, by us all.

ISBN-13: 978-1979871358
ISBN-10: 1979871353
Kindle ASIN: Not yet available

This is the companion volume to *Living and Breathing Romans to Galatians*.

Living and Breathing Romans to Galatians

Living and Breathing Romans to Galatians is an easy reading paraphrase of the Epistles. Here are Paul's early letters to these embryonic early churches.

Guarded, and carefully copied through the centuries for us, they are now unravelled in a fresh way, in the everyday language of today. They are here amplified to explain the revelation Paul personally received from Jesus that he was so concerned to share with all who would receive it. Here is Paul's heart revealed, alongside the price he paid to share this Good News of Jesus.

Here is the Good News that the same Holy Spirit who anointed Jesus wants to live in you, to strengthen you and demonstrate with signs and wonders through you that Jesus is our Redeemer and Father God's Anointed Son.

The reality of the promises, the prayers and the truths of this wonderful Good News that Jesus paid such a high price to bring us, is vibrantly brought to life. While Holy Spirit's life-changing, heart-changing, healing power to comfort, to save, to deliver, to restore, and to bring hope is here laid out for us.

Alongside the text, are thought provoking study questions, notes and cross references, to unveil the enormity of all that Jesus won for us, and to reveal our Heavenly Father's wondrous heart of love; His longing to know and be known, by us all.

Available from Amazon   Print
ISBN-13: 978-1727130621
ISBN-10: 1727139626
Kindle ASIN: Not yet available.

This is the companion volume to *Living and Breathing Hebrews to Jude.*

Your Invitation

Now where should a Passion Play end?
Good Friday is over and the tomb closed and sealed.

Eavesdrop on a group whose play doesn't end where their scriptwriter intended.
Join them for their Easter service, and travel with them, as they experience for themselves the resurrection appearances of Jesus.
Did Jesus really rise from the dead? Does it matter? Is it of any relevance for us? How would you recognize Him? What would it look like, if He were to come back today? How could He help you?
Then share in their very personal invitation to a life-changing encounter.

    This is *Your Invitation.*

Edwards Family Publishing:

ISBN-10: 1497403081
ISBN-13: 978-1497403086
ASIN: B00BTNGYM0

Mercy—God's Mighty Covenanted Assistance for You.

Mercy is covenant assistance, and its roots tell us a lot about the nature and character of our Heavenly Father, and His commitment to His covenants.

God is a God of Covenant, so this book illustrates and explains what a 'blood covenant' actually is and compares and contrasts the different covenants God has made, and why He makes them.

God has repeatedly bound Himself with covenants. Why? Because He wants to bless people outrageously. Would you like to be included?

Jesus cut a very binding 'blood covenant' with His Father, on our behalf, at the cross. This book spells out just what is included for you and I and how we are to draw on it.

Edwards Family Publishing:
    ISBN-13:   978-1523342068
    ISBN-10:   15323342064
    ASIN: B01LWBKJRC

MERCY

GOD'S COVENANT ASSISTANCE

Jim Edwards

Coming Soon

Summoned:

to a life of intimacy with the King of Glory

You are summoned to a life of intimacy with the High King of Heaven.
You! Yes *YOU*!
Why and how do we respond to such a call and what does it look like?
He only knows to love at any cost; will you too give up anything less.
He only knows to trust in hope and faith, and *you*.

It takes the blink of an eye and it takes a lifetime.
You gain—your destiny—your dreams—your significance.
It costs nothing, but yet it costs everything i.e.
Your destiny—your dreams—your significance
What does it cost Him, and what does He gain?
He is not thirsty for worship, but He is thirsty for relationship with you,
and for you and me freely wanting to relate to Him.

Do you accept His summons and your assignment?
Sounds impossibly hard? It starts with you simply saying 'Yes'.
He will make the next move—trust me!

As the best of fathers, He will speak so that you hear,
And every response, He always gives you the awesome freedom to choose.

ISBN-13:978-1536912357
ISBN-10:1536912352

John316Network

For other independent Christian authors, search for the John316Network, founded by Lorilyn Roberts.

These authors cover every genre, with members from many nations, but all with a Christian worldview.

Check out Lorilyn's award winning 'Seventh Dimension' series. This series is just so much more than a YA Fantasy.

While unable here, to endorse all of their books, or even all of the network, such authors, in totally random order, include

Lisa Lickel	Jerry Jenkins
Emma & Guy Right	Tracy Krauss
Nicola Taylor	Katherine Harms
Martin Roth	Carol Brown
Dana Rongione	Alice Wisler
Angelique McGlotton	Pamela Carmichael
Barbara Derksen	Elizabeth Paige
Roberto Roche	Randy Kirk
Carole Brown	Cheryl Colwell
Laura Davis	Joseph Young
Trish Jenkins	Carol Round
Janis Cox	Malo Bel
Anita Estes	Deborah Bateman

Made in the USA
San Bernardino, CA
20 March 2019